Moved
by the Past

European Perspectives:
A Series in Social Thought and Cultural Criticism

European Perspectives:
A Series in Social Thought and Cultural Criticism

Lawrence D. Kritzman, Editor

European Perspectives presents outstanding books by leading European thinkers. With both classic and contemporary works, the series aims to shape the major intellectual controversies of our day and to facilitate the tasks of historical understanding.

For a complete list of books in the series, see pages 243–245

Moved
by the Past

Discontinuity and Historical Mutation

Eelco Runia

COLUMBIA UNIVERSITY PRESS *NEW YORK*

Columbia University Press
Publishers Since 1893
New York   Chichester, West Sussex
cup.columbia.edu

Library of Congress Cataloging-in-Publication Data
Runia, Eelco.
Moved by the past : discontinuity and historical mutation / Eelco Runia.
pages cm.   — (European Perspectives)
Includes bibliographical references and index.
ISBN 978-0-231-16820-5 (cloth : alk. paper) — ISBN 978-0-231-53757-5 (ebook)
1. History—Philosophy. 2. Historiography—Philosophy. I. Title.

D16.8.R895 2014
901—dc23
2013045313

Columbia University Press books are printed on permanent and
durable acid-free paper.
This book is printed on paper with recycled content.
Printed in the United States of America

c 10 9 8 7 6 5 4 3 2

COVER DESIGN: Archie Ferguson

To Carol Gluck,
a muse

Contents

We must . . . proceed from a vulgar metaphysics.

—Giambattista Vico, *Scienza Nuova*

Introduction

Weshalb studiert man Geschichte? Ohne Zweifel um das Leben der
Menschheit in seiner Totalität zu erkennen.

—Leopold von Ranke[1]

Sometimes, in unguarded moments, I mutter to my students that
"historians don't think." I usually add that there's nothing wrong
with their mental abilities but that the discipline puts a premium on
"sorting things out," and that consequently the history departments
spit out specialists in *organizing* things who have somehow lost the
capacity to tolerate messiness. And "thinking," I go on, is turning
things upside down, is awakening dogs that lie sleeping, is taking
things apart, is, in short, willfully making a mess. In most disciplines,
of course, being allergic to messiness is no issue at all—in history,
however, it is. For whereas in other disciplines results are valid only
if they can be replicated by your colleagues, in history validity is a
function of the extent in which results can *not* be replicated by your
colleagues. And there is no escaping it: in order to fabricate something
that is robustly and distinctly *personal*, you have to resist the neat Pow-
erPoint slides that offer themselves to your clueless mind, to get your
teeth in what you are tempted to take for granted, and to create a nice
little mess.

When pressed, I tell my students that there are two antidotes to
historical hosophobia. The first is, much to their surprise, *popularization*. Good popularization starts from scratch, and taking your subject
apart leaves you with all the scratch you need. The second antidote is

to do what Lord Byron said a good workman shouldn't do: to "quarrel with your tools." I spell out that because history—like psychotherapy—belongs to the disciplines where you "are your own instrument," quarreling with your tools means quarreling with yourself. In history "quarreling with yourself" is nothing more—or less—than a sustained attempt to focus on what you bring to your subject rather than on what your subject brings to you, or, as psychoanalysts would say, on the countertransference rather than on the transference. For historians, "not thinking" goes under the name of "positivism" and takes the form of allowing yourself to become wrapped up in your subject. It implies consenting to be a vehicle for what Hayden White has called prefigurations—and, as I will show in the second chapter of this book—to the extent you succumb to prefigurations you only replicate your subject.[2]

In writing the essays on which this book is based I have struggled out of the grasp of the belief that we "own" the past. In each essay my premise has been that in fact we are part of a field that is bigger than ourselves, a field that includes what we fancy to be "our" history. As Hans-Georg Gadamer has said: "In Wahrheit gehört die Geschichte nicht uns, sondern wir gehören ihr."[3]

One of my guiding principles has been that "creating a mess" is opening yourself to the field to which you belong. That, by the way, is why theory is so important for everyone who is trying to engage history: theory, not as a body of concepts and categories, but as the process of quarreling with the tools of the trade can create the mess you need to open yourself to what is not already included in the preconceptions and prefigurations you bring to what you write about. My second guiding principle follows naturally from the first: I have tried to make the most of the fact that the surprises that befall you when you're opening yourself to the field are structurally equivalent to the contingencies of history. I have used this isomorphy as an antidote to the pitfalls of prefiguration and as my own brand of Giambattista Vico's *verum et factum convertuntur*—the principle that you can only really understand what you have made yourself.

In the form I employ it the equivalence of opening yourself to the field and history's openness to the future is especially useful for fathoming *discontinuity*. Discontinuity is perhaps the single most important issue that historians deal with. In theory, that is—for in practice they go to great lengths to not have to stare it in the face. Historians are amazingly smart, and brilliantly creative, in chasing monstrous discontinuity away and establishing continuity. Right after the fall of the Berlin Wall, George W. Bush's invasion of Iraq, and the introduction of the euro, historians rolled up their sleeves and set out to explain why these events were, after all, bound to happen and logical continuations of what preceded them. And though historians tend to loathe postmodernism, their repugnance of discontinuity was conveniently stiffened by the postmodernist notion that "il n'y a pas de hors-texte"—that, in short, everything we fancy to be new is contained in, and can be deduced from, what already exists. But there is no escaping it: history progresses by unforeseeable leaps and bounds—leaps and bounds that are neither implied nor determined by what the actors—that is, ultimately, we ourselves—bring to the diving board. As manifestations of, as Goethe said, "Im Anfang ist die Tat," leaps and bounds spring from a *dehors-texte*, and after 9/11 brought down the postmodern twin towers of language and meaning it is, I think, about time to focus on how, in history as well as in historiography, the new—the exhilarating, frightening, sinful, sublimely new—comes about.

That is what I try to do in this book. Though the nine essays of which it consists were written separately, and address an array of issues and topics, they are thematically coherent to an extent that surprised me. As I was reworking them for inclusion in this book, they reminded me of the ice floes we tried to run upon when we were children. It was an exciting game. When the ice in the canals was broken into floes we tried to run over the ice as far as we could, attempting to jump from a floe that was sinking, toppling, or sliding away to a next one just before it went down. Likewise, in the essays in this book, I tried to drive my arguments—and my intuition—as far as I possibly could, leaving my floe, and jumping to a next one, when I lost my balance and was in danger of going down. I do not know whether my single-minded scramble has brought me anywhere, but something of the excitement and the urgency as well as of the irresponsibility and waywardness with which I wrote the pieces collected here still shines through. And though I definitely do not reach another shore, I somehow haven't drowned, either. So at least it seems to me.

In the chapters that follow I show that being "moved by the past" comes in two modalities: a "regressive" and a "revolutionary" one. In both the "regressive" and the "revolutionary" mode the linearity of time is adjourned and a primordial "circularity" reclaims its rights. In the second chapter, I demonstrate that "moved by the past" can be a form of regression: I describe how we may act out a necrophylic relationship with a past that is more dead than we suspect—and in which we consequently reproduce a past that is more alive than we think. In the second half of this book the emphasis shifts to the way we may be "moved by the past" in a revolutionary sense, via situations in which a fresh and living past takes possession of us and gets us going again, in which Kairos gives birth to a new Chronos, in which time is created anew, in which—so to speak—a new linearity is rolled out. As a form of regression, being moved by the past entails inhibition, stasis, and a lack of creativity. Revolutionary *Schicksalwende* on the other hand—not just the French Revolution and the First World War but also the discontinuities I just mentioned: the fall of the Berlin Wall, George W. Bush's invasion of Iraq, and the introduction of the euro—involve "exhibition," frenzy, and a transgressive excess of creativity. In both the regressive and the revolutionary mode, the march of chronicity is interrupted, and past, present, and future start to play hide and seek: being moved by the past begins with being stuck in the present. Being stuck in the present begins with having lost the future. And losing the future begins with estrangement from the past.

Having come to the end of my book, I asked myself what the essays it contains add up to. It's a question I much preferred to dodge. I've always sympathized with the dancer Isadora Duncan—who replied when she was asked what she "meant" by a particular dance: "If I could say it, I didn't have to dance it." On a sunny Sunday in May, however, on the train to Groningen, somewhere between Zwolle and Meppel, it occurred to me that I could in fact "say" what I had, on my wooden shoes, danced all along, that my dance could be broken down (or up) into a couple of "vectors" that, though interconnected, could be named and identified separately. When I wrote them down there turned out to be ten of them: from continuity to discontinuity, from historiography to history, from meaning to presence, from metaphor to metonymy, from representation to incarnation, from story to monument, from epistemology to ontology, from identity to estrangement, from *allopoiesis* to *autopoiesis*, and, finally, from imagination to invention. Though some of them may puzzle you, I will not here, in what for you is the beginning but for me the end of this book, make up for what I didn't do in the pages that follow and explain them systematically. Taken together, however, my themes approximate my program for a new and up-to-date philosophy of history and they animate the book you are going to read.

There are a few persons and institutions I would like to thank. First I want to express my gratitude to the Netherlands Organization for Scientific Research—who gave me the generous grant that enabled me to pursue my interest in the economically worthless ideas expounded in this book. I thank *History and Theory* for printing some of the essays on which this book is based and for the permission to use them as/for chapters 1, 2, 3, 4, 6, and 8. I have always felt very fortunate that somewhere out there a venerable institution was eager to publish the things that in my own country were frowned upon. I also thank *Rethinking History* for printing the essay that in this book is chapter 7. Finally I want to express my gratitude to the anonymous reviewers of Columbia University Press—from now on I'm living in the state Pip lived in in Dickens's *Great Expectations*—that of having secret benefactors without knowing (though certainly suspecting . . .) who they are. Among the many people who inspired me just by believing in the things I did I want to single out Sepp Gumbrecht, Brian Fay, and Carol Gluck. Something of the kind is also applicable to my students. Quite a few of them were intrigued by what I was up to—and they stimulated me with their enthusiasm, their questions, and their offhand (but much appreciated) remarks that my ideas caused them sleepless nights.

I will end by expressing the hope that this book creates enough of a mess to open up the field of history to what to my mind is the historical question par excellence: the question of how, in an endless series of metamorphoses, we have transformed and continue to transform ourselves into who we are.

Moved
by the Past

1

Burying the Dead, Creating the Past

The object [of the historian's work] must be of such a kind that it can revive itself in the historian's mind; the historian's mind must be such as to offer a home for that revival.

—R. G. Collingwood[1]

The earth in Beaumont Hamel, just northwest of Thiepval, is an undulating green. The trenches have been partly filled up, the ridges of the bomb craters are eroded, and patches of grass and moss cover the softened contours like the down on the antlers of a stag. I ask myself: why would someone like me visit the place where the twentieth century was born from Flemish mud and French debris, the site of the battlefields of the Somme, Ypres, and Verdun? That descendants of the soldiers who perished in the Great War make pilgrimages to where it all happened may, perhaps, not need an explanation. But why would someone who didn't lose any of his forebears in either of the World Wars leave his books behind and wander over these inexorable fields? Do I not know that, though sources—as historians rightly call them— may "speak," the earth, grass, and moss will not yield up a single shred of knowledge that is not to be found in what was recorded in letters, photographs, diaries, and books? Is nature, however charged, not just a mirror that reflects, contorts, and—at the very most—revaluates what we already know?

But whatever I say to myself, the lure of these foreign fields persists. And, evidently, not just for me: the battlefields of Flanders and northern France, and the museums of Ypres, Péronne, and Verdun are major tourist attractions. Nor is the attraction restricted to the backdrop of the First World War. Scores of people are drawn to sites of memory, sites of mourning—on the condition that the events of which they bear witness are truly unimaginable. The Gettysburg battlefield draws one and a half million visitors each year; the Normandy Tourist Board recommends the "Historical Area of the Battle of Normandy" as "an open air museum in itself";[2] the House of Terror is one of Budapest's main assets; Berlin's "unique selling point" is the fact that it was the capital of the age of darkness; Auschwitz, Dachau, and Buchenwald have become (I hesitate) "popular destinations"; and the site of the World Trade Center is a must-see for the savvy visitor to New York City. I will not apologize for my, and others', penchant for visiting sites where unimaginable things did "in very deed occur." My point of departure is that battlefield tourism is not the perverse inclination to fondle sore spots, or the toffee-nosed alternative to freak shows and horror movies, but, rather, one of the most straightforward manifestations of our desire to *commemorate*.

This desire to commemorate is, in my opinion, the prime historical phenomenon of our time. I will not even attempt to give a catalogue of all its manifestations. Let me just mention the fact that people not only flock to battlefields, but also have an irrepressible urge to erect monuments. A Dutch newspaper recently gave a far from exhaustive list of the public monuments that have been unveiled in the Netherlands in the past few years: to children who died unbaptized, to Rotterdam policemen who were killed while doing their job, to the ten or twelve people who died of Legionnaires' Disease after visiting a flower show, to the "unknown" (that is, stillborn) child, to the abomination of slavery, to young traffic casualties, to the victims of a fire in a bar in Volendam, to the soldiers who died (mostly, by the way, because of accidents) during peacekeeping missions, and so on.[3] Professional historians tend to treat this monumentomania a little condescendingly. In fact, however, they have jumped on the bandwagon of what the lay public does so much more wholeheartedly—they fight the windmills of "collective memory" and conscientiously unearth the traumas of minorities.[4] And, of course, aspiring and up-to-date historians duly take stock of the "lieux de mémoire" of their respective countries, write tepid little pieces about them, and are happy that, for once, they don't have to bother about footnotes.

It keeps puzzling me. Claude Lanzmann once said that when you write about the Holocaust "the worst moral and aesthetic mistake you can make is to approach your subject as if it belongs to the past." But that mistake, it seems, is precisely what is being made: the discipline of history is pervaded with the desire to commemorate, but the infected historians hardly, if ever, commemorate the things they write about. It seems to be a neurotic inhibition: the discipline does want to commemorate but is held back by the fear that somehow it is a bit improper to give in to that wish. As a result commemoration is all over the place but is never taken as seriously as it should be. The predicament is perhaps best expressed by Pierre Nora himself. In "L'ère de la commémoration," the coda of the *Lieux de mémoire* project, Nora writes that the work "was intended, by virtue of its conception, method, and even title, to be a counter-commemorative type of history." But, Nora continues, "commemoration has overtaken it."[5] The intention of the *Lieux de mémoire* was "to make commemoration itself one of [the] primary specimens for dissection," but the "bulimia of commemoration" has devoured the attempt to dissect the phenomenon.

If Nora is right, if indeed we overindulge ourselves in commemoration without ever being satisfied by it, then, surely, the discipline is in the grip of a phenomenon it doesn't quite understand. One of the things I want to do in this book is to free myself from this devouring monster. I will start my project by offering ten theses about the desire to commemorate—the desire that brought me to the fields of Beaumont Hamel and that, I think, may well reveal how we, nowadays, relate to past, present, and future.

History and Memory

Let me begin by defining the issue somewhat more precisely. There can be little doubt that within the discipline the feeling is widespread that a tension exists between two very different and perhaps incompatible approaches to the past. In the wake of Nora's 1984 introductory essay to the *Lieux de mémoire* project, this crossroads is usually described in terms of "history" and "memory." "Memory and history," Nora says, "far from being synonymous, are . . . in many respects opposed.

Memory is life, always embodied in living societies and as such in permanent evolution. . . . History, on the other hand, is the reconstruction, always problematic and incomplete, of what is no longer."[6] The antithesis of "history" versus "memory" has caused a great deal of controversy, much of which can be reduced to the fact that it is a confusing and unprofitable way to refer to an opposition that is, of itself, fundamental indeed. The main problem with pitting "memory" against "history" is that memory is an extremely complex phenomenon and that anybody can find anything in it to suit his or her taste or purpose. Consequently, positing an antithesis between "history" and "memory" is about as helpful as positing an antithesis between "history" and "consciousness" or, for that matter, between "history" and "love."

To be able to evaluate the two diverging approaches to the past we'd better start with giving them proper names. This brings me to my first thesis:

FIRST THESIS: There really exists a "fundamental opposition" between two diverging approaches to the past, but instead of "history" and "memory," the poles of this opposition should be called "history" and "commemoration."

By "history" I mean the traditional, "botanizing," "positivist" conception of history Nora describes so eloquently. It is inspired by the belief that by bringing one's professional capacities to bear on a subject out there, one adds a little something to a very valuable, transpersonal, and ultimately transcendental goal. In this traditional, "botanizing" conception of history, each article, yes, each book review, contributes to the ever more truthful biography of a nation, a city, a regiment, an institution, a discipline, or a culture.

In order to explain what I mean by "commemoration" I have to make a distinction between "acts of God" (as they are called in American insurance policies) and the things people do for, and to, their kin—which I might as well call "acts of people." Acts of God are natural disasters: hurricanes, volcanic eruptions, tsunamis and so on. Acts of people, on the other hand, are the Prometheus-like things with which people willfully make a difference. A prime example of this urge is the wish to make history; thus among the most prototypical "acts of people" are the historical catastrophes humans inflict upon one another. Commemoration hinges on the idea that acts of people are committed by *us*—not, of course, in person, but as members of the group, the nation, the culture, and ultimately the species that brought the catastrophe about. Calamitous acts of people are made by us, because they *could have been made* by any one of us—if, by chance, we had been born a couple of hundred kilometers farther down or if we hadn't been blessed with—as the former German chancellor Helmut Kohl has expressed it—"the grace of late birth."

This brings me to my second thesis:

SECOND THESIS: Commemoration is trying to answer the question "Who are we that this could have happened?"[7]

The idea that, ultimately, "commemoration" is *self-exploration*—typically the fruit of an era obsessed with therapeutics and spiritual welfare—is not as new as one might expect. In fact it is at the heart of the philosophy of the incomparable Giambattista Vico. In a famous passage in the *Scienza Nuova*, Vico exclaims that he cannot understand why brilliant men like Descartes allow themselves to become completely engrossed with what they will never be able to fathom—nature—and ignore what is within reach of their genius: history.[8] We can only understand, Vico argued, what we ourselves have made, and because nature is made by God, we can never unveil its secrets. History, on the other hand, is made by ourselves—and therefore history lies within our grasp. We can understand history because we have *made* it, because we *are* history.

In the soft-headed brand of commemoration that is by far the most widely practiced nowadays, the question "Who are we that this could have happened?" is answered in an identity-enhancing, yes, self-celebrating way. If taken seriously, however, commemorative self-exploration is a confrontation with what we don't like to be confronted with: with the fact that occasionally we behave in utter contradiction to what we regard as our identity. In fact, it might be argued that it is precisely events in which we did things we didn't think we were capable of doing that we later want to commemorate. To the extent we don't like to face behavior that is at odds with our identity, commemoration tends to get stuck in a state of mind in which we, as commemorators, consider ourselves as beings slightly, but fundamentally, different from the ones who did the things we commemorate. Heterodox, "monstrous," and therefore *Gedächtnisfähig* behavior comes in three varieties: things we are proud of, things we are ashamed of, and the sublime "mutations" in which we "commit" history and embark on the unimaginable. Commemorating shameful behavior, demanding as it may be, only poses psychological problems; "sublime" behavior, on the other hand, confronts posterity with almost insuperable epistemological difficulties as well.

The question of how shameful events are commemorated not only illustrates the tendency to attribute them to "others," but also demonstrates that it is impossible to come to terms with a past event as long as we evade the question "Who are we that this could have happened?" As long as France didn't accept full responsibility for the Vichy regime, and pretended that Vichy *c'était les autres*, it couldn't come clear of that shameful episode. The Netherlands kept being haunted by the "police actions" in the Dutch East Indies as long as it maintained that the cruelties committed were just "incidents" perpetrated by some unrepresentative "rotten apples." And in order to come to terms with the *Guerra Sucia*, the Argentines will have to acknowledge that Jorge Videla and Alfredo Astiz were Argentines like themselves. This is my third thesis:

THIRD THESIS: Coming to terms with a historical trauma is the result of answering the commemorative question "Who are we that this could have happened?"

This doesn't mean that coming to terms with a historical trauma should be the *goal* of commemoration. Rather, coming to terms with a historical trauma is the free by-product of a sustained attempt at commemorative self-exploration.

Sublime Historical Events

Quintessentially memorable, or, as I should say by now, "*commemorable*," events are not, however, the events that make us ashamed, but are the sublime "acts of people" Goethe had in mind when he wrote: "Nur allein der Mensch / Vermag das Unmögliche." In such "impossible" acts we leave the beaten track and embark upon the unknown—as we did in events like the American Declaration of Independence, the French Revolution, the secession of the Confederation of the South, Bismarck's unification of Germany, the First World War, the Holocaust, and the redrawing of the map of what used to be Yugoslavia. What makes these events "sublime" is that no right-minded person could foresee them—and yet, disturbingly, it was supposedly right-minded persons who "made" them. This is just another way of saying that these events were at odds with the worldview from which they emerged. Sublime events are the "unimaginable" events that draw people who have no personal stake in the matter to the places where it all happened—as I have been drawn to Beaumont Hamel. Because sublime events effect a change in worldview, they not only are very hard to stomach, but also confront us with a major epistemological problem. For how can we ever answer the question "Who are we that this could have happened?" if the "we" who *made* the event is qualitatively different from the "we" who want to *commemorate* it?

What such an unfathomable discontinuity feels like was poetically expressed by the Prussian statesman and scholar Wilhelm von Humboldt. In calamitous events such as the French Revolution, Humboldt said, we destroy our "homely huts" and find ourselves back in "palaces"—unexplored universes we ourselves have somehow made. "When we start to do things beyond our confinements," Humboldt lamented, "the current often takes us up, we go beyond our habitual selves and destroy the homely huts in us. And in the palaces we erect outside ourselves we will remain forever foreigners."[9] That, indeed, is exactly what is at stake. After having committed a sublime act we find ourselves "in a palace"—or, as I prefer to call it, with a "monster" of our own making—and we wonder: how could such a ghastly creature ever have been nurtured by well-meaning, right-minded, and peace-loving people like us? In contrast to earthquakes or volcanic eruptions, anomalous "acts of people" confront us with the task of adapting our worldview so that it can encompass what we have actually brought about.

It is the prime feature of sublime historical "acts of people" that when we look back on them we cannot really imagine the position from which we came to commit them. The acts themselves have changed everything. We cannot deny that we did what we did, but was it really us who did what was done? This incommensurability is partly due to the sense of loss that inevitably sets in after we have burned these bridges behind us. After a sublime historical mutation this sense of loss expunges the thought that we could ever have jumped upon it— and it miraculously transforms agents into victims. The main reason, however, for our unwillingness to consider ourselves agents is that the things we did were "underdetermined," that we had insufficient reasons to do what we did, that—as Joseph Conrad said—we just gave in to the question "Why not?" Yet, as I will show in chapter 9, in each of the sublime "acts of people" we now want to commemorate, a willingness to go "*va banque*" was a vital ingredient. Whether we like it or not, a readiness to put a way of life, a culture, on the line, is a necessary component of sublime historical events. This is my fourth thesis:

FOURTH THESIS: People start to make history not *despite* the fact that it is at odds with—yes, destroys—the stories they live by, but *because* it destroys the stories they live by.

I would like to remark in this connection that we routinely assume that our history is *behind* us. In the sense, however, that after a sublime historical event our worldview lags behind with what was all too possible, our history really is *before* us.[10] We have to "catch up with it"—as the nineteenth century tried to catch up with the French Revolution, and as we, at the moment, are still trying to catch up with what the dual World War of the first half of the twentieth century has shown to be possible. I do not think—as Humboldt did—that we remain forever foreigners in the palaces we erect. Rather, we try to make them habitable. If the event we have brought about is too conspicuous to be smuggled away, catching up with it may even be a psychological necessity.

In fact, Daryl Bem's "Self-Perception Theory" nicely describes the process. According to Bem, individuals do not have privileged access to themselves. They do not derive their identity from somewhere "within." Rather, they do so by examining their own deeds, and by subconsciously answering the question "What kind of person am I, that I could have done the things I did?"[11] In my book *Waterloo, Verdun, Auschwitz* I have shown that societies strive for "dissonance reduction" in much the same way that individuals do.[12] Historians try, as Ranke said, "um die letzte und nächste Vergangenheit mit der früheren in Einklang zu bringen" ("to bring recent history [i.e., the French Revolution] into harmony with what happened before").

Making a palace habitable, "taming a monster," has, however, a rather annoying consequence: it obliterates its most salient feature, namely, the fact that it was an underdetermined answer to the question "Why not?" This can perhaps be seen most clearly in the American Declaration of Independence. The famous phrase "we hold these truths to be self-evident" suggests that these "truths," though perhaps unrecognized and unfulfilled, had always been there—and that the revolutionaries only gave them their due. But that, of course, is a typical ex post facto account. The decision to throw off the British yoke was not the result of "self-evidence." On the contrary: only after the irreversible step had been taken did it occur to Thomas Jefferson that the reasons for doing so were not contingencies but "truths," and not just truths but "self-evident truths." The "self-evident truths" didn't create the event, the event created "self-evident truths." Sublime "acts of people" like the American rebellion transform consciousness to such an extent that the *status quo ante* becomes unimaginable the moment the *status quo post* becomes self-evident. Differently put: the one thing without which the sublime historical event could not have taken place—our acting upon our impulse to make a difference—evaporates in the process of coming to terms with it. This, in fact, is my fifth thesis:

FIFTH THESIS: The more we commemorate what we did, the more we transform ourselves into people who did not do it.

As Henri Bergson wrote in his *Évolution créatrice*: "Precisely because it is always trying to reconstitute, and to reconstitute with what is given, the intellect lets what is *new* in each moment of history escape. It does not admit the unforeseeable. It rejects all creation."[13]

Consuming the Future

Before I turn to the questions of how we can, do, and should commemorate sublime "acts of people," I will have to say a few words about the supposition that the current "memory boom"—as Jay Winter calls it[14]—is a unique phenomenon. It is not. Surprisingly, today's memory historians somehow fail to historicize the phenomenon of which they are a part. The recent upsurge in the "desire to commemorate" can be pinpointed rather exactly: it started in the mid 1970s. The irresistible force that the phenomenon eventually acquired may well have been caused by the fact that this particular period saw a confluence of two strands of commemoration: the "hot" desire to commemorate the Holocaust and the somewhat "cooler" desire to commemorate the First World War. The first grew to full stature somewhere between Marcel Ophüls's 1971 movie *Le chagrin et la pitié* and the epochal 1978 Hollywood soap opera *Holocaust*. But I will not recount here how the willingness—yes, passion—to have oneself confronted with the reality of the extermination camps came to be expressed in literature, philosophy, history, and cultural studies. Let me just point to the fact that in the second half of the 1970s Primo Levi's *If This Is a Man* suddenly began to sell.[15]

The ambition to pay homage to the First World War may have been more subdued, but reveals at least as much about what is certainly a key issue: the transformation of the memory of those who actually witnessed a conflagration into a commemorative response of their descendants. This transformation was effected largely in the mid 1970s. On Armistice Day 1976 the *London Daily Telegraph* ran an article with the title "Memory of the Fallen Begins to Fade Away."[16] A year earlier, in 1975, Paul Fussell had published *The Great War and Modern Memory*. The *Daily Telegraph* article and Fussell's book are landmarks in a process in which testimony is replaced by commemoration. By the way, the intermingling of the World War I and World War II strands of commemoration is epitomized by the fact that Fussell dedicated his book "To the memory of Technical Sergeant Edward Keith Hudson . . . Killed beside me in France, March 15, 1945."

The dates are significant—for history progresses by generations. The period between the death of Fussell's brother-in-arms and the dedication in the book happens to cover precisely the twenty-five to thirty years that a generation is supposed to last. That history, as a discipline, does not evolve smoothly and incrementally, but by leaps and bounds prescribed by, or at least suggested by, generational issues, has a sound psychological reason. Not only do generations reexperience their past in and by means of their offspring, but later generations also tend to get interested in what their begetters have "fathered" the moment they realize that, whether they like it or not, now *they themselves* are fathering the future. This is my sixth thesis:

SIXTH THESIS: The focus of our desire to commemorate is prefigured by generational issues.

So the question is not so much why the mid 1970s suddenly started to commemorate the destruction of European Jewry, but why the same period also witnessed a revival of the commemoration of the First World War. The answer, I think, is simple: a generation after the First World War we were too busy *making* history to be able to commemorate it.[17] The commemoration of that war got going not one but two generations after the fact. But once on its way it kept gaining ground, so that right now, three generations after the First, and two after the Second World War, my bookseller has more new books about the First than about the Second World War.

That commemoration is (at least partly) a matter of generation is confirmed by the fact that it is never a steady trickle, but always comes in waves. Preoccupied as we are with the way the First World War is commemorated, we tend to forget that a particularly big wave overran Western Europe in the two or three decades *before* that War[18]—a period, incidentally, that (like ours) was obsessed with memory.[19] In the 1890s, "heritage" came very much into vogue and many Western European countries took initiatives to protect their patrimony. Britain's National Trust, for example, dates from 1895. In France, the Third Republic had Paris sprinkled with public monuments. In his 1912 *La statuomanie parisienne*, Gustave Pessard did some arithmetic:

> if we take into account the 335 mythological or assorted statues . . . the 328 illustrious Parisians of both sexes which ornament the façades of our Hôtel de Ville . . . if we add the 180 other monuments devoted to the memory of individuals . . . without forgetting the 72 statues which are at the moment just at the project stage . . . we come up with the fantastic figure of more than nine hundred-odd statues.[20]

In Germany, thirty years after Bismarck's stunning successes, building monuments became a kind of cult—a cult that inspired Alois Riegl to write one of the first books on the subject, *Der moderne Denkmalkultus* (1903). In fact, so many monuments were erected in Wilhelmine Germany that the effort backfired: the public got bored. Robert Musil remarked: "Das Auffallendste an Denkmälern ist . . . daß man sie nicht bemerkt."[21]

Though the infatuation with commemoration that started in the 1970s is not exceptional, it has one unique feature, which has caused a lot of confusion: whereas in most periods it is quite clear whether the desire to commemorate is inspired by either "excess" or "scarcity," in our time—which commemorates the Holocaust as well as the First World War—the two are out of step. One might say that the prime concern of a generation that has participated in a traumatic event is to be delivered from an "excess" of memories. This wish is best exemplified by Primo Levi. "For many of us," Levi said, "to be interviewed was a unique and memorable occasion, the event for which we had waited since liberation, and which gave meaning to our liberation."[22] For a generation, however, that has not lived through a traumatic event, commemoration means the reverse: to remedy the scarcity or, rather, absence of memories. The wish to acquire something as inalienable as a memory is beautifully explored in Geoff Dyer's *The Missing of the Somme*—an "essay in mediation"[23] in which Dyer submerges himself in the excess of memory of the war generation in order to remedy the blank in himself. Arthur Danto has remarked: "We erect monuments so that we shall always remember, and build memorials so that we will never forget."[24] At the moment we often seem to be at a loss as to what to do: to build monuments or memorials, to "remember" or "not forget."

The distinction between commemorating, on the one hand, from "excess" and, on the other hand, from "scarcity" of memory is not just a matter of "quantity." "Commemorating from excess" is primarily a *psychological* issue—motivated as it is by the wish to overcome trauma. "Commemoration from scarcity," however, is first and foremost an *existential* or, perhaps better, an *ontological* phenomenon. Generations that have nothing to weigh them down tend to regard the survivors of horrendous and sublime "acts of people" in a way not unlike the way we regard the astronauts who walked on the moon.

These "champions" have stared at the face of "truths" that normal life keeps hidden from us. Annette Wieviorka has said that the witness of the Holocaust "resembles the model of the early Apostles who brought the word of the Gospels to the people."[25] This gospel, I would like to add, has a name: reality. "Commemoration from scarcity" is the prime symptom of a "desire for reality," of an ontological homesickness (*Heimweh*), of a wish to commune with the numinosity of history. This is my seventh thesis:

SEVENTH THESIS: Commemorating from "scarcity of memory" springs from ontological homesickness and is a manifestation of a desire to get into contact with the numinosity of history.

Taking this line of reasoning one step further, one might speculate that ontological homesickness is connected with the impulse to make history, with the urge, that is, to commit "sublime historical acts of people." From such a perspective the human is the animal that has taken its evolution into its own hand. The mutations in this evolution take place at moments in which we no longer have "a history before us," or, perhaps better, in which we have "consumed" the future that a former sublime historical event has given us. In such a state, we are in danger of getting to know ourselves, and a state in which we are in danger of getting to know ourselves leads to what Heidegger called *Seinsvergessenheit*. In order to regain the blessed state in which we once more, though on a different level, do not know who we are, we have to do something that is truly at odds with what we regard as our identity—we have to destroy, to recall Humboldt's memorable phrase, our homely huts and erect a palace in which we once again are able to feel not at home at all. This is my eighth thesis:

EIGHTH THESIS: Every now and then we create new pasts for ourselves by committing fresh "original sins," by fleeing forward in horrendous, sublime—in short, historical—"acts of people."

This is a rather distressing thought. Can it be that the First World War was a consequence of having consumed the future with which the French Revolution had provided us? Can it be that right now we have consumed the future that the excesses of the first half of the twentieth century have given us?

Burying the Dead

In the final part of this chapter I will draw some conclusions from my attempt to regard commemoration under the aegis of human evolution. It's worth noticing in this connection that most thinkers about the subject take it for granted that our desire to commemorate, and our infatuation with memory, are caused by the "acceleration of time," by the "rapid change of society," by the "fact" that, as Pierre Nora said, "things tumble with increasing rapidity into an irretrievable past."[26] In fact, the idea that we have to go all out to hold our own in the present, and that, consequently, we have to put the past at a distance, is the cornerstone of the *Lieux de mémoire* project: *lieux de mémoire*, Nora says, "arise out of a sense that there is no such thing as spontaneous memory, hence that we must create archives, mark anniversaries, organize celebrations."[27] Nora's view—that the present is too full to accommodate the past—has been widely adopted, and echoes through the discipline, as in, for example, John Gillis's introduction to his *Commemorations*: "What we can no longer keep in our heads is now kept in storage."[28]

The view that the present is too full to accommodate the past suggests that we only take leave of the past when we *have* to, that, indeed, we have no "spontaneous memory." This, it seems to me, is a thoroughly anthropomorphic, or, rather, "historiomorphic," point of view. From an evolutionary perspective, humans are animals who have an absolutely amazing capacity to "externalize" things—to invent strategies by means of which what is truly theirs can be split off and placed at arm's length. Through its invention of language, writing, printing, and digitalization, humankind has brought about, in complete contradistinction to what Nora writes, marvels of "spontaneous memory." It might even be maintained that evolution took place *by means of* these mutations in externalization. Each new strategy of externalization presupposes a transformation, and each transformation makes room for a new proliferation. The process is nicely, if rather tendentiously, described in the famous passage in Plato's *Phaedrus* where the Egyptian king Thamos has a go at Theuth—the man who proudly advertised his invention of writing to the king. "If men learn this [art of writing]," Plato makes Thamos say, "it will implant forgetfulness in their souls; they will cease to exercise memory because they rely on that which is written, calling things to remembrance no longer from within themselves, but by means of external marks. What you have discovered is a recipe not for memory, but for reminder."[29] This brings me to my ninth thesis:

NINTH THESIS: Commemoration is not—as Platonists like Nora think—an epiphenomenon of some basic fault of humanity, but the necessary concomitant of the exquisitely human faculty of externalization.

One of the earliest, and most fundamental, externalizations is our custom of burying our dead. According to Vico, burying the dead is one of the things that makes humans human—and indeed, even our closest relatives—bonobos and chimpanzees—do not bury their dead. Humanity, Vico says, "had its origins in *humare*, to bury. The Athenians, who were the most human of all the nations, were . . . the first to bury their dead."[30] And, elsewhere, somewhat more graphically: "What a great principle of humanity burial is . . . imagine a feral state in which human bodies remain unburied on the surface of the earth as food for crows and dogs. . . . Men will go about like swine eating the acorns found amidst the putrefaction of their dead."[31] Vico may be right. By burying the dead—or, as in southeast Asia, by burning them—humankind may well have created a prime condition for traditions, for stability, for transcendence, for religion, for, in one word, culture. Burying the dead is an ambivalent practice, and an advantageous one at that. It is ambivalent because it combines things that seem to preclude each other: *closure* and *perpetuation*. Burying the dead is a means to take leave of the deceased without giving them up. It's an evolutionarily advantageous practice because it enables humans to bring much more to bear on the present than what their consciousness can contain.

Commemoration is the complement of burial, the creative—nay, *inventive*—recapitulation, the sacramental recelebration, of a particular act of externalization. It is a necessary complement in cases where there is an "excess of memory." That's why the *Madres* kept going to the Plaza de Mayo, that's why after World War I we invented "the unknown soldier"—which is really nothing more than an ingenious strategy to bring about the vital combination of closure and perpetuation even when there were no bodies to bury. But it is also necessary in cases of "absence of memory." Committing history is a form of externalization: by committing sublime historical deeds, by doing things that are at odds with our identity, we place history outside ourselves. Committing history thus is a kind of burial: we take leave of ourselves as we have come to know ourselves and become what we as yet do not know. In the process we come to see what is lost forever: what we are no longer. This is my tenth and final thesis:

TENTH THESIS: By burying the dead we create not our future, but our past.

2

"Forget About It"

A good metaphor implies an intuitive perception of the similarity
in dissimilars.

—Aristotle[1]

On April 10, 2002, in a live television broadcast, the director of the
Netherlands Institute for War Documentation (NIOD) presented
the first copy of the long-awaited NIOD report about the "events prior
to, during, and after the fall of Srebrenica" in 1995 to the Dutch minister of education, culture and science. In three massive volumes (total-
ing 3,394 pages), four book-length "partial studies," and a CD-ROM
containing another eleven such studies,[2] the NIOD described and analyzed the inability of a battalion of Dutch peacekeepers to protect the
Bosnian Muslims herded together in the "safe area" of Srebrenica. The
contract between the NIOD and the Dutch government, which had
commissioned the study and paid the costs, stipulated that the aim of
the project was to be to "increase our understanding . . . of the causes
and events which led to the fall of Srebrenica and the dramatic developments which ensued."[3]

One of these "dramatic developments" was the murder—by Serb
militiamen—of probably as many as eight thousand Bosnian Muslims. From the beginning it was quite clear that the raison d'être of
the NIOD investigation was to ascertain whether Dutch politicians,
military, civil servants, or peacekeepers were in any way to blame.
The report with which the NIOD came forward after more than five
years of research was critical about the eagerness with which the

then-government had sent a battalion of peacekeepers on an "impossible mission," but did not indict any Dutch politician (nor indeed any other Dutch individual or institution). Nevertheless, less than a week after the publication, and only a few weeks before the next general election, the Dutch cabinet resigned—because it "broadly subscribed" to the conclusions of the report. Wim Kok, the Dutch prime minister from 1994 till 2002, didn't specify exactly to which conclusions the cabinet—or, for that matter, he himself—subscribed but explained to the parliament that *somebody* had to take on political responsibility for the inability of the international community to prevent the mass murders, and that he had decided that he would be the person to do so.

In the weeks that followed, the report was duly reviewed in newspapers, talk shows, and magazines. Though the NIOD study had toppled a cabinet, it proved extraordinarily difficult to fathom the value of the document. Political journalists had their shots; historians supplied authoritative sound bites; commentators, editorialists, and other pundits ventured tentative evaluations—but behind the coquettish opinions shimmered bewilderment. What to make of this huge number of words about—or at least triggered by—one fatal week in July 1995? In November 2002 a symposium was held at Leiden University in which historians and philosophers of history tried to get some grip on the theoretical underpinnings of the report and, what is more, could discuss their findings with NIOD director (and head of the project team) Professor J. C. H. Blom.[4]

Because (as a historian who is also a psychologist) I had written about the way historians deal with traumatic events, and because I was in the midst of writing a novel about Srebrenica,[5] I attended the Leiden symposium. As I was listening to Professor Blom, it struck me that the words in which he described, explained, and defended his project closely resembled the words in which back in 1993, 1994, and 1995 the political and military authorities had talked about the Dutch mission in and to Bosnia. "We knew," Blom said, "that ours was a very hazardous enterprise." And: "We risked a highly unfortunate result," "We had to build things up from scratch," "It was unsure whether we could muster adequate resources," and so on.[6] This resemblance between *report* and *event*—or, to be more precise, between "what happens in the reporting environment" and "what happened in the environment about which the report is purportedly to report"—reminded me of a phenomenon I had often encountered in my work as a psychologist: the "parallel process."

Dominick LaCapra has remarked that "when you study something, at some level you always have a tendency to repeat the problems you are studying."[7] From a theoretical as well as a societal point of view, parallel processes are important manifestations of this tendency. Broadly speaking, a parallel process is going on when difficulties experienced in one environment are replicated in another environment. The concept originates in psychoanalytic supervision, is used in medical and psychotherapeutic settings, and refers, typically, to instances in which problematic interactions between residents and their patients are mirrored in the teaching encounter, in, that is, the interaction between residents and their tutors. System theorists speak in this respect of "isomorphism"—a term borrowed from mathematics. In general, says Douglas Hofstadter, the term "isomorphism" "applies when two complex structures can be mapped onto each other in such a way that to each part of one structure there is a corresponding part in the other structure, where 'corresponding' means that the two parts play similar roles in their respective structures."[8]

In this chapter I will introduce this phenomenon, examine the way Blom and his fellow NIOD researchers unwittingly replicated several key aspects of the events they studied, and discuss some instances in which paralleling highlights precisely those features of the object of the NIOD study that are hard to come to terms with. I will do this in some detail because the case of the NIOD historians not only raises embarrassing questions about how societies come to terms—or fail to come to terms—with traumatic historical events, but is also completely at odds with how we like to conceive the relation between historians and what they write about. When I tried to clarify what Blom's replications might signify, I realized that the situation I found myself in was rather exceptional. I had written about historical trauma before, but it had always been about painful events that lay far back in the past, about (as the poet says) "old, unhappy, far-off things, / And battles long ago." But now it was all here: a trauma that really was very painful, a nation that somehow had to come to terms with the unacceptable event, and historians (eleven of them) trying to put the catastrophe into perspective. I was (in short) in the midst of my own subject! I even participated in it, for—as I'd better confess here—the trauma was also very much *my* trauma.

The Parallel Process

As a psychologist I used to teach medical doctors to reflect upon their dealings with their patients—because doctors who are able to do so are less likely to stumble into unprofitable antagonisms or, as happens much more often, counterproductive symbioses with their patients. One of the methods I employed is group-supervision, in which physicians discuss unsatisfactory doctor–patient interactions with their peers, while the group-leader signals subconscious group-processes. Using this method, I was time and again struck by similarities between what is observable in the supervision-group, and the ostensible difficulties the doctors have with the patients about whom they are talking. Typically, some aspects of what had happened between the doctor and his or her patient were not verbalized in the story the doctor tells but, as it were, "played out" in the group.

In an article about the Dutch general practitioners training programme I gave the following, rather straightforward, case:

> In the second month of the training, K, a junior GP who has substantially more clinical experience than most other group members, tells the group about a patient who has visited him because of frequent headaches. He reports having examined the patient carefully and having made an effort to help the patient to the best of his abilities: "I even hinted at the possibility that his complaints might have some psychosomatic origins, but he wouldn't go into that." After some consideration he had decided to ask the patient to monitor for two weeks under what circumstances his headaches did in fact occur—to which the patient had responded: "That's all very well, but I'd rather have a referral to a neurologist." K reports that he had felt annoyed, but had nevertheless, "because of the time," consented to the patient's question. In the group K's story is ardently discussed, and a lot of interesting observations and valuable considerations are

made. Initially K listens actively, but in time he seems to lose interest and at the end he shows no signs whatsoever that the discussion has clarified anything. During the ensuing coffee-break K asks the group-leader—within earshot of his fellow group-members: "By the way, what do *you* do in cases like the one I told you about?"[9]

In taking it higher up, K behaves—on another level—in the same way as his patient. Doing so, he evokes the same emotions as he had experienced himself: by his question to the group-leader K humiliates the group, just as he had felt humiliated by his patient. He had unwittingly enacted the aspect of the behavior of the patient that had most infuriated him.

In K's case, at least four things stand out. First: it is not just a random aspect of the reported event that is omitted, but the spot where the shoe really pinches. Though he hadn't realized it, for K, his feeling of having been humiliated by his patient was much more of an issue than the origins of the headaches, the pros and cons of his advice, or the propriety of the referral. A second characteristic is that the parallels are so pervasive: not only the humiliation, but also the exertions (by K as well as by the group) and the time pressure are mirrored. Third, drawing attention to parallels is a way to overcome deadlock. When in the next group session the "coffee-break event" was discussed, K, though initially protesting, acknowledged the parallel and experienced it as a real eye-opener. The fourth feature is that in parallel processes, acting out is wedded to—and hides behind—conventionality. K's behavior was not so conspicuous as to provoke his colleagues to protest, yet conspicuous enough to affect them. His question to the group-leader aroused feelings of embarrassment, of having witnessed something that, though elusive, was definitely off-limits, but these feelings were swamped in the urge to go along with the flow of events. To address K's behavior required the unconventional, "unsociable" act of returning to the subject of his (coffee-break!) question in the next group session—something people are not easily prepared to do.

Parallel processes—like K's question to the group-leader—are subconscious reenactments of past events. They differ in two ways from Collingwoodian reenactments: they do not refer to *in vitro* representations but to real—*in vivo*—interactions, and, second, they are not the intended result of a conscious effort but the unintended ripples of sub-conscious processes. In a sense, a parallel process is a compulsion to repeat. When therapists do not understand what is going on between them and their patients, and consequently are not able to give a satis-factory report about it, they may, by parallel enactment, transmit the elusive aspect of the relationship with the patient to their supervisor. LaCapra's adage that "when you study something, . . . you always have a tendency to repeat the problems you are studying" thus gets a spe-cial twist. When, like K, you are caught up in a parallel process, your behavior repeats key aspects of what there is to know about the prob-lem you study—in a way, however, that you yourself don't understand.

The explanation of this remarkable phenomenon ultimately derives from Freud, who theorized that what is not adequately remembered may be repeated in the therapeutic situation through unconscious enactment.[10] In a groundbreaking article, Harold Searles, elaborating on Freud's idea, stated that enactments are not the prerogatives solely of patients, but occur within the supervision (that is, in the interaction between therapist and supervisor) as well.[11] Searles's supposition that the therapist was a kind of medium through which the enactment of the patient was flawlessly "transmitted" to the supervisor was, how-ever, rather quickly discarded. Since the 1970s most theorists in the field[12] take the position that it is not just idiosyncrasies of the *patient* that may be transmitted to the supervisor, but also (some say: pre-dominantly) idiosyncrasies of the *patient–therapist interaction*—that, in other words, the therapist is not a transparent medium, but part and parcel of what is transmitted to the supervisor. Accordingly, Sachs and Shapiro state that most parallelisms do not refer to the content of the therapeutic process, but to "treatment alliances"—to the tacit rules that form the basis of the therapist–patient relationship.

When a parallel process is operative there is always a dual set of transferences and countertransferences involved—the one, the patient/therapist set, as it were *in absentiae*, and the other in the here and now of the supervisor.[13] Yet parallel processes are not reducible to transferences or countertransferences. Key to parallel processes is a 180° turn of the "middle man"—the therapist. Paralleling occurs when therapists, in the supervision setting, unconsciously identify with their patients, enact this identification, and elicit responses from the

supervisor that replicate the difficulties they themselves have encountered—as *therapists*—in the therapy. This, of course, is a highly ambiguous gambit: the therapist brings up the "itching" relationship she has
with her patient in order to *change* it, but by eliciting the responses
they themselves have got caught up in, also seems to want to *perpetuate* it. But in this respect too, the supervision often mirrors the therapy. In K's case, it would be a good guess that just as K himself wants
both to remain the omnipotent doctor he fancied himself to be *and* to
find more satisfactory ways of dealing with his patients, the patient he
talks about wants *both* to get rid of his symptoms *and* to retain them.

That the therapist presents his case in such an ambiguous way
should not be taken to mean that the underlying problem is not a serious one. It almost always is. In most cases it is even so serious that
the therapist somehow is convinced that "he or she cannot do without it." In fact, parallel processes often point to problems so bound up
with the identity of the therapist that he (or she) feels he (or she) has
no other option than to try to have it both ways: to simultaneously
address the problem and evade it. In their being bound up with identity, the problems feeding into parallel processes resemble (psychological) traumata.[14] Like traumata, they want to be left alone just as much
as they want to be overcome. Unfortunately, when not addressed, this
strategy of having it both ways tends to be self-defeating: it engenders numbness, apathy, and deadlock, and generates an atmosphere
of "Forget about it."

The Ossendrechtse Heide

Remarkably, these were precisely the feelings the NIOD Srebrenica
report generated. In the weeks after the study was published there
was an initial burst of attention—from newspapers, TV stations, week-
lies, and so on—followed a short while later by a welter of articles
in specialized and professional journals. Then there were some con-
ferences and congresses, and finally the two most prominent Dutch
historical journals, the *Tijdschrift voor Geschiedenis* and the *Bijdragen
en Mededelingen betreffende de Geschiedenis der Nederlanden*, devoted
special editions to the NIOD report. Many points were made, many

issues raised, many hypotheses suggested—and there was, on the whole, remarkably little pedantry. Yet, the issues raised did not get any follow-up. Instead, as a Dutch weekly wrote, "silence set in."[15]

That the report led to an atmosphere of "Forget about it" was hardly to be expected. In the first place, because the NIOD study—eagerly awaited and long overdue—addressed the urgent question of how the Dutch could have failed to protect eight thousand Bosnian Muslims from being massacred, it was widely believed that the publication of the report would be the starting signal for a clarifying discussion on why, back in July 1995, things went so terribly wrong. On the basis of the thoroughgoing documentation and informed analysis of the NIOD there would be a kind of collective self-examination from which insights and conclusions would be drawn. That instead of this, apathy set in, was also remarkable because, second, the researchers themselves professed that discussion and reflection were what they had been after. They had taken care, they said, not to steal someone's thunder, and repeatedly declared that now that they had done their job, there could be a blossoming of well-informed discussions.

On consideration, what in fact did happen was not unlike what happened in K's supervision group. After K had talked about his interaction with his patient, the group members eagerly ventured questions, opinions, advice, and interpretations—each to the best of his (or her) abilities, each expecting that his (or her) remarks would be taken up, so that, eventually, K could gain enough insight into himself and his patient to overcome the impasse he had become locked in. Needless to say, the contributions of the group-members—however involved— were not intended as definitive statements. They were provisory inducements meant to get things going. But when nothing really *got* going, when there was no indication that K was seriously considering what was brought up, the group lost focus, and the discussion petered out into a melancholy coffee-break.

Though in the case of the NIOD report there was no single, clear-cut, K-like acting out, there were enough "provocations" to suspect that the report was indeed surreptitiously trying to have it both ways. I hasten to remark that by using the word "provocations" I do not in any way want to suggest that the makers of the report enjoyed putting cats among the pigeons. What I *do* want to say, however, is that they

unwittingly drew enough attention to what they unwittingly wanted
to hide as to merit the hypothesis that a parallel process was going on.
The tendency to "forget about it" that their report engendered might
have been the result of their wanting *both* to explore *and* to evade the
question of what in fact did happen in 1995 in Srebrenica. Were that
indeed the case, then, according to parallel-process theory, the issues
evaded could be expected to be bound up with identity. Chances are,
moreover, that the issues at stake would have been encapsulated in the
"provocations" occurring in and around the report.

Before turning to these "provocations"—and considering the question of what they might both hide and reveal about the Dutch mission to Srebrenica—I will pause for a moment and ask, first, whether
object (the Dutch role in Srebrenica) and subject (NIOD) had enough
in common to enable the subject to identify with the object, and, second, whether identification did in fact manifest itself in the opera-
tional modus of the research group. The questions are crucial, because
a substantial amount of identification is a precondition for parallel
processes to take place. In psychoanalytic supervision this communal-
ity is hardly problematic: the supervision is structured along roughly
the same lines as the therapy. In both settings there is a person seek-
ing help and a person offering help, a person stating a problem and a
person trying to make sense of it, a person presenting disjunction and
a person suggesting conjunction. As a matter of fact this is rather less
unlike the situation in historiography than might have been assumed.
A reader of a historical work—or, to be more precise, the public to
which that work is addressed—is in the same "tertiary" position as a
supervisor: historical reality communicates something to historians,
and historians communicate it to their public.

On top of this, there was, in the case of the NIOD, a more specific
inducement for identification. Surprisingly, in 1996, the year the
NIOD got the assignment to investigate the Dutch role in Srebrenica,
the institute was in roughly the same position the Dutch army was
in 1993, the year in which the United Nations asked the Netherlands
to provide a battalion of peacekeepers for the UNPROFOR-mission to
Bosnia. This similarity sprang from the circumstance that, in the early
1990s, both army and NIOD had to face the fact that what for decades
had been their raison d'être was irremediably gone—both had to find

new tasks, new challenges, new legitimacies. The army, after the end of the Cold War, began to shift its attention to participation in United Nations missions. In 1991, the Dutch minister of defense proclaimed a major reduction in the size of the army, coupled to the creation of an elite "Air Mobile Brigade"—intended as a component of a NATO rapid-deployment force, but tailor-made for politically attractive peace-keeping operations.[16] In 1993 the seriousness of the new orientation was put to the test, when decisions had to be made as to whether the expensive equipment (as, for example, Apache attack helicopters) the army wanted for the Air Mobile Brigade would indeed be purchased.[17]

When, in this climate, the secretary general of the United Nations, Boutros Boutros-Ghali, reminded the Dutch government of its promise to furnish troops for the Bosnian peacekeeping mission, several high-ranking military officials—including the commander of the Air Mobile Brigade—began to maneuver to put the Air Mobile Brigade on offer. Was a mission to Bosnia not an excellent opportunity to show what the brigade was capable of? The commander of the First Army Corps, Lieutenant-General Schouten, declared that it would be "very bad for the attractiveness" of the Air Mobile Brigade "when after two and half years it would not have left the Ossendrechtse Heide other than for a small exercise in Greece."[18] The politicians, headed by the minister of defense, jumped upon this idea, the skeptics were overruled, and—after some juggling and wriggling—the Air Mobile Brigade, though not fully up to strength (there were recruitment problems), not having completed its training, and as yet still provisionally equipped, got its golden opportunity. The feeling was that "Srebrenica" would be a diffi-cult mission, but this feeling was outweighed by the confidence that—with the famous Dutch hands-on approach—the job could be done.

The NIOD, meanwhile, was also in an unprecedented process of transformation. Established in 1945 as the Rijksinstituut voor Oor-logsdocumentatie (RvO, later RIOD),[19] the institute had, by the early 1990s, outlasted its task of collecting, disclosing, and studying the documentary evidence of the history of the Netherlands during the Second World War. The last (twenty-seventh) volume of *Het Koninkrijk der Nederlanden in de Tweede Wereldoorlog*—which had become the mainstay of the institute—was published in 1988, and with the com-pletion of this monumental work the question arose as to whether the institute had a future. Wasn't it time to move its archives to the National Archive, its other collections to the appropriate museums, and its research to the universities—and to close the institute? Or could the NIOD be transformed into an "Institute of Contemporary History"? The discussions hadn't yet reached a satisfactory conclusion[20] when in 1996 J. C. H. Blom, a successful and ambitious professor at Amsterdam University, was appointed the new director. Three days before he was to take up the directorship, Blom was phoned by the minister of education, culture, and science and asked whether he would contract for an "independent and historical-scientific study" of the Dutch role in Srebrenica.[21] Blom, not wanting to get stuck in his own version of the Ossendrechtse Heide, weighed the risks, counted his beads—and jumped on the opportunity the Dutch government so unexpectedly had offered him.

Replications

This identification-inducing origin was planted in identification-enhancing circumstances: the fact that Blom got carte blanche[22] gave him and his group a blank space in which identifications could easily be projected. It was, I think, this unique constellation that caused the Srebrenica researchers to replicate several key features of the Srebrenica mission with such uncanny precision.

In the first place, they took the same moral high ground as the one from which the Dutch Srebrenica policy had been conducted. The moral posture of the then–Dutch government was based on an obliteration of the fact that it had voluntarily taken on the assignment— and might be characterized as a combination of a sense of duty and a sense of being just the right entity to fulfill this duty. Both were copied. Government as well as NIOD presented their task as a "societal imperative,"[23] and both accepted what they saw as their lot with a dissimulated, subdued pride. Rather unsurprisingly, the similarity in posture led to a similarity in consequences. By insisting, for example, that they had taken on the Srebrenica study not because they had wanted to, but because it was a societal imperative, the researchers made Dutch society an accessory to their project in the same way the

Dutch government had enrolled Dutch society in its Srebrenica policy. Consequently, the question of whether—in the case of Srebrenica—this sense of duty deteriorated into a feeling of having to do someone else's dirty work, and to a concomitant erosion of responsibility, had to be answered by researchers who ran comparable risks.

Second, the researchers copied the mode of operation. From the beginning, Blom, like the Air Mobile Brigade and the Dutch cabinet that sent the brigade on its mission, systematically relied on the Napoleonic principle "On s'engage, puis on voit"—or, rather, on the Dutch equivalent of this principle, "de mouwen opstropen,"[24] a combination of willful unpreparedness, lack of interest in the big picture, improvisation, and a hands-on approach. The reliance on this mode of operation might be regarded as the corollary of the fact that neither Blom nor the NIOD had any expertise in their subject when they grabbed the opportunity to study it, but was certainly not inevitable. In the manner of the Air Mobile Brigade—that had not been too interested in the experiences of the Canadian unit it replaced—the NIOD preferred to start with a clean slate and didn't look for, or build upon, expertise that was already available. So, right from the acceptance of the job, the project was pervaded with the "can do" mentality that also determined the Dutch mission to Srebrenica. And in this respect too, what in fact had been a choice felt like a necessity. As the NIOD researchers later said: they had had to "wrestle" with the fact that they "had to build everything up from scratch."[25]

Then, third, the research group replicated the logistic predicament of the Air Mobile Brigade. Because, as an enclave, Srebrenica was completely surrounded by territory controlled by Bosnian Serbs, and because supply by air had been vetoed by the Bosnian Serbs, the brigade was in the position of having to protect prisoners against their jailers while at the same time having to ask these very same jailers permission to enter and leave the jail. The Srebrenica research group ended up in an equivalent logistic dependency when it accepted that access to foreign sources could not be guaranteed. With that acceptance, Blom and his associates made themselves totally dependent on the cooperation of the Dutch government—the government, that is, they might have to criticize. Of course, the Dutch government promised not to interfere in any way, to be forthcoming with documents, and to grant military and government officials permission to talk to the researchers—promises that were subsequently laid down in the contract Blom negotiated.[26] This contract offered enough safeguards to make questioning the independence of the research group—as has repeatedly been done[27]—a dead-end street. The question is rather whether the research group, being in the same logistic predicament as the brigade, might not have been misled by the decency with which the Dutch government refrained from abusing its logistic monopoly. Might this decency not have desensitized the group to the rashness with which the then-government had acquiesced in placing the brigade (and itself) in the logistical nightmare that was Srebrenica? There are no indications that it was a conscious strategy, but given the fact that logistically the research team was in a position equivalent to that of the Brigade, the Dutch government could not have chosen a more potent and vicious way to influence the research group than it did in fact choose: to be decent and forthcoming. Had the Dutch government behaved more "like the Bosnian Serbs"—and used its logistic monopoly more aggressively—it probably would have made the research group more perceptive of the misappraisals on which the Srebrenica mission was founded.

Fourth: Having embarked on his mission, Blom recruited a battalion—not of peacekeepers, but of experts. The Air Mobile Brigade had had major—and increasingly serious—recruitment problems, and consequently, Dutchbat III, the battalion that was in Srebrenica when the Serbs attacked the enclave in July 1995, had to be assembled from personnel of many different units. Dutchbat III therefore was a rather heterogeneous lot: some were very idealistic, some were in it only for the money, some were seasoned, some were green, some were the tough professionals the Air Mobile Brigade had wanted to attract, and some had neither military experience nor ambitions. Because nobody at the NIOD was qualified for the Srebrenica study, Blom also had to bring a team together—and out of all the available options he chose the recruitment policy that most resembled the one the Air Mobile Brigade had employed. The heterogeneous group of specialists Blom assembled (on an ad hoc basis, and in different batches) comprised a journalist, a former Navy officer and military historian, a London-based anthropologist, a specialist in foreign affairs, one of his former students, a teacher in Serbo-Croatian, and a former employee of the Organization for Security and Cooperation in Europe.[28] Of course, the point is not that these people weren't capable—most of them were—but that, by replicating the recruitment policy of the Air Mobile Brigade, the research group came to embody some of the very problems it was supposed to study.

I will mention just two. The most obvious problem springs from the fact that because of its heterogeneity and because it was too new to have traditions, the Air Mobile Brigade lacked esprit de corps. Loyalty was at company—or even platoon—level. The lack of esprit de corps might well have been the reason that Dutchbat III, and especially the Potocari-based staff unit, was afflicted by serious tensions (some of them—as, for example, the bitter feud between an army and a navy medical team—attributable to cultural differences). The question of to what extent these tensions influenced the effectiveness of the battalion when, in July 1995, the Serbs attacked, had to be answered by a research group that, according to several sources, was also plagued by strife and controversy.[29]

Another, perhaps more important, problem has to do with the fact that "recruitment policy" is not a neutral input factor, but points forward to what eventually will count as a good job. The way the NIOD research group was assembled predisposed it to an end result in the form of a collection of individual contributions. Blom and his group seem to have operated on the assumption that as long as all the relevant specialties were represented on their team, and as long as the fruit of everybody's toil found its way into the final report, the group had acquitted itself of its task. Consequently, accumulation, and not synthesizing, distillation, or just plain writing, provided the formal structure of the report. As one of the researchers remarked: "cutting and gluing, that's the way to do it."[30] The supposition that an assemblage of individual contributions could count as a good job may well have led the NIOD group to the perspective from which they assessed the Srebrenica mission: that there is no one to blame when everybody has done his (or her) own individual job to the best of his (or her) abilities.[31]

This conception of duty is inseparable from the fifth way in which the research group replicated their object: the style of leadership. The fact that the title page of the report mentions (apart from the names of the researchers) not one but two persons with whom the "final responsibility" rested,[32] suggests that the group replicated the peculiar dual leadership of Dutchbat III. In Dutchbat III, Lieutenant-Colonel Karremans concentrated on the contacts with the "outside world" (higher UN-echelons, Dutch army headquarters, Serb and Muslim leaders) while his deputy, Major Franken, effectively commanded the battalion on a day-to-day basis. Though this division of labor certainly resembled the one between Blom and his deputy, the dual leadership was probably introduced too late (in 2001) to have influenced the way the group treated their object.

Far more pervasive was, I think, the extent in which the research group replicated Dutch cabinet-style decision-making. Dutch cabinets are—as they are called—"collegial." Ministers have a dual task: each of them is responsible for a department, but together they discuss, decide, and defend the common policy. This common policy is supposed to be monolithic: there is no voting, there are no minority views, discussions are secret, and neither parliament nor public is ever permitted to have a look at cracks or fissures. The task of the prime minister—who has no "spending department" himself—is to chair the cabinet meetings, to take care that the ministers exercise their dual task in a balanced way, and to embody the indivisibility of the common policy.[33] This description neatly describes the method of working the NIOD group chose to employ. The researchers, like ministers, each had to run their own "department," but were to discuss the work of their peers during weekly meetings, and intended to juggle their findings and opinions into common conclusions. Like ministers, they promised not to spill the beans, and like ministers they agreed to keep their mouths shut even when their days in office were long over.[34]

What Blom disclosed about his leadership style suggests that he, for his part, had meant to lead the group in the collegial manner of a Dutch prime minister. Science, remarked Blom (who consistently presented the Srebrenica study as a scientific endeavor), should not take place in "hierarchical surroundings." "Scientists should do their research in freedom, without someone saying at the end of the trajectory: I am right, because I am the boss."[35] In addition to some of the advantages, the cabinet style of doing research also had some of the pitfalls of its governmental counterpart. One of the risks is that when tensions run high, and time begins to press, there is a tendency to neglect the second component of the task: to communicate with your colleagues. This, in fact, happened in the final stages of the making of the report: the researchers became so absorbed by their own "department" that they virtually stopped reading each other's texts.[36] Something of the kind may also have happened in the Dutch cabinet, when in 1993 it had to decide whether to send the Air Mobile Brigade to Bosnia, and in July 1995, when the enclave was overrun by the Serbs.[37] The replicated leadership style almost inevitably led to the replication of the yardstick with which leadership was to be assessed. The NIOD group evaluated the performance of Kok, the prime minister, against the yardstick with which Blom himself wanted to be assessed:[38] the quality with which he had exercised his "regiefunctie" (an untranslatable word, meaning a leadership-style somewhere in between "coordination" and "steering").

LaCapra's remark about researchers repeating the problems they study is rather crassly illustrated by the sixth way in which the NIOD group replicated its object: it created its own enclave. Under the supervision of the AIVD (the Dutch State Security Service), the third floor of the NIOD building was converted into a stronghold that effectively kept outsiders out and insiders in. The doors of the researchers' rooms were strengthened and provided with combination locks and judas holes. To prevent the occupants of the houses on the other side of the canal from peeping in, the windows were covered with curtains. The computers the researchers used were disconnected from the Internet.[39] Not only were the borders with the outside world made as impermeable as possible, but the researchers also *behaved* as if they were surrounded by enemies.[40] They were as anxious about being diddled out of their information as the common Dutchbat soldier was about being robbed of his equipment. The rationale for their locking themselves in was, of course, that the information they worked on might be politically sensitive. They had to imprison themselves, as they themselves afterwards said, because they had to operate "beside and in . . . the political-journalistic complex."[41]

Through the creation of this enclave, a dynamic came into being in which the outside world of Dutch politics, on which the researchers were in any case logistically dependent, began to count as "Serb" (with the journalists as its irregulars) while the research object, with which the researchers had locked themselves in, was "Muslim." The rules of the game implied that as long as the researchers had not acquitted themselves of their "Muslim" research task, the "Serb" "outside world of Dutch politics"—though culturally familiar[42]—was to be distrusted.[43] By making an enclave in the Herengracht NIOD building, the researchers replicated not only the relation with the "enemy," but also the relation the Dutch back in 1995 had had with the Muslims who were entrusted to their care. Behind the perimeter of the strengthened NIOD doors, the troublesome relation of Dutchbat (or rather, the Dutch government) with the Muslim population of Srebrenica was engrafted on the relationship between the researchers and their (unfamiliar) object.[44]

Seventh (and last), the research group copied the combination of protraction, exhaustion, and frenzy that characterized the time frame of the Srebrenica mission. Dutchbat III had had to be relieved on July 1, 1995, but because the Dutch government had got itself into a jam with the United Nations,[45] and because the Bosnian Serbs had intensified their policy of obstructing replacements and blocking supplies, the battalion was in a state of exhaustion when, on July 6, crisis struck. Not surprisingly, this exhaustion, aggravated by severe shortages, impeded the functioning of the battalion and induced, in their headquarters at the Hague—probably even more so than in the field—a feeling of "Let's get it over with." The NIOD research group worked itself into a comparable sequence of protraction and exhaustion when, after having missed the summer 2001 deadline, it also missed the November 2001 deadline.[46] They *had* to be ready on the next date agreed upon: April 10, 2002. Pressure from parliament, public, and press mounted: in May there were to be general elections. It was in these circumstances that a great part of the report had to be written. A "crisis staff" worked from 8 in the morning till 11 in the evening, at dinnertime pizzas were brought in, and some researchers slept in a nearby hotel. "We went along the abyss," Blom later said, "some threatened to collapse."[47]

By replicating the crisis, the research group also replicated the exhilaration of the participants in the original Srebrenica crisis. Blom later compared it to a "pressure cooker"—and its ingredients were similar to the ingredients of the pressure cooker of those hot days in July 1995: apprehension, adrenalin, professionalism—and a wish to get it over with.[48] So, the NIOD campaign ended in an orgy of writing, a delirious "flow" of competency, determination, and improvisation in which in an incredibly short time an impossible number of pages were produced—a number that (when appendices and so on are included) was roughly equivalent to the impossible number of Muslims killed in 1995.[49]

Staying on the Surface

How did the way in which the NIOD research group identified itself with its object affect the content, tenor, and/or conclusions of its work? Before I answer this question, it might be remarked that identifications in themselves are neither good nor bad. They may *diminish* as well as *enhance* the quality of an analysis—depending on the way they are used. Arthur Mitzman has shown how Jules Michelet's identification with the fate of France during the French Revolution went as far as his replicating, in his life, some of the key events he had to describe. In order to narrate the fall from grace of Danton, Michelet orchestrated his own falling from grace. According to Mitzman, Michelet subconsciously brought himself to a position in which he could be fired from the Collège de France, dismissed as the head of the Archives, and sent into exile to Nantes[50]—where he subsequently wrote the famous Danton pages of the *Histoire de la Révolution française*. Being in themselves neither good nor bad, identifications may, however, *diminish* the quality of description and analysis when—as happened in the case of K— their metaphorical provisionality (enabling the subject to understand the object in terms of the subject) somehow gets lost. In such cases, the identifications submerge and assume a life of their own (that is, are taken up in parallel processes)—only to emerge, sooner or later, as acting out or, as I have called them, "provocations."[51]

The best way to identify such unfruitful identifications is not by scrutinizing the story, but by tracking the provocations. However, scrutinizing the story—hermeneutics—is what literate people instinctively do: in the case of K, the group members (working on the hypothesis that because K brought up his interaction with the patient something must be amiss) seized upon the story K told, only to discover that their interpretations, whether sensible, judicious, "true," or not, didn't make any difference. Instead of delving deep, one had better stay at the surface. The important thing, as Freud said, is to conceive of the illness "nicht als eine historische Angelegenheit, sondern als eine aktuelle Macht"[52] ("not as something of the past, but as a force that influences the present"). When acting out takes place, attention should not gravitate to the stories about the "historical" there-and-then before the *actuality* of the here-and-now is clarified. "Staying on the surface" means resisting the temptations the words of the patient, the therapist, or, as in the present case, the historian offer, and trying to concentrate on what in and by the telling is brought about in the encounter between, in the present case, historian and public. "Provocative" acting out is taking place when the rules that determine that encounter (or the relationship in general) are transgressed. Sometimes the rules that are transgressed are *explicit*, but in the majority of cases the *aktuelle Macht* of the unacknowledged identification is brought to bear upon the tacit rules that form the basis of the relationship. Acting out, in other words, usually manifests itself in the "treatment alliance."

Acting out in the form of surreptitiously mocking the treatment alliance[53] is difficult to handle. Addressing the transgression of an explicit rule is relatively easy: addressing the transgression of one of the tacit rules that form the basis of the relationship in which the transgression occurs is very difficult.[54] Technically it is difficult because such "provocations" always have a Janus face: they are "conventional" as well as "subversive," sanctimonious as well as sacrilegious, "constructive" as well as "destructive." If you address the one, you risk being shown the other. In the case of K, attempts to address his coffee-break remark in the next session might seriously backfire because K might profess having forgotten the incident altogether, or he might play to the gallery and say: "What's wrong with being curious?" or "We are here to learn, aren't we?" Addressing such remarks is technically difficult because it means keeping in touch as well as being steadfast, without drifting into a zero-sum game in which either the transgressor, or the person addressing the transgression, feels denuded. On top of this technical difficulty, there is the problem that having to say things about things that should go without saying is literally unsettling. It means that a discussion about *historische Angelegenheiten* (or, more broadly, a discussion on the level of representations) is supplanted by a discussion about the preconditions that regulate and determine that particular discussion. It means, in short, focusing on *function* instead of *intention*—which (as, for example, the reception of Foucault among historians has shown) is a very threatening thing to do.

So, in order to answer the question of to what respect the NIOD–Srebrenica report was influenced by the way the researchers unwittingly identified with their object, one has to resist the temptation to plunge into the text. Instead it is necessary to "stay at the surface" and track the "provocations" in and around the report: where and how did the researchers transgress the tacit rules of the relation between historians and their public? Chances are that in their provocations the researchers repeated, in LaCapra's words, the problems they studied. It might be supposed that in these provocations they enacted those aspects of the "dramatic developments" of July 1995 that were too bound up with themselves—be it as historians, as men and women, or as Dutch citizens. What exactly did the NIOD researchers enact? In this section I will sketch three provocations that, in my view, point to paralleling. I will do this rather cursorily—in order to gain some space to discuss, in the next section, one instance of paralleling at somewhat greater length.

One of the provocations that immediately created a lot of disturbance was the fact that the NIOD research group delivered its 3,394 page report (and the thousands of pages of appendices) with the message that, though the report contained the facts the group had assembled and the "explaining analyses" it had performed, the judgments weren't included (whereupon everybody read the fifty-page "epilogue" to scan for whom the report would mean trouble). As Blom said in his presentation speech: "making judgments is up to others."[55] By its stubborn refusal to pronounce judgment, the NIOD group enacted, I think, the obsessive impartiality of the Dutch policy in Srebrenica. For the researchers impartiality meant withholding judgment on the politicians, the military, and the civil servants who had played some role in the catastrophe. For the Dutch in Srebrenica impartiality had meant that no sides would be taken for or against either the Bosnian Muslims or the Bosnian Serbs. Consequently, in Srebrenica the official policy had been that, while the Serbs had to be kept *out* of the enclave, the Muslims *in* the enclave had to be disarmed.

This policy was paralleled in the report. The NIOD researchers, who in their Herengracht "safe area" had come to regard the outside world of Dutch politics as "Serb" and the research-object with which they were locked in as "Muslim," consistently tried to keep their distance from Dutch politics, while at the same time "disarming" their report by depleting it of (potentially dangerous) judgments. On the face of it, the one might have been a consequence of the other. The more effort it took for the NIOD group to keep the "familiar" world of Dutch politics at a distance (and the better it succeeded in doing this), the more the group felt obliged to fulfill what it saw as the other side of its mission: to disarm the "unfamiliar" research object. Reproaches that the NIOD researchers had purposely spared Dutch politicians therefore are, I think, beside the point.[56] Paradoxically (or, from the perspective of parallel process theory: quite logically), it was precisely their sense of having upheld their "incorruptibility" vis à vis Dutch politics that led them to disarm their report.

A second provocation was the fact that a report that took months (full-time) to read[57] was presented as something that no citizen wanting to join the debate about what had gone so terribly wrong could afford to leave unread. "Historians," said Blom, "have to present their findings in such a way that every citizen can join the debate about moral judgments on the basis of reliable knowledge and analysis."[58] The message was that every participant in the debate had to found his or her opinion on the basis of the "reliable knowledge and analysis" that the NIOD had provided, but that this inexorable substratum of facts could not *itself* be the object of debate. Convinced that the facts they had assembled need not be spoken for, the researchers felt themselves excused to, as Ranke famously put it, "sich gleichsam auszulöschen und nur die . . . mächtigen Kräfte erscheinen zu lassen" ("to vanish as it were into thin air and to let . . . the potent forces speak for themselves")—leaving their public to stare at their report as at the grin of the Cheshire cat. It might be argued that by delivering their (potential) readers to their unmanageable text, by insisting that they (despite its unmanageability) base their decisions on it, and by suggesting that their report was really all there was to know, the researchers placed the (potential) readers in the same position as the Dutch political and military leaders had been vis à vis the original events.

Both in 1993 (when decisions about the participation in the UN mission to Bosnia had to be made) and in July 1995 (when the Serbs attacked), the Dutch leaders acted as if they were at the mercy of events. They felt obliged to take so many facts and circumstances into account that they lost their room to maneuver. This (quasi-)inexorable face of events is paralleled in the (quasi-)inexorable face of the report. The inexorable face of the report is, in turn, a result of the fact that the NIOD group consistently worked under the assumption that the workmanship of the historian yields a body of, as Blom said, "verified facts" and that out of these verified facts "the story as it were forces itself on the researcher."[59] In the same way, in 1993 as well as in 1995, the Dutch politicians acted as if the events in which they were taken up had a "logic" (or a "dynamic") of their own, as if, in other words, "policy forces itself on the politician."[60]

The suggestion that "things just happen as they happen to happen" manifests itself right down to the style of the report. The description, in the "Epilogue," of how the crucial decision was taken to put the Air Mobile Brigade at the disposal of the UN is a case in point.[61] The passive form is profusely used, people "support" some policy, other people are "informed," things are "discussed," people "subscribe" to some "line of policy," people are "strengthened in their views" (whereas other people "strike critical notes"), "foundations for decision-making are laid," points of no return are passed, occasionally somebody even "takes the lead" in something—but in the whole passage nobody ever *decides* something. Nevertheless, a course of events is embarked upon—or, in the words of the report: "The political–journalistic constellation had far-reaching consequences. In fact, the Netherlands put an Air Mobile Battalion at the disposal of the UN without preconditions."[62] This indefiniteness *might* be a characteristic of what is described, but because it *certainly* is a characteristic of the way of describing, it would be a safer bet that the way the researchers present the events mirrors the way the protagonists saw them, that—in other words—the dissociation of doer and deed is paralleled in the dissociation of writer and text.

The third provocation was the fact that on the one hand the Srebrenica study was presented as a scientific endeavor, but that on the other hand the researchers publicly declared that, insofar as they had elucidated the numerous incidents they assumed their public had wanted them to elucidate, their project had no scientific value at all. At the Leiden symposium, Blom called the dozens of pages the report devoted to one of the most publicized issues—the destruction, in a Dutch army laboratory, of photographic evidence of Serb atrocities—"from a scientific point of view totally irrelevant."[63] What, according to the researchers, *was* scientifically relevant, however, was to put research findings in a context "in such a way that the inherent dynamic of the historical process becomes visible."[64] It was to be a recurrent theme in the report: for a "clear understanding" (as the researchers used to call it) events had to be "contextualized" by competent historians.

In their interpretation of what their mission as professional historians was, the researchers enacted, I think, the way the Dutch back in 1995 interpreted their task as peacekeepers. In Srebrenica, the Dutch had taken their task to mean that they shouldn't bother too much about provocations and humiliations as long as they succeeded in their job of keeping the Serbs *out* and the Muslims *in*. The responsible Dutch politicians and diplomats for their part had, during the year and a half a Dutch battalion was in the enclave, operated on the assumption that they shouldn't bother too much about the ("incidental") Srebrenica abscess, as long as they were taken seriously in the international political arenas where a solution for the Bosnian problem was to be found.[65] By regarding incidents not *as* their mission, but as peripheral to or even distractions *from* their mission,[66] the NIOD paralleled the way back then the Dutch—by not bringing their full weight to bear on incidents—were sent barking up the wrong tree.

The inclination of the Air Mobile Brigade to regard incidents as peripheral to its mission was, I think, bound up with its professional identity. In the brigade a distinction was made between on, the one hand, operating in a military mode ("green") and, on the other hand, operating (counterintuitively) in a peacekeeping mode ("blue"—after the color of the UN). It was quite clear that in the "blue" mode you couldn't make full use of your "green" military resources—but how to command respect in a "blue," nonmilitary way was rather less clear. Instead of thinking this problem out, the Air Mobile Brigade from the start interpreted its mission in an ambiguous manner: on the one hand it chose as its prime objective a task that left ample room for its congenial, "greenish," professional identity: to man a perimeter (not quite to defend, but to "observe" it). On the other hand, the brigade tried—by being friendly, helpful, facilitating, and generous—to find a nongreen way for everyday, peacekeeping use.

The consequence of this ambiguity was that as a peacekeeping unit, the brigade did not succeed in becoming authoritative. It did not even gain respect—not from the Serbs, not from the Muslims. It never occurred to the brigade (let alone to the politicians back home) that to respond authoritatively to the daily incidents and humiliations *was* the mission, and not a nuisance that unfortunately was included in the bargain. The predicament of the Air Mobile Brigade was that where its professional identity was (at the perimeter) there was no mission, and where its mission was (in the incidents) there was no professional identity. Not surprisingly, the inability to deal honorably with the daily incidents eventually undermined not only the brigade's belief in itself as a peacekeeping force, but its "green" professional identity as well. Consequently, when in July 1995 the Serbs attacked—and the perimeter was overrun—Dutchbat could not come up with an adequate "green" response. Instead the battalion resorted to a caricature of the way it had interpreted its "bluish" mode of operation: it threw itself on being friendly, helpful, facilitating, and generous to the Muslims who were herded together at Potocari and held at gunpoint by their Serb enemies.

For the NIOD researchers, the congenial "green" mode of operation consisted in being able to bring their "scientific" competency as professional historians to bear on the Dutch role in Srebrenica, whereas investigating incidents (like the destruction of photographic evidence) was mere "blue" peacekeeping. Like the Air Mobile Brigade, the researchers chose a task that was as "green" as possible, and like the Air Mobile Brigade they decided to man a perimeter—in their case the "perimeter" was called "context." Right from the start the researchers

began to work on an ever-expanding perimeter of spatial and temporal context—until the small kernel of the ten days in July 1995 was
surrounded by so many layers (thousands of pages) of context, that,
in the eye of the public to which the report was addressed, it became
almost totally incidental. By acting out, instead of thematizing, the
tension between mission and incident, the NIOD group drew attention to (as well as evaded) what may well have been a major deter-
minant of the Dutch policy to, and conduct in, Srebrenica. Insofar as
the report became yet another instance of a "tragedy in the Balkans"
becoming an "affair in the Netherlands," it perpetuated it.

"To Deter Attacks by Presence"

A provocation I would like to discuss at somewhat greater length is
the peculiar way the NIOD researchers[67] reacted to the historians who
took their report seriously enough to write an article about it. In these
reactions[68] the researchers invariably exhorted their colleagues to
engage in "serious scientific discussions" while showing their teeth to
anyone who did not completely identify with the way the NIOD had
defined its task. I shall not try to demonstrate and tabulate the more
subtle stratagems the researchers used to intimidate their colleagues,
and will restrict myself to the ones that best survive quotation: one of
the historians was called "small-minded," and another "sour"; a whole
group of historians (those interested in theory) was called "arrogant";
there was talk about the "self-appointed detectives of the theoretical
police"; some historians were said to revel in "ostentatious learning";
and so on. All the while the NIOD researchers, in their reactions, did
not yield a single inch on a single issue raised by a single historian.
Instead, they reiterated, explained, and justified what they had done
in their report, and, second, availed themselves of the opportunity to
lecture their colleagues about how to conduct a historical investigation, how to conceive of the societal mission of the discipline, and how
to behave in scientific discussions. This was accompanied by professions of modesty. Time and again the NIOD researchers proclaimed
that neither they themselves nor their report had any "theoretical pre-
tensions" and that they hadn't written their report for the "(historical)

theoretical connoisseur."[69] The only critique the group accepted focused on irrelevant details[70] and the error-laden index.

My point here is not that this pattern of reaction is remarkably similar to the way the Dutch government reacted to the Srebrenica catastrophe[71] (which makes it a replication) but that by transgressing the rule that in professional discussions you play the ball and not the man, it was a provocation of their fellow historians. The ad hominem remarks of the researchers cannot, I think, be attributed to personal characteristics of the researchers or the project leader. Neither can it be maintained that they were polemical responses to polemical attacks. On the contrary: all the intimidating remarks were made in professional journals in response to professional articles written in professional turns of phrase. In fact, Blom and his group did not react at all to reviews in newspapers, magazines, or other "lay" publications, or to articles whose authors had (in the eyes of the NIOD group) insufficient professional credentials. So, though their report was commissioned by the government and intended as a "discussion paper" for a nationwide debate, their peers—being the only ones they wanted to interact with—constituted their real public. The insistence of the researchers, often in the very same paragraph in which they showed their teeth, that they wanted to engage their colleagues in "serious scientific discussions" gives their reactions the Janus face that is so characteristic of parallel processes. By simultaneously calling for and discouraging discussion, the Srebrenica researchers prevented both what they did *not* want (their peers attacking them) and what they *did* want (elucidation). Instead, they instilled an atmosphere of "Forget about it" even they themselves came to deplore.

What did the NIOD group simultaneously want to address and evade in its provocative pattern of reaction? The answer is, I think, that in the way they reacted to their fellow historians, the researchers enacted the Dutch mandate in Srebrenica. This mandate was "to deter attacks by presence." In Srebrenica, the Dutch battalion, too small and too lightly armed to withstand a full-scale attack, had the task of deterring the Bosnian Serbs from overrunning the enclave by being conspicuously present. The assumption was that the Serbs would not dare to harm the Muslim population of Srebrenica because doing so would mean harming Dutchbat, and harming Dutchbat meant incurring the wrath of the international community Dutchbat supposedly represented. The Dutch acquitted themselves of their task by building exposed, uncamouflaged observation posts along the perimeter of the enclave: they calculated that the Serbs would not dare to violate the line demarcated by the Dutch posts. By not yielding an inch, by refusing to compromise, by declining to evacuate positions once taken, by showing their teeth and firing intimidating warning shots when anyone approached too near, by taking up blocking positions when inroads seemed imminent, the NIOD researchers enacted the options that in July 1995 were open to Dutchbat—or rather, to the Dutch government. One might say that right down to its intimidating materiality, the three bulky, closely printed volumes of the report repeat what Dutchbat was supposed to do: to deter attacks by presence.[72]

As in the case of K, the parallels are uncannily pervasive—and point to aspects of the Srebrenica mission that are rather hard to stomach. The professions of modesty may be said to reflect the low-profile approach of which, at the time, Dutch peacekeepers were uncommonly proud. Whereas American, French, or British peacekeepers (like, perhaps, the "self-appointed detectives of the theoretical police") were regarded as a bit trigger-happy or, at least, a bit too heavy-handed to tame passions effectively, the "unassuming" Dutch prided themselves on their ability to pacify animosity in a much more natural way.[73] Moreover, the way the NIOD group appealed to "science" is similar to the way Dutchbat was supposed to represent the international community. Both were "outposts" (the researchers even designating their study "an extreme case of contemporary history"),[74] both (felt they) had to bolster their position by referring to what they felt they represented—a dependence that, in the case of Dutchbat, was utterly betrayed when, in July 1995, the international community left the enclave in the lurch. Further, the wish to stay on speaking terms at all costs was reminiscent of the original Srebrenica mission. Up to the very end the Dutch didn't want to antagonize the Serbs—no matter how crassly those very same Serbs violated the rules and humiliated the Dutch. The researchers, for their part, always wanted to "discuss" things with their peers—no matter how abused they felt when those peers didn't identify with their plight.[75] Then, finally, there were the ambiguous attempts to "civilize the barbarians": the way the NIOD researchers lectured their unimpressed colleagues reflecting the way Dutchbat—or, rather, the Dutch—tried to breathe some civilization into the Balkans.[76]

The peculiar manner in which the NIOD researchers tried to deter attacks by their mere presence also reflects an unflagging belief in the rule of law—or, perhaps more accurately, a belief in the unassailable priority of the "law of rules." This belief—which was a key feature of the Dutch Srebrenica policy—betrays itself in the provocative inappropriateness with which the NIOD researchers employed Dutchbat "rules of engagement" in a scientific setting. The Dutch attitude with regard to rules showed itself both in the content of the "rules of engagement" the researchers chose to apply, and—perhaps more importantly—in the extent to which they made themselves dependent on them. As to the rules per se, the NIOD group made it unmistakably clear that they would refuse to join battle with "irregulars"—journalists or other nonacademics alike. Moreover, it unilaterally defined the terms on which it was prepared to fight—and only with the persons who happened to have the right marks and badges—and backed up its conditions with an appeal to an absent higher authority. Then, it didn't accept arbiters, which of course was a logical concomitant of its unilateralism—and which, incidentally, made it essential that "theoretical historians" be provoked out of their proclivity for addressing rules, conditions, presuppositions, and other things that go without saying. Finally, it chose the terrain—which was to be not inside, but at the perimeter of, the enclave of the report. The researchers bluntly stated that, "as a rule," "in the report there was to be no discussion with earlier publications."[77]

The most conspicuous parallel, though, was not the substance of the rules, but the degree to which the NIOD group made itself dependent on them. Macaulay relates in his *History of England* that Lord Galway was beaten in the Battle of Almanza because he preferred losing by adhering to the rules to winning by disregarding them. In Srebrenica, in 1995, the Dutch did something of the same. Right to the time of their retreat, when around them the Muslims they had undertaken to protect were massacred by the thousand, the Dutch felt bound to "rules of engagement" by which they had much to lose and nothing to win. It was a dependence on two levels: in the enclave (in their dealings with the Serb attackers), and in the international political arena (in their relations with the UN and the UNPROFOR command and control system). It is an ugly and painful fact that—though on both levels their opponents did not live up to, disregarded, or transgressed the rules agreed upon, and though adhering to the rules is far more disadvantageous to the weak than to the strong—the Dutch persevered to the very end in upholding rules that had lost any validity. This dependence is completely reiterated in the descriptions, analyses, and conclusions of the report. "In the given situation," the NIOD writes about the Dutch obligingness in the face of the Serb attack, "it wasn't reasonable that Dutchbat—on its own accord or pressed by the Dutch government—would have gone against the grain of the line that was agreed upon. Such an initiative to a different way of acting should have originated from the higher UNPROFOR echelons or from the ultimately responsible UN."[78]

The uncritical reiterations of rule-dependency[79] are, I think, consequences of the way the NIOD paralleled the Dutchbat mandate to deter attacks by its mere presence. In their report the NIOD researchers were just as "reasonable" as the Dutch had been in 1995—and they wanted, in turn, to have their report measured with the same yardstick—that is, in terms of the same "rules of engagement." Naturally, the historians who wrote articles about the report, not knowing the rules of engagement they were supposed to apply, couldn't help violating them. Rather than inferring from the critique of their colleagues that they had been unconsciously dependent on a narrow and inappropriate set of rules, the researchers interpreted criticism that didn't comply with "their" rules of engagement as "smoking guns" that justified retaliation.

Conclusion

To take stock of the NIOD Srebrenica study by means of parallel process theory raises enough questions to justify ending on a meditative note. In the first place there is the question of validity. As I write, I am still amazed by the extent to which what happened in and around the NIOD study can be accounted for by the parallel processes that revealed themselves in the casual remarks of Professor Blom at the Leiden symposium. But is the extent to which the NIOD study can be interpreted in terms of the events it describes as an artifact of a meta-phoric way of looking at things, as an epiphenomenon of something else (as for example "Dutch culture" or "Dutch national character"), or as what I think it is: a genuine, logical, and comprehensive—albeit also an unsettling and a bit eerie—manifestation of unconscious identifica-tion processes? In the context of psychiatric supervision the validity of a parallel process interpretation can be ascertained by asking, Does it work? In supervision there always is a dual check: a valid interpreta-tion leads to a sense of relief by the group members that the (factual and emotional) phenomena they have experienced can be so parsi-moniously explained; it breaks deadlock and occasions the group to resume its work in a productive manner. A second check is that a truly valid interpretation starts a process of significant behavioral change in the therapist who brought the case up. Though, of course, the opera-tionalization differs in the case of history, the test of the interpretation put forward in this book also has to be: Does it work? Which, in the present case, means: Does it fit the facts? Is it convincing? And, per-haps, does it eventually break the deadlock of "Forget about it"?

Second, there is the question of representativeness. In some respects the NIOD Srebrenica study may have been atypical. The similarity between, on the one hand, the psychological position from which Blom and his group embarked on their project and, on the other hand, the position from which the Air Mobile Brigade went to Bosnia was quite exceptional. The same holds true for the unique, identification-enhancing blank space into which the infrastructure of the study could be projected. Then: the scarce information that leaked out of the research group suggests that right from the start an uncommonly compelling kind of group-think was operative. Group members dissuaded themselves and their colleagues from reflecting on what in fact they were doing—both as individuals and as a sys-tem—and if they did, they dared not address the matter and so pre-cluded the group from altering the course it had hit upon. The extent to which the NIOD group replicated its object may finally have been augmented by incomplete and tricky conflict resolution. LaCapra has identified two extremes in trying to come to terms with emotional response. On the one hand there is "full identification, whereby you try to relive the experience of the other"; and on the other hand there is "pure objectification, which is the denial of transference, and blockage of affect as it influences research, and the attempt to be as objectifying and neutral an observer as possible—whether as an empirical fact gatherer or as a structural-formal analyst."[80] The articles by Blokker and Van der Horst suggest that in the NIOD group there was a conflict between "identifiers" (who tended to identify with the Muslim victims) and "objectifiers" (who wanted to historicize the Srebrenica event). The identification that eventually came about (not with the *victims*, but with the *research object*) may have been the (unintended, unconscious, and ultimately invalidating) "compromise" between these two factions.

But favorable though circumstances may have been in the NIOD case, they do not, I think, fully explain how the event came to be so surprisingly faithfully enacted in and around the report. The circumstances may account for the *scope* of the identification, the *flagrancy* of the provocations, and the *comprehensiveness* of the parallels, but can hardly be held responsible for the *tendency* to identify, the *urge* to provoke, and the *propensity* to enact the things that are too hard to tell. This, of course, raises the question whether parallel processes are common phenomena in the history of historiography. They may well be. In fact, I see no reason why they shouldn't arise when pervasive identification is accompanied by absence of reflection. Rather than an unfortunate blemish on the histories in question, this may be a happy opportunity, for, as I think I have demonstrated, parallel processes are not only real-life phenomena, but effective analytical instruments as well. Studying historical works from the perspective of parallel process theory may uncover mechanisms that otherwise are silently replicated. By making use of parallel process theory, "sources" can be tapped that otherwise stay outside the range of the historian or the historiographer of history—as, for example, the "surface-sources" of the responses evoked in and by the confrontation with a historical text. Finally, studying historical works by means of parallel process theory transcends the introversion of both postmodernist theory of history and the positivist practice of history. Studying the "surface" of the practice of history from a parallel process point of view is a fruitful and exciting way to reconnect words and deeds, representations and events, historiography and history.

I will conclude with what, I think, is the most troubling aspect of the phenomenon I have described. Historians like to believe that *if* there is any interaction between themselves and their objects, then it is surely a "Kantian" interaction, an interaction, that is, in which the research object is prefigured by what they, as subjects, bring to bear on it. I think the most disturbing consequence of this whole parallel process thing is that historical knowledge may be much more "Aristotelian" than we like to acknowledge. Historical knowledge may be determined—to a degree that is barely imaginable—by *the object* of research. Or to put it somewhat more succinctly: historians may be the plaything of their objects, instead of the other way around.

3

Presence

Erst wie eine fremde Gewalt [der Mensch] ergreift, ihm forttreibt, und . . . in ihm lebendig wird, kommt wirkliches und wahrhaftes Daseyn in sein Leben.

—Fichte[1]

Philosophers of history have long been led astray by the phenomenon of "meaning"—first by pursuing it, then by forswearing it. The story of how philosophers of history have read meaning *into* history ends somewhere in the 1960s. The story of how they have tried to read it *out of* it begins with Geyl and Popper and is—though there is not much of an audience left—still being told. The first story is much too long and much too fascinating to tell here, in this chapter, but there is no escaping saying at least something about how—in the last three or four decades—philosophers of history have tried to purge their—my—discipline of attempts to establish meaning. I might as well start this sketch by recalling that before it was kissed from its slumbers by linguistics, philosophy of history consisted of two parts: "critical" and "speculative" philosophy of history.[2] Speculative philosophy of history was about *res gestae* and endeavored to reflect from some elevated perspective on what had happened in the past. Critical philosophy of history was concerned with what historians in fact do, which, in the early 1970s, amounted to, as Arthur Danto has remarked, "bickering over the adequacy of the Covering Law Model."

The two parts have fared very differently. At the time philosophy of history became infatuated with linguistics—the early 1970s—speculative philosophy of history, compromised by ideological *parti pris* and undermined by the belief that statements had to be falsifiable in order to be taken seriously, was already thoroughly discredited. Critical philosophy of history, on the other hand, was an established—though not very exciting—academic discipline and (being engaged with history as it was or should be *written*) in a good position to benefit from what linguistics had to offer. The flowering of the new, "narrativist" version of critical philosophy of history was facilitated by, and contributed to, what may be called the "memory crisis" of the 1970s.[3] This crisis—characterized by a growing belief in the existence of "repressed memories" and a diminishing trust in recollections that are "at hand" in the stories we entertain—was not just a matter of how *individuals* relate to their past. It also pervaded the way *societies at large* relate to their pasts. So it is, I think, not just a coincidence that the year Flora Rheta Schreiber's book about the sixteen personalities of "Sybil" was a bestseller (1973) was also the year Hayden White's *Metahistory* was published. Both books bear witness to the emergence of what we nowadays take for granted: that there is a schism between what actually happened in the past and the way memories coagulate into (biographical or historical) plot.[4]

It was, I think, precisely because it concentrated on what lies on the near side of this schism—on, that is, the coagulations that are present in the form of historical texts—that the new philosophy of history came to prosper. Having freed itself from the burden of the past, it became, for a while, one of the most dynamic regions of the discipline of history. In the new philosophy of history there was no room for what in the old days had belonged to "speculative" philosophy of history.[5] It is one of the ironies of White's deeply ironic *Metahistory* that it was to become the major landmark in a process in which philosophy of history was emptied from reflection on what had actually happened in the past, from the search for "laws" and patterns, from questions about how history comes about, from—in short—all brands of metahistory. So, in fact if not in intent, *Metahistory* did away with the last vestiges of metahistory and inaugurated the heyday of "metahistoriography." The practice of putting historical reality within parenthesis surfaces, for example, in Saul Friedländer's introductory remarks in the seminal *Probing the Limits of Representation*: "It will be evident . . . that none of the contributors has forgotten the horror behind the words."[6] The debate *itself*, however, was not about the horrors but about the words, and it might be maintained that in discussing the "limits of representation" the contributors wittingly or unwittingly drew attention to the limits not of representation but of *representationalism*.

Even now it remains an article of faith: as a philosopher of history you don't "speculate." In his attempt to define an up-to-date mission statement, Aviezer Tucker reduces philosophy of history to "philosophy of historiography."[7] And though his counsel to ignore all "problems that cannot be decided by an examination of historiography, such as the logical structure of explanation and the relation between language and reality"[8] is evidently not taken to heart even in the pages of *History and Theory* and *Rethinking History*, few would disagree that the core business of philosophy of history is the study of "the nature of historiographical knowledge and the metaphysical assumptions of historiography." The taboo on metahistorical questions is even projected on the process of history itself. One of the *idées reçus* in philosophy of history (and a hallmark of cultural rectitude) is that "the time of the big stories is over"—a phrase that hypostatizes what philosophers of history *used* to do at the same time it canonizes their current timidity. Jörn Rüsen remarked some time ago that "the master narrative of the West is that we don't have a master narrative,"[9] although it is probably not primarily "the West," but the discipline of history that shuns big stories. Politicians and journalists talk without much reserve about jihads and clashing civilizations. And outside the history departments, political scientists, economists, and biological anthropologists do rather uninhibitedly what historians and philosophers of history have forbidden themselves to do—to the extent that Samuel Huntington's Department of Government of Harvard University has been designated "the world center of substantive philosophy of history."[10]

On consideration, even *within* the discipline of philosophy of history "speculation" is an ineradicable—though zealously dissimulated—phenomenon. I will pass over the fact that it is logically impossible to prove that something (weapons of mass destruction, the monster of Loch Ness, a master narrative) does *not* exist, and that, consequently, the (unfalsifiable) supposition that history has no master narrative is in itself speculative. More important is the fact that even on the level of their texts philosophers of history can hardly avoid "speculation." Just visit a conference, read a copy of *History and Theory*, or order a history book—and admit: speculative statements by the dozen. There's nothing wrong with this. On the contrary, philosophers of history are—like all professionals—"their own instruments":[11] they are in the business at all, and write what they write, because they bring what is a major ingredient of that instrumentality—their own historicity—to bear on what they gather from their objects. Purging this instrumentality *really*, instead of only nominally, of "speculative" ideas and suppositions about history and historicity would result in triviality, inanity, or even total aphasia.

There can be little doubt that the sense that it is somehow improper to establish *meaning* is a key ingredient in the ban on speculation.[12] It stands to reason that this almost phobic reaction to meaning has to do with the horrors of twentieth-century history. But however it is motivated, in the long run this abstinence doesn't agree well with a passion to account for the role history and historicity play in human life. And indeed, speculation, barred from the front door, is already coming in through the back door. Some recent trends in the philosophy of history may be comprehended as subconscious attempts to circumvent the prohibition to aim openly at meaning. The busiest and liveliest speakeasy of the "prohibition era" is, I think, the topic of "trauma." "Trauma" may be regarded as a kind of negative—and politically correct—equivalent to "meaning." Fathoming trauma caters to the same need to reflect on time and memory, failure and success, individuality and historicity, life and death, as more upbeat attempts at perspectivity. In this sense, exploring trauma—and its belatedly born twin brother, agency—is the substantive philosophy of history of modern days.

Remarkably, the taboo on openly looking for meaning in the sphere of *res gestae* coincides with an unprecedented knowledge about how in the sphere of *historia rerum gestarum* meaning comes about. Thanks to Whitean representationalism we have never known more about how historians wittingly and unwittingly construe meaning in, and by the way they tell, their stories. Whitean representationalism, however, is mainly a "negative," critical tool. Used in a positive, "substantive," "speculative" way, it creates—by being bound up with metaphor—continuity on wherever it lays its hands. And—after the unimaginable discontinuities of twentieth-century history—facile continuities are not the kind of meanings we can accept as appropriate, satisfactory, and convincing. In its "substantive" form, Whitean representationalism is like the man in the fairy tale who sees his wish fulfilled that everything he touches turns into gold—only to discover that the food he desperately wants to eat changes into precious, though uneatable, metal the moment he brings it to his mouth.

It's rather tragic: we want something badly, we know perfectly well how to *make* what we want so badly—yet we forbid ourselves to act upon our knowledge and keep wandering in the dark. Clearly something has gone wrong. In this chapter I take the position that, on consideration, it is not *meaning* we want but something else, something that is just as fundamental, something that outside philosophy of history, in society at large, is pursued with a vehemence quite like the vehemence with which philosophers of history believe only meaning can be pursued. For it is, I think, not a need for meaning that manifests itself in, for example, nostalgia and retro-styles, in the penchant for commemorations, in the enthusiasm for remembrance, in the desire for monuments, in the fascination for memory. My thesis is that what is pursued in the Vietnam Veterans Memorial, in having a diamond made "from the carbon of your loved one as a memorial to their [sic] unique life,"[13] in the reading of names on the anniversary of the attack on the World Trade Center, in the craze for reunions, and in a host of comparable phenomena, is *not* "meaning" but what for lack of a better word I will call "presence."

Presence, Discontinuity, and Metonymy

"Presence," in my view, is "being in touch"—either literally or figuratively—with people, things, events, and feelings that made you into the person you are. It is breathing a whisper of life and reality into what has become routine and cliché—it is fully realizing things instead of just taking them for granted. By "presence" I do *not* mean the fulfillment of a wish to stop time, and preserve, respect, and honor what you happen to possess. The need for "presence"—and the drive behind all brands of commemorations—is a veritable *passion du réel*—as Alain

Badiou has called it.[14] It is a desire to share in the awesome reality of people, things, events, and feelings, coupled to a vertiginous urge to taste the fact that awesomely real people, things, events, and feelings can awesomely suddenly cease to exist. Artists who take care that their work is as incontrovertibly *there* as it can possibly be strive for presence. So do people who do away with the conventionalities, the emptiness, and the spuriousness of daily life in order to establish or reestablish contact with, as Fichte said, "wirkliches und wahrhaftes Daseyn." Presence—being in touch with reality—is, I believe, just as basic as meaning. Whereas meaning may be said to be the connotative side of art, of consciousness, of life, presence is the denotative side. Both meaning and presence are antithetical to another drive, the drive to be taken up in the flux of experience. But, again, opposition to this drive, however heartfelt, doesn't necessarily have to take the form of a struggle for meaning. It may also be a quest for presence or, as in a work of art, an attempt to create an endurable and enjoyable intersection of both meaning and presence.

What I call the need for presence has been recognized—or at least acted upon—for quite some time *outside* philosophy of history. It has also left its mark on the domain of history. It inspired Pierre Nora's *Lieux de mémoire* project; caused the spate of books and articles about monuments, commemorations, remembrance, and memory (collective or otherwise); and motivated the launching of the journal *History and Memory*. The attention is fully justified. The need for presence may be said to be the existential equivalent of one of the key issues in history and for historiography: the problem of continuity and discontinuity. It is a manifestation of the will to account for the fact that we are completely unchanged yet completely different from the person we used to be. It is a symptom of the determination to account for the fact that our past—though irremediably gone—may feel more real than the world we inhabit. But however urgent and relevant both the need for presence and the problem of continuity and discontinuity are, philosophers of history have refrained from trying to account for them—partly, I believe, because their focus on "meaning"—both as something to pursue and as something to oppose—put them on the wrong track, partly because they didn't want to be accused of speculation, and partly because the fact that they lacked the tools to deal with the phenomenon led them to believe that it wasn't there.

In this chapter I will argue that the concept of *metonymy* is a surprisingly suitable tool for coming to grips with discontinuity and with the need for presence. Or, rather, I believe that by exploring metonymy, a discourse of presence can be established that does not explain discontinuity away in some sort of "meaning," but gives it its due. The traditional discourse of meaning couldn't do this. Old-fashioned substantive philosophy of history was adept at suggesting meaning by constructing continuity—whereupon representationalism unveiled the mechanics of this process and so deconstructed the substantive attempts at meaning. But, unfortunately, discontinuity is not what is left when you have deconstructed continuity. Accounting for discontinuity requires addressing not primarily the question of how continuity is created, but how *discontinuity is brought about*. I think it is precisely here that the trope of metonymy can be helpful. Metonymy can teach us something about the "mechanics" of discontinuity—both on the level of *res gestae* (or as Spinoza called it, the *ordo et connexio rerum*) and on the level of *historia rerum gestarum* (Spinoza's *ordo et connexio idearum*).[15] Metonymy—the trope, as I will explain later, of "presence in absence"—illuminates the seemingly strange, but in fact very common, phenomenon of our being able to "surprise ourselves." My thesis is, to put it somewhat paradoxically, that metonymy is a metaphor for discontinuity. Or, rather, that metonymy is a metaphor for the entwinement of continuity and discontinuity. Whereas representationalism has given us an unprecedented insight into how continuity is created, metonymy can account for man's inordinate ability to spring surprises on himself.

This, indeed, is how, in my opinion, "discontinuity" might best be conceived: as our being surprised by ourselves.[16] I will have to say more about this particular conception of discontinuity later, but would like to introduce here, at this point, two distinctions. The first is the rather obvious one that humans can surprise themselves with their words as well as their deeds. Differently put: their ability to "spring surprises on themselves" is operative on both the level of the *ordo et connexio idearum* and the level of the *ordo et connexio rerum*. My second distinction is the somewhat less obvious one that on both levels surprise can be passive as well as active. Or, to put it more ceremoniously, humans' ability to surprise themselves comes in two modalities: retroactive and proactive. They can either (passively) let themselves be overwhelmed by what has been written or done before, or they can (actively) overwhelm what has been done before by fresh words or actions.

The brand of discontinuity with which historians are most familiar results from the "proactive" dynamism of historical actors. It refers to the fact that every now and then we, as historical actors, give in to the urge to make some nice little history, and flee and stumble happily forward into *terra incognita*.[17] It includes (among many, many other examples) not only the falling of the Berlin Wall, but also Leopold II's resolve to civilize the Congo, and George Bush's determination to bring "freedom and democracy" to the Middle East. At least as interesting, however, is the phenomenon that (on the level of the *ordo et connexio idearum) as historians too* we may sometimes proactively "flee forward"—in this case to approaches, books, or insights we hadn't even dreamt of. In both cases we find ourselves back in situations we couldn't foresee, yet which are unmistakably real and have an exhilarating presence—situations that confront us with the task to "catch up" with the history, or the view of history, we ourselves have somehow created.

Despite the prevalence of the proactive form of discontinuity, for philosophers of history the retroactive forms of discontinuity are perhaps the most fascinating. On the level of the *ordo et connexio rerum* retroactive discontinuity occurs when we are "overtaken by history" and start—regressively—to do things that are at odds with our identity. It is a kind of historical compulsion to repeat—as in, for example, the building, by the Israelis, of a wall to keep the Palestinians out, and the compulsion (on the part of Americans) to use Saddam Hussein's Abu Ghraib prison for the very same things it had wanted to eradicate root and branch by invading Iraq. Last but not least, there is retroactive discontinuity on the level of the *ordo et connexio idearum*. This anomalous variety of discontinuity includes all instances in which we, as subjects, are overwhelmed by the presence of the past—as in *Sehnsucht* and nostalgia, in Johan Huizinga's "historical sensation," in what Frank Ankersmit calls "sublime historical experience,"[18] and, finally, as we have seen in the previous chapter, in the mind-boggling cases where the object of their research controls and prefigures the histories historians write.

Here, in this chapter, I will try to account for discontinuity by addressing the question of how we spring surprises on ourselves, how we—as historians as well as historical actors—treat ourselves to unimaginable and unsettling historical or representational faits accomplis. I do not propose a return to old-fashioned, un-self-conscious "speculation." The modern, up-to-date philosophy of history I have in mind accounts for discontinuity not by being more inclusive, more creative, and more "speculative" on *one* level (as Spengler or Toynbee did), but by tying in with the fact that, as my definition suggests, discontinuity is a matter of different levels. For, in order to "spring surprises on yourself" you have to be on two levels. Or, to put it somewhat less graphically: you can only surprise yourself if you exist on different planes, and if the connection between these planes is less than open and transparent. Because in history there is no equivalent for what for the individual is the absolute discontinuity of death, historical discontinuity is always, I wouldn't say *relative*, but irremediably bound up with continuity. As soon as you try to solve the riddle of discontinuity by studying it in isolation, the phenomenon either vanishes or turns into the inedible gold of continuity.[19]

Walking the Plane of Time

To understand how continuity and discontinuity are entwined we had better start by forgetting about time and instead approaching the past in the manner Frederick the Great approached his enemies on the battlefield: obliquely. Coming to grips with discontinuity requires an adjustment many philosophers of history will hesitate to make: to focus not on the past but on the present, not on history *as what is irremediably gone*, but on history *as ongoing process*. It is an adjustment not unlike the momentous modification Freud came to make in his approach to the past of his patients. Somewhere around 1900 Freud stopped heading for that past *straightaway*. Instead of delivering himself to the alluring stories his patients volunteered to tell him, he opted not for a Rankean "turning to the sources," but for a radical (and

counterintuitive) "presentism." By sticking to the present as stead-
fastly as he could, by exploring the symptoms and the transferences
that made themselves *felt in the here and now* of the analytic encounter, Freud was able to come forward with much more "original," much
more "convincing," much more "effective," versions of the past of his
patients than they had entertained themselves.

Freud, in short, discovered that what looks like the royal road to
the past never takes you anywhere but to places within sight of your
point of departure, whereas exploring the present may have you,
somewhere, someplace, tumbling into depths you didn't suspect were
there. In the same way, innovative historical thinking does not *start*
with focusing on history, but *ends up* with it. It does not plunge into
history right away, but starts with trying to ascertain in what respects
the present cannot be understood *but by* turning to history. The past
that is easily accessible, that spreads its legs and offers itself to for-
nication, that circulates—as a kind of "shareware"—through society,
that past is, well, perhaps not exactly *dead*, but surely not much more
than a reflection of what we already know. The past, however, that is
absent from our own mythology, the past that is withheld verbally,
the past that is a subconscious *Aktuelle Macht* rather than freely cir-
culating "shareware," *that* is the past that waits to be made sense of.
And that was what the NIOD researchers I discussed in the previous
chapter failed to do.

Res gestae—or, to borrow Spinoza's phrase once more, the *ordo
et connexio rerum*—thus should be taken to mean "the cross-section
through time that presents itself at any one moment to consciousness," to mean, in other words, "the reality we live in." In the same
way, *historia rerum gestarum*, Spinoza's *ordo et connexio idearum*, may
be conceived of not as what some dead white males have written,
but as the assemblage of texts, methods, codes, habits, topics, trends,
and fashions that we *now* regard as the praxis, or discipline, of history. Defined in this way, both structures—"present-day reality" as
well as "the discipline of history"—offer themselves to the eye as *surfaces*—surfaces consisting of elements of different historical "depths."
To scan, with an "evenly suspended attention," the *surface* of what
happens in the therapeutic session was what Freud advised his colleagues to do.[20]

Both surfaces—"present-day reality" as well as "the discipline of history"—may be compared to a *city*. There are "structures" of all kinds of sizes and functions, some very old, some relatively new, some still under construction. Some parts of the city are booming, and others lie fallow. Some parts are carefully restored, while others are dilapidated. There are areas that once were destroyed by war (which may or may not have left traces), areas that have been completely transformed by public works, areas in which "time has stood still." There are ghettos and prime locations, stations and malls, monuments and no-go areas, garbage dumps and sanctuaries, and, of course, there is an endlessly complicated, though more-or-less working, infrastructure, partly visible, partly subterranean, partly even wireless. I wouldn't call such a city a palimpsest: a city is not *uniformly* written over, but locally, irregularly, opportunistically, erratically. The point I want to make is that both surfaces, "present-day reality" and "the discipline of history," are, *at one and the same time,* a tightly knit, "organic," functioning whole as well as a jumble of things that are genetically, ontologically, and existentially separate. Both are—and I repeat: *at one and the same time*—a wonder of continuity as well as an orgy of discontinuity.

"Continuity" and "discontinuity" are to be considered, that is, *not* in a historical, temporal, "vertical" sense, but in the spatial, "horizontal" sense of "being thoroughly interwoven" and "radically contiguous." Trying to envision continuity and discontinuity in its temporal sense is so hard as to be virtually impossible. To understand continuity and discontinuity requires being able "to walk around" the events in question—but as soon as we start to look backward, the second dimension needed for approaching events from different angles somehow gets lost. It seems that the difficulty in experiencing time as "planular," let alone "spatial," comes with modern culture. Henry Glassie mentions that until recently in rural Ulster, time was experienced relative to "Great Days which rise out of time like hills off the land, signaling centers, letting boundaries drift from attention."[21] We moderns, however, have disciplined and straightened time so thoroughly that it requires an enormous, almost Proustian effort to "unthink" the linearity to which we have accustomed ourselves.

Interestingly, from Saint Augustine to Pierre Nora, writers fascinated by the problem of continuity and discontinuity have translated time into space. Some of the most perceptive of them were novelists and wayward geniuses who have not been taken very seriously by historians and philosophers of history. Analyzing how, for example, in the literary imagination problems of time have been transformed into, and treated as, problems of place, would require a study of its own, but such a study would surely have to include Walter Scott. Scott frequently likened his books to "journeys,"[22] and in *Waverley* the landscape of Scotland is not just a scenic backdrop, but the dense, laden, and multifarious presence of what had happened in Scottish history between the mid-seventeenth and the mid-eighteenth centuries. Wandering through this present past, Edward Waverley hits upon history in the places he visits and the people he meets, and the bodily felt spatial relations make him realize that, for example, the abominations of a civil war are simultaneously very close and very far away. "It seemed like a dream," Scott writes, "that these deeds of violence should be familiar to men's minds . . . as falling within the common order of things, and happened daily in the immediate vicinity, without his having crossed the seas, and while he was yet in the otherwise well-ordered island of Great Britain."[23]

More visionary still than Scott was Balzac, a novelist obsessed with recent revolutionary history, but one who, after *Les Chouans*, refrained from writing historical novels. Balzac is not just "the chronicler" of Restoration France, but the prime example of the writer who translates time into space. The reader of the *Comédie humaine* gets the impression that Balzac was unable to experience the past other than as actual presence—and that he could not experience the present other than as a potential past. Balzac "sees" the places he describes by, on the one hand, fathoming their historical depth, and by, on the other hand, wondering how they will look as "history" to later generations. In the *Comédie*, Balzac performs his trick of translating time into space on different levels. On the most general level, he treats the continuities and discontinuities between the ancien régime and post-Napoleonic France in terms of the relations between the countryside and Paris. On a medium scale there is that "most philosophical city," Paris.[24] For Balzac, deciphering Paris is fathoming history. The *quartiers, faubourgs,* and *hôtels* of the Parisian metropolis embody, in Balzac's universe, the actual presence of the revolutionary period *itself*—with himself as its historian turned *secrétaire*.[25]

Smaller still is the scale in the book that may be regarded as the "navel" of the *Comédie, Le peau de chagrin*. In *Le peau de chagrin* (1831) so much history is crammed into so small a space that the reader cannot help but feel a bit claustrophobic. In three rooms of an antiquary shop things from all times and places are assembled, the whole of history, secular, cultural, spiritual, without any order. In this "philosophical garbage dump"[26] the *peau* itself, the little ass's skin, embodies what for Balzac was the real heritage of the revolution and the ultimate challenge of his time: the fact that the process of history had lost its self-explanatory nature as something that was *given* (or taken care of by God or his earthly substitutes) and had to be taken in hand by taxpayers turned citizens. The exhilarating power of being able to plot a course into the future comes at a cost—the cost, as Balzac sharply observes, of life. Balzac characteristically describes the competing claims of history and life in the spatial metaphor of the size of the ass's skin. The magic of the skin is that "the circle of your days, represented by this Skin, will shrink according to the strength and number of your desires."[27]

A contemporary example of an author who translated time into space is W. G. Sebald, whose heroes (if such they may be called) roam and drift like modern-day Waverleys over the surface of a rebuilt but "superficial" postwar Europe.[28] For them, as for Waverley, only for one being on the spot does history acquire reality. Sebald describes the work of his colleague Peter Weiss as a "pilgrimage over the arid slopes of our cultural and contemporary history in the company of *pavor nocturnis*, the terror of night, and laden with a monstrous weight of ideological ballast,"[29] which, except for the fact that Sebald's characters travel with a rucksack that is much too small to contain any ideological ballast, is a good description of his own art as well. The protagonists of *The Rings of Saturn* and *Vertigo* sense the horrors of twentieth-century European history in and by the places they visit, and in their wake, we readers find ourselves back with the history we ourselves have somehow committed.

Sebald's project of translating time into space is perhaps most spectacularly realized in *Austerlitz*, a book in which the history of Jacques

Austerlitz is mapped out as a journey that brings him to Fort Breen-
donk, Llanwddyn, Prague, Theresienstadt, and Paris. The turning
point of this journey is the ladies' waiting room in London's Liverpool
Street Station, where, "fifty years since," Austerlitz had been handed
over to his stepparents and where, figuratively speaking, he now hands
himself over to the real parents he never knew. The outward-bound
journey of a life without memory thus collapses into a homeward-
bound journey of a memory without a life. "I felt that the waiting
room where I stood as if dazzled contained all the hours of my past
life, all the suppressed and extinguished fears and wishes I had ever
entertained, as if the black and white diamond pattern of the stone
slabs beneath my feet were the board on which the endgame would
be played, and it covered the entire plane of time."[30] Starting from this
Proustian sensation of "presence," Austerlitz sets out on the journey
that brings him to the places that have made him into the person he is.

Typically, Sebald's characters explore this "plane of time" by *walking*. True, they use public transport to move around, but in the immediate vicinity of history they "descend" and rely on their legs. Of course,
as a means of traveling time, "walking," as a method, doesn't cover
nearly so much ground as the historian's practice of gathering things
from books, of touching things lightly, of hovering ironically above
an object. But for Sebald, that's just an advantage. For him, "walking"
entails the epistemological wonder of being, at the same time, *both*
maximally personal *and* minimally subjective. Walking is: meeting a
landscape on its own terms (and so making it your own), as well as
conquering it step-by-step with your whole body (and so experiencing
it as it is). Walking determines not just the content of Sebald's novels,
but also constitutes their form. Stylistically, "walking" ensures maximal presence—it means that you are present *in toto* in every phrase
you write, that you don't hitch on the cheap with what you didn't
imagine yourself, and that you discard words and phrases that merely
sound good.[31]

But surely the most maddeningly brilliant, poetically concrete, and
proudly self-conscious attempt to translate time into space is Giambattista Vico's *Scienza Nuova*. In fact, the book is not an "attempt" at
all: Vico's metamorphosis from a Cartesian "digger" to an Aristotelian
"walker"[32] took place in the decades before he sat down to write the

Scienza Nuova. The first (1724) *Scienza* sprang quite well-armored from Vico's head, and in its ultimate, third, edition (1744) the form of the book is fully in accord with the perspective it explores. It dissimulates its own origin and presents itself as a well-ordered warehouse in which thousands of insights, discoveries, theories, and hypotheses are shelved. Most of these stored thoughts are about history, yet they result from Vico's ability to "divine" past worlds in what he gleaned from the plane of the present.

So, though the *Scienza Nuova* gives the impression of being a compendium about the historicity of humankind, I cannot but agree with Donald Verene when he calls Vico "above all a philosopher of place, not time."[33] How to conceive of this unique topical philosophy isn't made any easier by what Vico himself has to say about it. In a famous passage, he describes his science as "a rational civil theology of divine providence . . . , a demonstration . . . of what providence has wrought in history."[34] Now, rather perversely, with Vico "providence" does *not* mean that God, let alone humans, foresaw what was "wrought in history." Instead it means what for us, seculars, looks like its opposite: the amazing but ineluctable fact that somehow history ended up with precisely the world as we know it, rather than with a different one.[35] Accordingly, the project of the New Science is: trying to fathom "the institutions by which, without human discernment or counsel, and often against the designs of men, providence has ordered this great city of the human race."[36]

The all-important point is that these institutions (by which the "great city of the human race" is "ordered") are actually present in the present and can be walked. They lie open for examination, for, as Vico says, "though this world has been created in time and particular, the institutions established therein by providence are universal and eternal."[37] But it is not just because Vico takes the position that the whole of history is present in "places" (that is, "institutions") that can be "visited" that his philosophy can be termed "topical." It is topical first and foremost because Vico radicalized the ancient rhetorical concept of "*topoi*," widened its scope, and made it the framework of his new science of the humanities. In rhetoric, "*topoi*" refers to the "places" where arguments can be found, to systems of discourses, to "areas of appropriateness." The idea of *topoi* had traditionally included both retrieval and storage—and for Vico indeed, "topics" is at least as much about "finding" as about "shelving." The concept therefore doesn't have the modern connotation of "the collection of clichés we can fall back on when we are too lazy to think something up by ourselves."

On the contrary: in his *Autobiography* Vico defines "topics" as "the art of finding in anything all that is in it."[38] It is an art not unlike Sebald's skill of making the places he visits "speak" of the unspeakable things that happened there. So, the "places" Vico comes across "on the plane of the present" are "common" places in the sense that anybody can visit them, that they lie open for examination, that they can be walked. But they are not "commonplaces"—they are not empty but full, not shallow but deep, not dead but alive. They are the repositories of time—or, perhaps even better, the places where history can get a hold of you. Places are, in short, storehouses of "presence." Thinking ought not to stop, but to *begin* there. For Vico, "topics" is the opposite of Cartesian criticism (which may be described as "the art of finding in anything *the least* that is in it") and refers, in its aspect of *inventio,* to the creative principle itself.

Inventio may be regarded as the keystone of the *scienza nuova.* The more so because Vico boldly declares that the creative principle is operative on both the level of referentiality and the level of reality. He claims that the places we can visit on the plane of the present are "invented" in just the same way as we walkers may "invent" their contents in order to experience "presence." In his *Autobiography* Vico reports with a characteristic dissimulated exhilaration about his invention of the principle of invention. Talking about himself in the third-person singular, he writes: "Vico finally came to perceive that there was not yet in the world of letters a system so devised as to bring the best philosophy . . . into harmony with a philology exhibiting scientific necessity in both its branches, that is in the two histories, that of language and that of things." And he immediately goes on to state the goal of his *scienza nuova*: "to give certainty to the history of languages by reference to the history of things; and to bring into accord the maxims of the academic sages and the practices of the political sages."[39]

So, "topics," for Vico, is not just about *exploring* the plane of the present, but about how it is *made* as well. Vico, in fact, presents his "art of finding in anything all that is in it" as the driving force behind human evolution, as the motor of the process in which, as he said, the *orribile bestioni* of prehistoric times have been modified into the civilized human beings we meet in the streets. Vico thus completely reverses the traditional view that we owe our culture to a surplus, to, for example, the "matchless wisdom of the ancients." According to Vico, Caesar would rather *not* have crossed the Rubicon, and poetry, in his view, doesn't flow from a horn of plenty but is "born entirely of poverty of language and need of expression."[40] The wonder of Vico is that he keeps his eyes firmly trained on the perplexing fact that the more sophisticated can spring from the less sophisticated, that, as he himself said, our forefathers somehow "brought forth from their bestial minds the form of our human minds."[41]

The gist of Vico's new science is his conjecture that the endless series of metamorphoses by which we have become what we are is powered by the use we have learned to make of *topoi*. Topics, he says, "has the function of making minds inventive."[42] The art of topics is the mechanism by which mind transcends itself, by which consciousness emerges, by which, out of nature, culture comes into being. This, indeed, is what Vico's *topoi* ultimately are about: in order to find in any "place" "all that is in it," you have to find *more* in it than you *think* there is in it. And after having found in it more than you thought there was in it, you cannot imagine that there was less in it than you actually found: consciousness has changed. But not only consciousness has changed: the place itself has changed as well. It is transformed into something that couldn't have been imagined, yet was somehow entirely present in the place that is left behind.[43]

Metonymy as Transfer of Presence

Vico thus achieves philosophically what Scott, Balzac, and Sebald practice in their novels: he translates time into space and so creates the conditions to account for the *simultaneousness* of continuity and discontinuity. I think this simultaneousness can be comprehended amazingly well in terms of *metonymy*. In the beginning of this chapter I defined discontinuity as "humans' ability to spring surprises on themselves," and I have indicated that this notion involves the existence of different planes and a less than open connection between these planes. Metonymy—or rather: the interplay between metaphor and metonymy—goes a long way in conceptualizing what happens on and between these planes.

But before I expand on my thesis that metonymy is a metaphor for the simultaneousness of continuity and discontinuity, I will pause for a moment and examine the concept of metonymy itself. How to conceive of this little known, heavily underrated, disquieting, and Protean trope? How to account for the fact that metonymy—though it is, as I will argue, not only the *primary*, but also the most *historical* trope—plays virtually no role in modern, representationalist philosophy of history, is hardly ever mentioned even by literary critics, and is taken seriously only by some obscure linguists and semiologists? Why, finally, are (as I maintain) the Berlin holocaust monument, the paintings of Jackson Pollock and Barnett Newman, the plaster cast of the left hand of Métilde Dembowski on Stendhal's writing desk, the diamond you may have had made out of the ashes of your loved one, the phrase "the gall bladder in room 615 doesn't want to eat," the photographs in the work of Sebald, the exclamations of Robespierre, Danton, and Saint-Just in the Assemblée nationale, and Colonel Chabert in Balzac's story with the same title all metonymies?

Any attempt to come to grips with the concept might as well start with the *Shorter Oxford English Dictionary,* which defines metonymy (lit. "change of name") as "a figure in which the name of an attribute or adjunct is substituted for that of the thing meant, e.g. *sceptre* for *authority.*" Since the days of Aristotle there have been hairsplitting discussions as to what kind of "attributes and adjuncts" may be substituted[44] for what kind of "things meant." The list includes: maker for product ("Jim reads DeLillo"); part for whole ("a flotilla of fifteen keels"); attribute for property ("finally the king handed the scepter over to his son"); place for event ("Arthur goes to Wimbledon"); controller for controlled ("Bush invaded Iraq"); container for contained ("Fred smokes a pack a day"); behavioral reaction for emotion ("Sheila gives me the creeps"); physiological effect for psychological affect ("Dick is a pain in the ass"); institution for the people who are responsible ("the Red Cross underestimated the damage"); and so on.[45]

These instances not only show how deceptively common metonymy in fact is, but they also demonstrate the importance of *context*. Metonymy might be described as the willfully inappropriate[46] transposition of a word that belongs to context 1 (for example, the domain of proper names: DeLillo) to context 2 (the domain of books), where it subsequently stands out as just slightly "out of place." I will return to the fact that this conspicuousness is liable to wear. Here I want to stress that metonymies are, as Cicero said, *mutata*: "displaced words."[47] In the displaced word or phrase, different "contexts," different "spheres of appropriateness," or, as Vico would say, different "places," are connected as well as juxtaposed. In fact, a displaced, metonymical word might be visualized as a "fistula"—an "abnormal passageway"— between two different *topoi*. The phrase "the gall bladder in room 615 doesn't want to eat," for example, is a "fistula" between the *topos* of (reductionist) medicine and the *topos* of (holistic) care.

Three things need to be commented upon. The first is that metonymy is not an exclusively linguistic phenomenon. The plaster cast of the left hand of Métilde Dembowski on Stendhal's writing desk meets the criteria just as well: it is a "willfully inappropriate transposition of something from one context to another," and is in its new context "slightly out of place" indeed. Curious specimens of nonverbal metonymies in a linguistic context are the illustrations in the novels of Sebald. These illustrations—in *Austerlitz* only photographs, in *Vertigo* also train tickets, receipts, postcards, advertisements, and so on—function as fistulae or holes in which the past discharges into the present. In an insightful article, Heiner Boehncke has argued that each individual hole is what Roland Barthes has called a "punctum"[48] (a snip, a little blemish, a pinhole)—and indeed, Sebald's illustrations are a kind of "leak" in time through which "presence" wells up from the past into the present. In fact, Sebald was obsessed with what I have called presence, and because his metonymical illustrations play a major role in bringing it about, he took care to maximize their out-of-place-ness. They are not on separate pages and there are no captions to frame the metonymies and lessen their abrupt contiguity. These "disturbing remains"[49] have no "meaning"—they simply stand for the ineluctable fact, as Sebald said in an interview on German radio, "that we live on thin ice, that every moment we can fall through the ice."[50]

Sebald's illustrations have been described as "kernels of reality" surrounded by "expanses of nothingness."[51] Sebald insists that the artifacts they depict are washed ashore on the plane of the present, and that they deserve to be cherished like fossils. The plaster cast of Métilde's hand on Stendhal's writing desk may also be regarded as a fossil or a relic of—or, perhaps, as a private monument to—the woman who was the prime love of Stendhal's life. In fact, *all* fossils and relics are metonymies, and *all* monuments have at least a metonymic strand. That fossils and relics are metonymies goes without saying—they are prototypical instances of the brand of metonymy called *pars pro toto*. That many monuments may also count as metonymies is perhaps somewhat less self-evident. Monuments are—like all works of art— idiosyncratic compounds of metonymical denotation and metaphorical connotation: they *say* something (connotation) about what they *stand for* (denotation). Monuments are *Fremdkörper* that make past events present on the plane of the present, fistulae that connect and juxtapose those events to the here and now.

Modern monuments are predominantly metonymical: denotation far outweighs connotation. Whereas an early nineteenth-century monument like François Rude's *Marseillaise* (on the Arc de Triomphe) says a lot about what is hardly presented (the departure of the volunteers of 1792 to the front), a modern monument like Peter Eisenman's Berlin Holocaust Memorial has little to say, but much to stand for. Modern, metonymical monuments function not by giving an account of an event, but by forcefully "presenting an absence" in the here and now. In fact, a modern monument consists of a metonymical operation that is metaphorically "loaded"—in such a way that it accomplishes the opposite of what Balzac and Scott did: it transforms space into time. A modern monument entails, first of all, a metonymical transposition of "substance"—like the concrete slabs of the Berlin Holocaust Memorial—from one "place" to another— where it tries to occupy space in such a way that there is no escaping it. Then, second, in an act of artistic transubstantiation, this metonymical *Fremdkörper* is metaphorically associated with what is to be commemorated: it is claimed that the way the monument is present in the present "is like," or equals, that particular part of the past that deserves to be "presented."

It should be remarked that while a modern monument *presents* a past event in the here and now, it can hardly be said to *re*present it. A monument like the Berlin Holocaust Memorial is a repository of what haunts the place of the present, a refuge for what has always (or at least since the event in question took place) been there. It is closer to a relic than to a painted, written, or sculpted pictorial account of what happened—though, of course, it differs from a relic in the sense that presence is transferred to a new, and willfully made, object. So, whereas premodern, metaphorical monuments are primarily engaged in a transfer of *meaning*, modern metonymical monuments concentrate on a transfer of *presence*. This transfer of presence comes in many forms: from the incorporation of original material (soil, wreckage, dust) in the monument to the naming of names—as in the Vietnam Veterans Memorial and the projected monument to the victims of 9/11. Because the representationalist philosophy of history of the past decades was geared to grasping how metaphor is instrumental in establishing satisfactory representations, it could account for transfer of meaning, but not for (metonymically achieved) transfer of presence.[52]

The second point I would like to make is that the phenomenon of metonymy cannot be apprehended without keeping in mind that individual metonymies have "careers." These careers come in two modalities. In most cases metonymy is absorbed by the context in which it is placed. What starts as an eye-catching, disconcerting, and ineluctable presence ends up as something so inconspicuous that it cannot even be called a cliché. Language is replete with metonymies that have long lost their capacity to attract attention—you have to be very tenacious in your worship to prevent the plaster cast of the hand of your onetime lover to be lost in the bric-a-brac on your writing desk. A fresh metonymy is like a strange new building in the city—first nobody quite knows what to do with it, then all kinds of interactions get going by which it is integrated into the tissue of the city. In Sebald's novels the illustrations virtually compel the reader to fill the "expanses of nothingness" that surrounds them with, as Boehncke says, "hypotheses, fictions, and histories"[53] that diminish their unbearable introversion. With monuments, this incorporation process takes a paradoxical twist. Unlike normal buildings, monuments are especially *designed* to get—and keep—such interactions going: it is in these interactions, after all, that the event the monument stands for is "commemorated." But, unfortunately, the more the monument is interacted with, the more it loses its "presence" and the faster it becomes a platitude. Therefore, to maximize their life span, monuments have to be as avant garde as possible.

How metonymical strangeness loses its pungency and becomes incorporated into the context in which it is placed is a central theme in the novels of Walter Scott. In *Waverley* the hero is transposed from the context of civilized England to find himself in a Scotland in which he is metonymically "out of place"—a condition Scott called "romance." Edward Waverley savors the strangeness of the context into which he has ventured, and he sits down "to give himself up to the full romance of his situation. Here he sat on the banks of an unknown lake, under the guidance of a wild native, whose language was unknown to him, on a visit to the den of some renowned outlaw, a second Robin Hood perhaps."[54] Modern linguists claim that each metonymy has a source-domain and a target-domain.[55] In *Waverley*, however, it is impossible to say what is the one and what the other. From the perspective of space, civilized England is Waverley's source-domain, whereas Scotland is the target-domain. From the perspective of time, however, it is the other way around: as past, "romantic" Scotland is the source, whereas England, as present, is the target. What one can say is that Edward Waverley is a metonymical fistula between Scotland and England, past and present, and that in and by his journey he not only juxtaposes but eventually also *connects* the planes. At the end of the book—when he is happily married to the bride he has picked from the past—Waverley has integrated Scotland and England, past and present, and has ceased to be a *Fremdkörper*.

Though most metonymies end up, like Waverley, as "honorable citizens" of their environment, sometimes one is so powerful that it infects the context in which it is placed and transforms its setting "in its own image." This is, I think, the career of the abstract art of, for example, Jackson Pollock and Barnett Newman. Jean-François Lyotard has argued that abstract art aspires to musicality; I think a far more persuasive case can be made that it aspires to metonymy. Abstract paintings are "all presence and no meaning." These "relations of color and shape largely divorced from descriptive connotation,"[56] as Clement

Greenberg said, transpose something to the context of art and leave little doubt that their raison d'être is to be as "out of place" as they possibly can. Abstract art thus highlights a key feature of metonymy: its out-of-place-ness generates presence. But the fact that abstract paintings are about nothing doesn't necessarily mean that they are about themselves—like, as cultural folklore has it, musical compositions. By claiming to be art, abstract paintings insist that they perform a very precise operation—they maintain that, though *Fremdkörper*, they are definitely not *random Fremdkörper*. In this sense their metonymical presence is, like that of modern monuments, secondarily loaded with metaphor. It's a frustrating metaphor though. Abstract paintings posit a kind of algebraic equation in which what is on the right side of the "=" is spectacularly present, while what is on the left side is conspicuously absent. An abstract painting is a metonymy loaded with an empty metaphor.

The fact that abstract art is "all presence and no meaning" may explain its impact. Whereas metaphor "gives" meaning, metonymy insinuates that there is an urgent *need* for meaning. Metaphor (as, for example, my "city" metaphor) weaves interrelations and makes "places" habitable. Metonymy, on the other hand, disturbs places. When fresh, it questions meanings, awakens us from what we take for granted, and draws attention to what we don't like to be reminded of: that the implicit rules of the place are far from natural and self-evident, are indeed a system of habits and conventions. Because it disturbs the peace, a fresh metonymy gives rise to an impulse to jump upon it. This in fact is what happened with abstract art: these paintings about nothing generated a torrent of books and treatises that were about *them*. When it proved to be impossible to interpret the paintings in terms of the context in which they were placed, the context was interpreted in terms of the paintings. Critics like Clement Greenberg undertook to reinterpret painting in terms of the metonymical *mutata* by Jackson Pollock, retrospectively instaurating traditions—as Greenberg did with his idea of a tradition of "flatness"—in which the *Fremdkörper* could be incorporated. All this is rather strange: abstract art originates from a desire for decontextualization, and precisely because of that generated an unprecedented process of contextualization. By refusing to create images of its environment, it had its environment recreated in its own image.

In both careers—*incorporation by* context and *recreation of* context—metonymy ends up as "just a place" on the plane of the present. Discordance inevitably erodes. One might say that as long as a metonymy is out of place, it has presence, but that thereafter it is just present. Yet, even as a place that is taken for granted, its presence is not irremediably gone. It's still there, but it has turned its face downwards—you don't see it when you don't walk the plane of time, the "great city of the human race," very, very attentively. Consequently, a metonymy is a "presence in absence" not just in the sense that it presents something that isn't there, but also in the sense that in the absence (or at least the radical inconspicuousness) that *is* there, the thing that isn't there is still present. Metonymical "presence in absence," in other words, works both ways: upward *to* the present, and downward *from* the present. These two ways correspond to the two aspects of *topoi*: invention and storage. As *inventio*, metonymy transposes something to the present, or, more correctly: as *inventio*, metonymy has *made* the surface as we know it; the present consists of metonymies that once were *Fremdkörper* but now are taken for granted. As "storage," metonymy contains what was left behind. But what it stands for can still be found in—or, as Vico would say, "invented" out of—what we may find on the plane of time.

This brings me to my third point: the question of invention. All metonymies are invented, and invention requires first of all decontextualization. Writers know that this is no easy matter. Most words lie, as a Dutch expression has it, "in de mond bestorven" (lit. "in the mouth as if they are dead"): they trigger the discourse in which they are buried—or, conversely, *are* triggered by the discourse that's going on. Each word and every phrase has its own sphere of appropriateness, and it requires quite a bit of literary talent to tear it away from the context in which it is at home and implant it in a context in which it is inappropriate. For a writer, metonymies, though hard to "find," are extremely valuable. By means of metonymies authors can transcend themselves and can suggest that what they describe has a reality independent of them. This is, I think, what Robert Musil had in mind when he said that the "casual mentioning of a hair on a nose is more valuable than the most momentous thought."[57] The key word here is "casual": Musil is not advocating meticulous precision or competent description—he is, I think, not even referring to the "imagination." For a writer, the important thing is, according to Musil, not to reproduce a picture he has in his mind (a picture including a hair on a nose) as faithfully as he can—but to admit *Fremdkörper* in his text that are beyond his scope, that he could not have imagined himself. Whereas a purposeful description—a *re*presentation—of the nose with the faithful inclusion of the hair would have required some imagined picture, *casually mentioning* the hair doesn't need an imagined picture at all. Quite the contrary: it establishes—"presents"—a reality that is far too real to have been imagined. The hair on the nose is a metonymy that opens a reality outside the text. It gives rise to presence.

Casually mentioning a hair on a nose—and, by doing so, opening a reality—is on a textual scale what, according to Vico, also takes place on the scale of history. It is what he calls *inventio*. *Inventio* is not dabbling around a bit and picking the things that suit you, but, as we have seen, "finding in a place all that is in it"—which, as we have also seen, for Vico means finding more in it than you think there is in it. *Inventio* thus is not exploration, but a *mutation* of consciousness. Inventions are the proactive words and deeds—as I have called them in the introduction—with which we surprise ourselves. In a wonderful passage, Vico muses: "Rational [i.e., Cartesian] metaphysics teaches that man becomes all things by understanding them, this [i.e., Vico's own] imaginative metaphysics shows that man becomes all things by *not* understanding them; and perhaps the latter proposition is truer than the former, for when man understands he extends his mind and takes in the things, but when he does not understand he makes the things out of himself and becomes them by transforming himself into them."[58] What Vico means by his bold claim that "man becomes all things by *not* understanding them" is that in a true invention a new evolutionary level is reached, a level that is fundamentally discontinuous with the earlier one. To invent something is to create the beginning of a context that as yet does not exist, a bridgehead to the unknown. This bridgehead is metonymically connected and juxtaposed to what is left behind, and eventually becomes metaphorically connected to the context that grows out of it.

Why Vico maintains that we not just *create*, but truly *become* things "by not understanding them" can perhaps best be illustrated by what he says about the invention of the name of Jupiter. In Vico's view, *inventio* goes all the way down to the point where (by a heroic act of "finding in a place all that is in it") a thing is taken out of the context of prelinguistic reality and is given the name with which it is taken up in the context of language. "Naming things" is creating things by making a distinction—as, according to Vico, the forefathers of the Romans did when they distinguished the thing that was foremost of all the things they didn't understand—the thunder—from nature and called it "Jupiter."[59] In Vico's view, in the invention of Jupiter a kind of "master" *topos* was created. With the invention of the name of Jupiter, nature lost its old ontological supremacy and (paradoxically) became ontologically subordinate to what was invented "out of it." As Vico says, "nature is the *language* of Jove."[60] The moment the name was found, nature was seen in terms of "Jupiter." From the moment the Jupiter bridgehead was established, Jupiter was humanity's universe. From then on humans lived "in" Jupiter—"became" Jupiter in the sense that Jupiter constituted their consciousness. According to Vico, and I fully agree with him, "being" is always and irremediably one ontological and evolutionary level ahead of "understanding." We are what we don't understand; we can understand what we are not. The moment our interpretation of the world in terms of Jupiter threatens to be well on its way, *we begin to dare to not understand* Jupiter and we spring a fresh surprise on ourselves by fleeing—by means of *inventio*—forward to a new bridgehead.

In the same way as "nature is the language of Jove," metaphor is the language of metonymy. By this I do not just mean that you can only talk about metonymy in metaphors. What I mean is that you have to have a metonymical bridgehead before you can (on the level where that bridgehead has taken you) become metaphorical. In my opinion this was also Vico's point of view. Verene, in his otherwise admirable book, concludes that Vico attributes the primordial power of naming to metaphor: "The metaphor," says Verene, "is that through which a *topos* is originally formed."[61] I think he is wrong. It is true that Vico calls metaphor the "most luminous" and the "most necessary and frequent" of the tropes,[62] but from this it cannot be inferred that *topoi* are born from metaphor. On the contrary. Vico says: "In such a logic, sprung from such a[n imaginative] metaphysics, the first poets had to give names to things from the most particular and the most sensible ideas. Such ideas are the sources, respectively, of synecdoche and metonymy."[63] The question of which is more basic, metaphor or metonymy, cannot be answered. Metonymy is more basic than metaphor in the sense that it creates the "bridgeheads." But it invents them by finding all that is in the metaphors that are left behind. Metonymical presence and metaphorical meaning are locked in an evolutionary dance.

Adam, the Third Coalition, and a Hapless Stowaway

The fact that in its new context the transposed word rubs shoulders with neighboring words explains why metonymy is often designated as "the trope of contiguity."[64] Though in my opinion contiguity is an (intended or unintended) *effect* rather than the essence of metonymy, there can be little doubt that the trope is heavily dependent on our astonishing ability to intuit and employ "spheres of appropriateness." Surely, proficiency in using *topoi* must have, as evolutionary scientists would say, *survival value*. Otherwise, contributors to any scientific or academic debates wouldn't be able to comply, in their books and articles, with "rules of the place" of which they are not even conscious. Metonymy is also, in the second place, dependent on our ability to play with, and accept, transgressions of the rules of the place. It is precisely the combination of our ability to sense what is appropriate in a given context and our ability to tolerate and appreciate some juggling with what is appropriate that makes metonymy work—as in, for example, the gall-bladder sentence, and phrases like "the hamburger has left without paying."[65]

By connecting and juxtaposing contexts, metonymy distances itself from, as well as draws attention to, both the context from which it was taken and the context in which it is placed. Perhaps it is this ambiguity that gives metonymy its contradictory capacity of appropriating things at the moment of making them strange. The phrase "the gall bladder in room 615 doesn't want to eat" succeeds in making hospital routine strange[66] at the same moment that it capitalizes on it.[67] This coincidence of alienation and appropriation is perhaps most apparent in *naming* things. The primordial metonymical operation of giving things names is one of Vico's grand themes; it is aptly described in Genesis where God brings the animals he has created to Adam "to see what he would call them: and whatsoever Adam called every living creature that was the name thereof."[68]

What Adam does is not unlike what historical actors do. In a way, what historical actors do is even *more* metonymical than the job God put Adam up to: the things historical actors give names to are not *brought* to them, but have to be *invented* by them. Historical concepts are invented (by, indeed, a heroic act of "finding" cum "founding") *out of* the undifferentiated jumble of everyday reality, and *into* the domain of representation—as in the metonymical phraseology in the Assemblée nationale and the Constituante between 1789 and 1793. In the speeches of Robespierre, Danton, and Saint-Just the nineteenth century was invented. Whatsoever the revolutionaries called what they found in the place of the present, "that was the name thereof": "patrie," "France," "citoyen," "liberté," and so on. Of course, this kind of invention has nothing to do with naïve historical realism—with, that is, the belief that historical actors have some kind of privileged access to the reality in which they operate and they "just" communicate this reality to their public.[69] In much the same way as, according to Vico, with the invention of the name of Jupiter, nature came to be seen in terms of "Jupiter"—so the metonymical *mutata* of the Jacobins became the language of the *ordo et connexio rerum* of everyday politics the moment they were invented.

But, of course, inventing really new names (and thus, according to Vico, "places") is quite exceptional. Accordingly, most of the work done by historians is written in language drawn from the existing collection of "places" that constitutes the discipline of history. Even the most cursory glance reveals that this language is thoroughly metonymical. The metonymicality of historical texts is not simply a matter of style or vocabulary (as in "the king handed the scepter over to his son" or "the redcoats stood their ground"). Metonymy is deeply ingrained in how historians think, work, and write. Just leaf through a history book: "Germany declared war," "After Stalingrad . . . ," "Napoleon invaded Russia," "The Germans hated Versailles," "The Netherlands Indies, though remaining neutral, increased its output of foodstuffs,"

"All three imperial powers began to experiment with consultative bodies," "The British bombarded Satsuma,"—there is simply too much of it; metonymy is (no pun intended) all over the place.

It would be wrong, I think, to dismiss these metonymies as just a form of shorthand.[70] The metonymical principle of taking things out of one context and placing them in another is part and parcel of historical method. This is how Palmer and Colton, in their famous handbook, describe the forming of the Third Coalition in 1805:

> Alexander was . . . ready to enter a Third Coalition with Great Britain. The war aims of the Third Coalition, though not accomplished, suggest what was at stake in the ten years that followed and anticipated much of the final peace settlement of 1814. Alexander and William Pitt did not in truth commit themselves specifically to much. But Pitt did not reject Alexander's idea that, after the war, some kind of organized international body should enforce the peace. Alexander's interest in the "freedom of the seas," which in plain terms meant international controls on the use of British sea power in wartime, aroused no corresponding interest in London. It was somewhat vaguely agreed that French ascendancy in Germany and Italy should cease; that the French should be driven from Belgium, and Belgium combined with Holland in a strong buffer state against France; and that Prussia should be strengthened on the Rhine. It was understood that England should receive territory overseas, and Alexander revealed some of his plans for reuniting Poland. The tsar pictured himself the future arbiter of central Europe.[71]

Though at first sight it doesn't show, even in this randomly chosen fragment numerous contexts are metonymically connected and juxtaposed. There are all kinds of "fistulae" between all kinds of places. First, the passage contains a lot of metonymical *names* ("Great Britain," "London," "the French," " . . . against France," "Prussia," "England," "central Europe") in which the *topos* of diplomacy is connected to the *topos* of the nation-state. Then, second, in *phrases* ("the war aims of the Third Coalition," "some kind of organized international body should enforce the peace," "international controls on the use of British sea power") institutionalized or projected forms of cooperation between nations are substituted for calculations and intentions of people.[72]

Third, and more important, is the fact that, in Palmer and Colton's Third Coalition text *agency* is structurally metonymical. Look, for example, how the name "Alexander" is used. Even in autocratic Russia, the sovereign did not equal the country, so who or what does the "Alexander" of the first sentence stand for? *Who* exactly was "ready to enter a coalition" with Great Britain? The tsar himself—in the knowledge that his sentiment was sufficiently shared? The tsar and his coterie? The Russian upper class? A significant part of the Russian population? And how unified was Alexander even as a person? The text gives no clue, and the issue has to remain undecided—as it also has to remain undecided whether "Alexander" stands for the same thing in each of the five (or six, if the "tsar" of the last sentence is included) instances the name is used. The quoted fragment is finally metonymical because the sentences and subordinate clauses that stand contiguously side by side in Palmer and Colton's (con)text are taken from a range of wholly different "places." The first sentence originates from the "place" of psychological interpretation, the second is derived from the *topos* of historical analysis, the third belongs to the sphere of evaluative description, the fourth ("But Pitt did not reject . . . ") is a statement of fact, and the fifth is an ironic sequence of a strategic calculation ("Alexander's interest . . . "), an evaluative description ("which in plain terms . . . "), and a conflation of a statement of fact and an historical analysis. And so on.

Remarkably, the metonymical nature of historical texts tends to go unnoticed. I don't think Palmer and Colton's Third Coalition fragment strikes anybody as a collation of "loose and separate" sentences and disjointed interpretations. This is all the more amazing because, by definition, metonymy tends to highlight rupture: the two parts of the phrase "the gall bladder in room 615," for example, stand conspicuously cheek to cheek. Of course, one of the reasons that Palmer and Colton's thoroughly metonymical text doesn't *look* metonymical is precisely that it is so thoroughly metonymical. In a literary text, metonymical *Fremdkörper* stand out, whereas in a historical text—a text, that is, that wholly *consists* of *Fremdkörper*—contiguity is so general that it looks like continuity. The main reason, however, that the metonymical nature of historical texts tends to go unnoticed involves the surreptitious ad hoc emplotments that are so typical of how historians work.[73] Palmer and Colton, for example, present the forging of the Third Coalition as a kind of (mediated) dialogue between Tsar Alexander and Prime Minister Pitt. Because the authors knew full well that Alexander and Pitt in fact never met, the surreptitious dialogue-image is a metaphor—a metaphor by which they can organize this particular chunk of text, a metaphor, moreover, in which irregularities—as, for example, the metonymical uses of the name "Alexander"—may sink away.

My analysis of the Third Coalition fragment thus suggests that the continuousness that forms the surface of the historical text is of a particular kind: it is a succession of contiguous places of which the contiguity is blotted out. We readers are not supposed to continuously "walk" such a text—as Sebald walks the plane of the present. Historical texts invite us to read faster than at a certain minimum speed—on pain of noticing the cracks and fissures if we go too slowly. Indeed, it is one of the functions of metaphorical emplotment to keep reading going—to prevent our becoming hooked by and in a particular place. On the other hand, as every writer knows, a certain amount of supposedly irrelevant metonymic detail[74] is necessary to convince the reader that the story is "real." So, in actual fact, writing history is (like any writing) an oscillation between—as linguists say—a metonymic "syntagmatic" pole (which connects language to the prelinguistic world of events and impressions) and a metaphoric "paradigmatic" pole (which exploits the code of linguistic signs). It is impossible to say what predominates over what. Roman Jakobson argued that in the realist novel—which is genetically related to modern historiography—metonymy is predominant.[75] Indeed, in historiography metonymy *is* predominant in that in historical texts metonymies are "all over the place." But, on the other hand, *metaphor* is predominant in that on the surface of the historical text metaphorical continuity tends to suppress metonymical contiguity.

Now, the remarkable thing is that by veiling metonymical *Fremdkörper*, metaphor paradoxically enhances one of the key features of metonymy: its being a "presence in absence." The words "gall bladder" in the phrase "the gall bladder in room 615" make present in his or her absence a real and particular human being. In a historical text, however, the conspicuousness that signals "look, something's absent here" is suppressed. So, one might say that in a metaphorically emplotted historical text *presence is even more absent* than in a text in which metonymy is allowed to stand out. But, and this is a point that can't be stressed too much, *it is still there.* Below the surface of the text— in words and phrases we take for granted when we speed along, in expressions we happily forgive the historian, in the concepts and categories the author keeps so masterfully in the air, in the proper and improper names that fill up with color, sense, and meaning—below, I repeat, the surface of the text—the things the metonymies stand for are still present. In absence, but *present.* The words and phrases that have been woven into the texture of the text are metonymically connected to the places that are left behind—all the way down to the point where names have been substituted for *reality.*

One might say, then, that in those faintly glowing metonymies— hardly visible in the more brilliant light of metaphor—historical reality *itself* is "absently present." These metonymies are Vico's repositories of time. In fact, my account may be regarded as a variation of Vico's topical philosophy of history in which the whole of history is present in "institutions"—"places"—that can be "visited" on the plane of the present, places that can be walked and lie open for examination. The way historical reality is "absently present" in a historical text is, however, very different from the way an object may be hidden in a room. An object hidden in a room doesn't interact with, let alone *transform,* the person who eventually finds it—whereas we readers have been made into the persons we are precisely by the historical reality that is absently present in a historical text.[76] This "ontological drift" is the counterpart of human evolution and a consequence of the fact that consciousness mutates in exactly the same direction and in exactly the same "amount" as the concomitant historical mutation—so that the feeling of self-evidence remains constant.[77] Because of this ontological drift, historical reality is incomparably more absent and incomparably more inaccessible than we like to think, though it is also—in metonymy—incomparably more present and accessible.

"Accessible" isn't the right word, though. It suggests that one may enter historical reality at will and/or in accordance with the intention of the author, whereas my thesis is that the presence of the past does not primarily reside in the intended story or the manifest metaphorical content of the text, but in what story and text contain *in spite of* the intentions of the historian. One might say that historical reality travels with historiography not as a paying passenger but as a *stowaway*. As a stowaway the past "survives" the text; as a stowaway the past may spring surprises on us. A spectacular example of what I have in mind is Balzac's *Le colonel Chabert* (1832). In that quintessential metonymical story,[78] Chabert—who was supposedly killed in the Battle of Eylau in 1807 and who since then has been "absently present" only as a name—surfaces as a dirty, smelly, disagreeable, but very living and very palpable presence in Louis Philippe's Paris. Balzac takes care to contrast Chabert's horrifying reemergence to the continuity-suggesting legalism of the period. The colonel, who was buried in a mass grave and has worked his way to the surface by using a "Herculean" bone as a lever, is a metonymical fistula who connects the sedate Restauration era with the *grandeur et misère* of the revolutionary period, the military exploits of Napoleon, and the horrors of battles such as Eylau.

So, as a stowaway, as what is absently and unintentionally present on the plane of time, metonymy is a metaphor for discontinuity or, rather, for the entwinement of continuity and discontinuity. In countless surface names, countless "Colonel Chaberts" travel as stowaways with what we used to regard as our past. The reality of the past is present in "the great city of the human race," not in the metaphorical likenesses that represent, and intend to illuminate, the past, but in the eroded and introverted metonymies from which these likenesses were born and which—though very much on the surface—we are persuaded not to notice by all those alluring and illuminating metaphors. It is in this peculiar interaction between metonymy and metaphor that the simultaneousness of continuity and discontinuity resides. This is not to say that metonymy doesn't give access to historical reality. It does, but the accessibility of the past that goes with metonymy is of a discontinuous kind. It may occur when a metonymical "place" gives way and we fall through all those metonymical connections down to the epiphanic moment in which historical reality stops being *absently* present in words and phrases and stands before us as Colonel Chabert stands before the people who took his story for granted.

And So ...

The interplay between metaphor and metonymy I have sketched—which I propose to call "metonymics"—thus accomplishes what representationalism fails to do: to account for the relation between historiography and historical reality—to account for, that is, the relation between the *ordo et connexio idearum* and the *ordo et connexio rerum*. The wonder of a historical text is not—as representationalism implies—that it *fails* to bring us into contact with historical reality, but that it, despite its textuality, somehow, sometimes, *does* bring us into contact with historical reality. It is clear that this contact is not continuous, that it is not willfully and intentionally brought about by the undistorted mirror of the mind of the historian—as naïve historicism had it—but this doesn't alter the fact that the past *is* present in the present, that the past *does* spring surprises on us, that though we may not be able to get into contact with historical reality as intensively as we would like, historical reality is, as the case of the NIOD-historians shows, very able to get into contact *with us*. In a society busily—nay, frantically—engaged in looking for "places" where this "presence" can be found, it is, I think, the task of philosophy of history to elucidate—no—not *where* it can be found, but *how* finding (and founding) presence can be understood.

But I can hardly end without making clear how my interpretation compares to the view Hayden White proposed in *Metahistory*. White—as far as I know the only philosopher of history who has taken metonymy seriously—doesn't regard *all* historiography as essentially metonymic (as I do), but associates the trope with the mechanist reductionism of, for example, Karl Marx.[79] White's strategy of calling metonymy "reductionist" enables him to account for Marx's dialectical materialism. By metonymy, White argues, "one can simultaneously distinguish between two phenomena and reduce one to the status of a manifestation of the other,"[80] and "by such reductions . . . the phenomenal world can be populated with a host of agents and agencies that are presumed to exist *behind* it."[81] This, according to White, is precisely what Marx does: he reduces the phenomenal world to the economic realities *behind* it. But White's interpretation is a bit problematic. In my view even the part/whole and cause/effect metonymies upon which White concentrates cannot truly be termed reductionist. Of course, in the quintessential metonymical sentence "the gall bladder in room 615 doesn't want to eat" a person seems to be reduced to a gall bladder—but this apparent reduction is an epiphenomenon of the fact that in the metonymical words a shortcut is brought about between the level of medicine and the level of care. In much the same way, Marx's originality is not that he *reduces* the phenomenal world to the economic world, but that he metonymically *connects and juxtaposes* the harsh world of economic reality to the lofty world of culture.

It wouldn't be fair, however, to conclude that White's conception of metonymy as reductionist is an unwarranted reduction of the concept of metonymy. White uses the concept on quite a different level than I do. With him metonymy is—along with synecdoche, irony, and metaphor—one of the prototypical modes of emplotment. In my view, however, all strategies of emplotment, including the strategy White calls metonymy, belong to the sphere of "metaphor." They are metaphorical because they are in the business of the "transfer of meaning," whereas metonymy, by presenting an absence, is a "transfer of presence." Though it can, perhaps, not be maintained that a metonymical "transfer of presence" predates metaphorical "transfer of meaning," the latter is, in my opinion, not possible without the former. It might, finally, be argued that the concept of metonymy *itself* may count as a metonymy. Insofar as it is a *corpus alienum* that positions itself uncomfortably in what is taken for granted, it may well disrupt the "place" of philosophy of history.

4

Spots of Time

An unapparent connection holds more firmly than an apparent one.

—Heraclitus[1]

ost historians seem to believe that such a thing as the past exists. Of course, if you ask these historians straightaway they will admit that no, indeed, the past is just a thing of the past. The next moment, however, you can hear them talk happily about their—or, at least as probable, *our*—"relationship with the past." And there's no escaping it: if you define yourself as having a relationship with something or someone, you thereby indicate that you believe that that something or that person *exists* in a way that is on a par with the way you think you yourself exist.

There is another group of historians—a much smaller one, I believe, and a group in which philosophers of history are heavily overrepresented—who assert that the past does *not* exist. The historians belonging to this group maintain that the only remnants of the past that survive into the here and now are traces and inscriptions, papers and documents, pictures and footage, bytes and pixels—the venerable things, in short, that are designated by a remarkable metaphor, the metaphor of *sources*. The historians who maintain that only physical remains—but not the past itself—can be said to exist persuade themselves that it is their task to construct convincing views of the past by creatively *using* these remains.

In this chapter I will elaborate on what I said in the previous chapter and take the position that both categories of historians—the historians who believe that the past *does* exist as well as the historians who believe that the past *does not* exist—are wrong. My thesis is that the past is incomparably more absent than the first group of historians is prepared to think, and—at the same time—incomparably more present than the second group of historians is willing to admit. This is not a roundabout way of saying that in a sense both groups of historians—believers and nonbelievers—are right. The point I want to make is that the past is more radically absent from the here and now than even the nonbelievers suppose, and—once again, at the same time—more dramatically present than even the believers assume.

But I grant that my distinction between believers and nonbelievers is a bit too schematic. Actually, it is worse. Historians are inclined to combine a halfhearted belief that the past exists with an equally halfhearted belief that the past does not exist—and so they can be said to be doubly wrong. The past is, as L. P. Hartley nicely summarizes this ontological twilight state, a "foreign country." The discipline of history thrives on the brackish ontological status of its object. The ontological ambivalence of the past not only has psychological survival value, but also comes in philosophically handy. By burying ontological questions under epistemological answers historians are able to convince themselves that what holds true for other bona fide academic disciplines holds true for the discipline of history as well: that there are "subjects" and "objects," and that the former are neatly divided from the latter.

In history, however, there *is* no clear-cut distinction between subject and object. The past does not exist independently of the historian—as is proven by the simple fact that the better the work of a historian is, the less it could have been written by another historian. Yet—or (perhaps more correctly*) because of this*—the prototypical historian passionately denies that he coincides with his or her object.[2] Prototypical historians tend to depict themselves—with Rankean mock modesty—as supremely *un*interesting tools with which supremely *interesting* objects can be elucidated. These same prototypical historians, however, are not *that* different from some of the professionals they loathe to be compared with: psychiatrists, psychotherapists, or even religious leaders, persons who owe their effectiveness to their skill in bringing their subjectivity to bear on their objects, persons who specialize in—as psychotherapists call it—"being their own instrument."

Now, historians can keep claiming that they are self-contained subjects dutifully studying objects "out there" as long as they can cheat a bit regarding the ontological status of the past. It always reminds me of the frustrating game that in Dutch is called *balletje balletje* and in English a "shell game." When you address historians they point to what they write about, and when you address what they write about they take it personally. That this *balletje balletje* game can be played out at all is made possible by what it is supposed to hide: by the fact that history is an academic discipline where objects cannot be separated from the subjects who study them.

The concept of presence, introduced in the previous chapter, is, I think, a convenient way to put an edge on the issue of how exactly the past can be said to exist. But before I rush forward into a discussion of how to conceive of the past as existing *both* "more" *and* "less" than we are inclined to think, I will take a step backward, for I'm about to fall into the academic trap of starting off with what heuristically comes last: words and concepts. So, instead of performing some philosophical hocus pocus with the concept of presence, instead of discussing definitions, and instead of burdening the reader with the task of scratching up aspects of reality that might give some sense to the word, I will sketch three real-life phenomena. In fact, it was these phenomena that put me on track of what I now call "presence."

Turning the Tables

The first phenomenon is what I call my "Abba-sensation." In the beginning of this year—while I was zapping TV channels—I stumbled upon a documentary about the Swedish pop group Abba. Spellbound, I kept watching, and to my surprise I was—as I am still a bit ashamed to add—moved to tears. Just a bit of *Sehnsucht*, you might say—nothing wrong with that. But the strange thing was that at the time Abba scored its hits, I had not felt any interest in the band. I detested their music and I couldn't feel any enthusiasm for the band members. Abba, in short,

wasn't part of my identity. So I wondered: how could I *now* be moved
by something that *then* wasn't part of my identity? I tried to remember
if I had had comparable sensations about bands whose records I had
in fact bought and played, but as far as I remembered that had never
happened. What to make of this sensation? Had I fooled myself? Had I
subconsciously admired those predictable rhymes, those sticky melo-
dies, those dancing asses? Or was I moved by the Abba documentary
precisely *because* Abba had not been part of my identity?

The second phenomenon is the one I described extensively in chapter 2: the bewildering case of the group of eleven Dutch historians who
unwittingly *reproduced* the events they studied around the killing, in
1995, of about eight thousand Bosnian Muslims who were supposed to
have been protected by a battalion of Dutch peacekeepers. Apparently
the past intruded upon these historians in a way they couldn't—or
at least didn't—control. They may have been under the impression
that *they* were mastering the past, but, strangely and inexplicably, the
past turned the tables and mastered these historians. How can that
be? How to account for the fact that past events can have the power
to reproduce themselves in the way historians describe these events?
How to explain this uncanny power of history to take revenge on the
historians writing it?

The third phenomenon to which I would like to draw attention is
the fact that the Americans in Abu Ghraib prison in Baghdad couldn't
resist torturing their Iraqi prisoners. I think what happened in Abu
Ghraib is a medium-sized example of what can be called a "compulsion
to repeat." The compulsion to repeat is a very common phenomenon.
On the level of language it surfaces in our penchant for homonyms and
rhyme, and in our inclination to use words and phrases that are *related*
to words and phrases that are "in the air." Remarkably often, form is
contaminated with content. If a TV host is talking about agricultural
policy, chances are that she (or he) will do so in terms of "fruitful,"
"fertile," or "barren." A Dutch newspaper designated the plummeting
sale of Viagra with the word normally used for the weakening of an
erection.[3] And when, recently, a newspaper discovered that officials of
the Dutch ministry of defense were involved in corruption, a former
Dutch secretary of defense explained that the spasmodic reactions of
quite a number of employees of the department were understandable

because they were in the habit of reacting "defensively" when they felt they were "attacked"—an explanation that indicates that either the employees or the former secretary (or, presumably, both) replicated the task of the department in another sphere. Apart from being a linguistic and psychological reality, the compulsion to repeat also occurs on the level of history. There it can take the form it had in Abu Ghraib, the disturbing and embarrassing form of *acting out* the past. In the cells and corridors of Abu Ghraib, Saddam Hussein's past torture practices were present in the same way as a word permeates consciousness by a ban on thinking it. The American jailers in the Abu Ghraib would have had to be kept in check very carefully to prevent their giving in to what loomed so large—and, as we know by now, they weren't.

What happened in Abu Ghraib is even more unsettling than the way the Srebrenica historians reproduced the past in their writing. The Abu Ghraib case suggests that the past may operate like a kind of *locus genii*—that it may have such an irresistible power that it is able to express itself in what actually happens in the real world. It opens a perspective that is almost too disturbing to accept: that the past may have a presence that is so powerful that it can use *us*, humans, as its *material.*

The phenomena I have mentioned, freakish as they may be, have a common denominator. What they share is that they are thoroughly at odds with how historians nowadays conceive of the past, with how we think history is being made, and with how we interpret our efforts to transform history into historiography. Other phenomena that are equally hard to account for—like déja vu and Johan Huizinga's historical sensation—point in the same direction. They too cast doubt on the paradigm currently in force, according to which the historian can prefigure history but history cannot prefigure the historian. But I do not think that these freakish phenomena *as such* warrant taking a fresh look at how we conceive of the past. The main reason that we should do so is that the past affects each and every one of us in a manner not unlike the way the Srebrenica historians were mastered by what they were supposed to master.

"Presence," in other words, is a very common phenomenon. And it is not just a phenomenon to be afraid of. Actually, we *want* to be affected. As I said in chapter 1, we go to great lengths, and are willing to spend huge amounts of money, to *have* ourselves affected by the past. Unfortunately, most of the strategies we devise to have us moved by history don't work. They fall into the trap of brute force, of virtuality, of literalness. The new $90 million Lincoln Museum in Abraham Lincoln's birthplace of Springfield, Illinois, is a case in point. In this museum visitors are treated to stunningly lifelike scenes from old Abe's life. They see the as-yet-not-so-old Abe tending his general store in New Salem, composing the Emancipation Proclamation, and sitting in the theater moments before he is shot. The goal of this "experience museum"—as the museum's designer (who once worked for Walt Disney) calls it—is not "to fully explain all of the issues that confronted Lincoln, but to inspire in the visitor a deep sense of personal connection and empathy with the man."[4]

Yet despite the effort, the miracle only sporadically comes about. This is the fate of many museums that put their money on recreating the past. It's rather sad: even if *both* museum *and* visitor are heading for the coveted "deep sense of personal connection," the twain rarely meet. The reason for this mismatch is, so at least it seems to me, that most makers of "experience museums" take as their point of departure that the past they want to bring alive is not already present in the here and now. Makers of experience museums tend to treat the past as *ab*sence—and regard it as their mission to "fill in" the absence they think they perceive. The Lincoln Museum silently assumes that for most people Lincoln has stopped being a living presence and that that yawning void has to be filled as completely as possible by harnessing the newest techniques, the most prestigious historical advisors, and the most alluring dramaturgy. The main reason that this approach doesn't work—and that the public admires the verisimilitude of what it gets offered rather than being moved by the past—is that it relies heavily on "metaphoric" strategies.

For trying to fill in absences really is a metaphoric strategy. Each museum display is—like every form of communicated reflection— a conjunction of metonymic and metaphoric elements. A metaphor *creates* context. Every metaphor has the form of "A is like B"—and explains something in terms of something else. When I say "Linda eats like a hamster" I try to say something sensible about Linda's eating habits by comparing them to those of a rodent everybody is familiar with. Metaphor induces the sense that something is under-stood—it "generates meaning." Metaphor thus tries to dispose of strangeness—Linda's weird way of eating is made just a little less unfamiliar by the metaphoric comparison. A metonymy like "the club foot jumps the queue,"[5] on the other hand, highlights something by presenting it *out* of its context: the fact that a person has a club foot is underscored by identifying that person by his disability and presenting him in a situation that is more-or-less incongruous with his handicap. Metonymy has no interest in creating meaning—it draws attention to the fact that something *is* and by zooming in on what may be called "existential givenness" it establishes "presence." So, whereas metaphor tries to do away with strangeness, metonymy *makes* things strange. It accomplishes this by bringing about a short circuit between different contexts.

Traditional museum displays—objects in showcases—are predomi-nantly metonymic: objects that are torn away from the context of the past are shown in the context of the museum. The hundreds of funeral monuments I saw a couple of years ago in the Museo Etrusco in Volt-erra were forced into a museal order that was completely silent about the order from which they originated: "Urne semplice," "Demoni, maschera e simboli," "Animale fantastic e feroci," "Scene di congedo funebre," and "Ciclo eroico." Attributing meaning is in traditional museum displays (like the one in the Museo Etrusco) secondary and almost completely dependent on the textual explanations. In these texts the objects on show are "given context"—they establish meta-phorical connections between objects and public and between life as it was back then and as it is lived right now. So the museum game is that things that are on the one hand metonymically torn out of context are on the other hand metaphorically placed into a context. The objects on show are simultaneously made strange and familiar. Experience museums like the Lincoln Museum employ a completely different mix-ture of metonymic and metaphoric strategies than the Museo Etrusco: they are predominantly metaphoric.[6] Experience museums insist that the past was "like" the presentation it offers the public. They even want the public to forget the metaphoricality of the metaphors they employ—they very much want to dissimulate the fact that the past is not identical with what is on display. It would be a mistake, however, to conclude that this "identity" is of the same order as the existential givenness on which metonymy zooms in. Experience museums seem to have no inkling that presence—as I showed in the previous chapter—is not brought about by metaphor—let alone by the brute force of virtuality—but by metonymy. Presence is *not* the result of metaphorically stuffing up absences with everything you can lay your hands on. It can at best be *kindled* by metonymically *presenting* absences.

Some strategies for having ourselves be affected by the past, for having the past intrude upon us, actually *do* work. One of the most effective is the naming of the names of the dead—or, more specifically, of the victims of history.[7] As far as I know this strategy was first employed in Sir Edwin Lutyens's Monument to the Missing of the Somme in Thiepval. Later, Maya Lin had the names of all the Americans who were killed in Vietnam engraved on the monument that is misleadingly called the Vietnam Veterans Memorial. The strategy of naming names was so successful that by now it is routinely employed in the monuments and commemorations with which we satisfy our lust for presence. Its success depends on the fact that Lutyens and Lin had an intuitive sense for the power of metonymy. Another Lutyens monument, the London Cenotaph, is perhaps the quintessential metonymic monument.[8] As a *Fremdkörper* in the heart of London, it is just there, metonymically presenting the absence of the millions of dead buried on the other side of the Channel. With his sensitivity for metonymy, Lutyens may well have understood that names are the metonymies par excellence. By providing the names of the dead, these objects make absent lives present in the here and now. A name is a cenotaph for the person who once bore it, an abyss in which we may gaze into the fullness of a life that is no more. In the names of the dead, in short, we glimpse the numinosity of history. They have that effect, I believe, because ultimately they throw us back on ourselves. When we let our eyes travel over the names on the Monument to the Missing or the Vietnam Veterans Memorial, the past takes possession of us insofar as the awesome depth of life in ourselves opens up.

Though very common, and despite the fact that we put a lot of effort into pursuing it, presence—the living on of the past in the here and now—is hard to substantiate. It is strikingly undramatic, very elusive, and impossible to isolate. You can experience it, but you can't document it. It can move you, but you can only tell from its wake that it has been there. It has symptoms, though, symptoms from which we can infer that the past really has a presence that eludes our consciousness. One of them is the fact that we "know" far more of the past than can be accounted for by what we have consciously learned from the books we have read, the films we have seen, the paintings we have stared at, the music we have heard. If we did not possess such a mysterious surplus, how else to explain a phenomenon that I think every historian recognizes: that suddenly our sweating away at some historical "object," our rummaging and nitpicking, our plodding and tinkering, suddenly yields to a kind of luminosity, in which the past comes to our assistance and supplies our work with the life we ourselves couldn't provide. You may call it "inspiration," an "Aha-Erlebnis," or just plain "insight," but my point is that it is a kind of gift from regions whose existence we normally do not recognize.

The Noble Art of Slandering

The question, then, is how this subliminal, mysterious, but uncommonly powerful living on, this *presence* of the past, can be envisaged. What does it look like? How does it come into being? And how does it exert its influence? As we try to answer these questions, the first thing to be noticed is that presence is not brought about by *stories*—by, to be more precise, what stories are supposed to do, by, that is, the storiness of stories. My Abba-sensation suggests that the scope and the effectiveness of stories may be much more limited than we have talked ourselves into believing. Ever since the advent of narrativism in the early 1970s, up to the adverse, sulking, counterdependent narrativism of Derrida, we somehow were convinced that stories are what makes the world go round. In the wake of Benedict Anderson, scores of historians exploit the idea that the "identity" of an "imagined community" is a function of the stories that that community entertains about itself. And in much the same way, biographical identity is supposed to result from the stories we tell ourselves—and others—about what we've done.

But Abba was definitely *not* included in my story about myself—and yet, or, as I now think, *precisely because of this*, I was moved by the Abba documentary. This brings me to my first conclusion: my Abba-sensation suggests that what really makes me *me* is not my story about myself, but the variety of ways in which my past can force me—and enable me—to rewrite my story about myself. This, I think, is also valid on the level of the nation. What makes a nation a nation is not its story about itself, but the variety of ways in which its past can force it—and enable it—to rewrite its story about itself.

We encounter a problem here, though. One of the merits of narrativism was that it wasn't just a theory about how we (as nations, cultures, or persons) establish identities, but also about how we manage to lead more-or-less coherent lives. The idea was that we sort of "live" the stories that we consider to be valid, and that because of this the experiences we create tend to be in harmony with the plots in which they have to be assimilated. But if, as I have just proposed, what makes me me (and a nation a nation) is the "variety of ways in which my past can force me to rewrite my story about myself," how can I ever *acquire* the experiences that will eventually force me to do so? How, second, can it be that these experiences exist *without being taken up in some story*—that is, how can they exist and operate in an *unrepresented* form and yet not be blown away? And how, finally, can we imagine these experiences to *survive* in the mind for years, nay decades, on end, quite unchanged and, apparently immune to the wear and tear of time?

As I was thinking about these questions it occurred to me that my Abba-sensation was far from unique. A comparable observation was made by Italo Calvino in his *Invisible Cities*, where he draws attention to the mysterious fact that a city, a landscape, or a work of art may make an indelible impression *precisely* when you do not try to pay attention. Again, the Dutch writer Rudy Kousbroek remarks about this phenomenon that, paradoxically, you may *see* landscapes, cities, and works of art most clearly when you *do not look at them* consciously. As Kousbroek says: they have "stamped" themselves "on your memory when you were doing something else."[9] In fact, as I should have remembered earlier, my Abba-sensation was nothing but a miserable variation of Proust's grand theme in *À la recherche du temps perdu*—a theme that was aptly summarized by Walter Benjamin when he wrote "that only what has not been experienced explicitly and consciously, what has not happened to the subject as an experience, can become a component of the *mémoire involontaire*."[10]

How does this *mémoire involontaire* get filled? And can we say anything definitively about the kind of things it contains? In order for us to answer these questions it might be helpful to compare notes with the rhetoricians. For the question of how—and with what kind of things—our *mémoire involontaire* gets filled can be turned around into the question of how we can fill the *mémoire involontaire* of others.[11] The treacherous issue of what exactly goes on in *our* memory can be converted into the question of how we might smuggle things into the memory of *others* without their being aware of it—and this, of course, is a rhetorical question. In his *Topics*, Aristotle indeed has some things to say about this matter, and Schopenhauer's funny piece about "how to be put in the right" also contains some clues, but by far the most useful discussion about the question of how to influence the *mémoire involontaire* of others was offered by the Dutch writer Karel van het Reve.[12]

As I recall, in his essay Van het Reve attempts to outline the art of slandering. The main thrust of his argument is that to vilify someone really effectively you should cover up your tracks as well as you possibly can. This is important, Van het Reve says, because you should at all times avoid giving the impression that you are just avenging some personal grudge. Van het Reve recommends two simple rules for covering your tracks. The first is that you should suggest that the damaging things you say are common knowledge, and that you are just passing them on. The second is that you shouldn't amass all the damaging things about your victim that you can think of, but you'd be better to weave a damning remark about him or her into a text about *something else*.[13]

So if you want to blacken, say, Professor Zijderveld, the well-known Rotterdam sociologist, you can, of course, write a review of his latest book and enlarge on his megalomania, his vanity, his jealousy, his superficiality, and/or his willingness to go over dead bodies to get a real commercial publisher. And of course you can also, in this review, describe his crowing with pleasure when, instead of going to church, he spends his Sunday morning playing with his toy trains with a real ticket collector's cap on his head. But, according to Van het Reve, all this, no matter how irresistible, is to be avoided. Instead of writing a damning book review, it is much more effective to make use of a piece about something completely different—say "presence"—and to knit some damaging aside about the crowing ticket collector in a subordinate clause. *Then* it will stick—the more so when you succeed in giving the impression that what you say is common knowledge.

If Van het Reve's art of slandering works, as I believe it does, then it gives an inkling as to how, and with what kind of things, the *mémoire involontaire* might get filled. It tends to contain things that we believe are "common knowledge," "public secrets"—things, that is, that are not labeled, that seem to have no identifiable source, that cannot be referred to in a footnote, and, most important of all, that cannot be connected to how and with what stuff we have furnished our minds.

When you come to think of it, it's rather strange: the things that *stick*—the things, that is, that make their way into the *mémoire involontaire*—are the things that do *not* connect to how we have designed the interior of our minds. If you had received the impression that the person slandering Zijderveld had a bone to pick with the professor, the vilification wouldn't have worked. It wouldn't have worked because the slander would have been connected to something else, rendered harmless by the knowledge of "who had said it."[14] But, paradoxically, *precisely* because of that—precisely because the slander would have been connected to something already in the mind—you would also have been able to remember it. You would remember it, however, in an *innocuous* form: in the form that "person so-and-so has an axe to grind with Professor Zijderveld and said this-and-that about him." You would remember it in the form of a *story*.

To sum up: the things that stick do so because they do *not* connect to something already in the mind. As "common knowledge"—or "public secrets"—they just float around. The things that *do* connect to something already in the mind are "defused" by that connection, but can also, because of their being connected to the existing layout of the mind, be *remembered*.[15] Defusing and remembering go hand in hand.

Before I return to the question of how to conceive of a past living on in the here and now, I need to make a final point about the noble art of slandering. If effective character assassination requires that you don't use defamations that connect to things that are already in the mind of the listener, then the art of slandering has another rule, a rule that, as far as I remember, wasn't mentioned by Van het Reve. This third rule is that you should cast your defamations in *metonymies*. You should in any case refrain from witty, or not so witty, *metaphors*. You shouldn't, for example, liken Professor Zijderveld to the animals he makes you think of. Though they may never have troubled their minds about it, gossip writers instinctively know this. They know that effective slandering avoids metaphor — that metaphors provide intellectual entertainment on the level of *logos*, but that metonymies strike home on the level of *pathos*.

The reason that metonymy offers a much better road to the *mémoire involontaire* than metaphor is that metonymy is much better at communicating what I have called "common knowledge."[16] Or, to be more precise: metonymy is better at suggesting that what it conveys *is* "common knowledge." Metaphor, on the other hand, specializes in bringing about a sense of personal comprehension. A metaphorical text draws attention to itself, "simulates," parades its richness, shows off its possible meanings — and, by doing all this, *invites interpretation.*[17] By inviting interpretation, metaphor posits a subject as well as an object. As soon as a trope makes consciousness collapse into a subject and an object, it forfeits its ability to impart "common knowledge." This indeed is what metaphor does: it forfeits the possibility of instilling "common knowledge" and instead devotes itself entirely to inspiring the sensation that something "out there" is comprehended.

With metonymy, things are quite different. Metonymy is the trope of *dissimulation*. Metonymy wants us to believe that it imparts only one "meaning" — the truth — that this "meaning" lies right at the surface, and that this one "meaning" is all that it conveys. Because it suggests that it has nothing to hide, metonymy denies that it needs to be interpreted. Metonymy thus tries to situate itself before the subject/object split. It tries to prevent the milk from curdling into, on the one hand, somebody who has to interpret and, on the other hand, something that has to be interpreted. Insofar as it succeeds in doing so, the knowledge it imparts is "common knowledge."

Public Secrets

After this crash course in the art of slandering, I will return to my question of how the living-on of the past in the here and now can be envisaged. Can we, with the help of what I have said about how, and with what kind of things, the *mémoire involontaire* gets filled, say anything a little more definitive about how our past can force us to rewrite our stories about ourselves? I think we can. The way the past is present in the here and now is quite similar to the way effective slander floats around in the subconscious regions of our mind. Like effective slander, "presence" (for that's what we're talking about) is almost impossible to track down. It is an active force, we do not know it is there, it neither *is*, nor *connects* to, a story, and because it cannot be remembered, it cannot be forgotten either. Like effective slander, "presence" can be regarded as a form of "common knowledge," as a jumble of "public secrets," a huge sphere of—to modify a notion of Frank Ankersmit's—"ideas without a subject."[18]

"Common" knowledge does not mean *uninteresting* knowledge. On the contrary. Slander need not but can be quite informative: the picture of Zijderveld playing with toy trains with a real ticket collector's cap on his head (a blue one with two gold stripes) might be revealing for anyone who can only imagine him in a professorial gown. In much the same way, the "common knowledge" that goes into presence can be very rich. If a historian succeeds in making it conscious, and manages to put it to use in a historical work, this common knowledge (which from then on isn't common anymore) can have the effect of revelation and may give the impression of deep thought and original insight. Just think of the historical sensation that inspired Johan Huizinga's *The Waning of the Middle Ages*.

I think the art of slandering also gives an idea of where to look for "presence." We have seen that the "public secrets" in which successful slander is embodied tend to originate in metonymy. So it will not come as a surprise when I propose that presence resides in the metonymical region of language. In order to explain what I mean by "the metonymical region of language," I should say something about the concept of *representation*. For I believe that the concept of representation makes it virtually impossible even to *discern* this metonymical region, or, as I should say, this denotative level of language.

To reiterate a point I made in chapter 3, the concept of representation obscures the fact that all "pictures"—in paint, words, or marble—are amalgamations of "metonymical denotation" and "metaphorical connotation." Here, however, we immediately run into the ambiguity of the word "picture"—and of its Sunday-best equivalent "representation" as well. The word "picture" does not convey the fact that each picture achieves two things: it *presents* something and it *says something about, or does something with, what is presented.* Aristotle, I believe, sensed this as he also struggled with the shortcomings of the word "picture." In his book on memory he wrote: "A picture painted on a panel is at once a picture and a likeness—that is, while one and the same, it is both of these, although the 'being' of both is not the same, and one may contemplate it either as a picture or as a likeness."[19]

Aristotle's distinction between "picture" and "likeness," between what is "presented" and "what the writer or the artist does with what is presented" is, I think, especially relevant for history. Yet the fact that historians cannot avoid *presenting* a part of the past when they want to *do* things with that part seems not to have interested philosophers of history. That is to say, the denotative level of historiography is sometimes *mentioned,* but it is the level of what historians *do* with what they present that always steals the show. In fact, one of the few thinkers about history who takes "metonymical denotation" seriously is the early twentieth-century German historian Karl Heussi. In a little book published in 1932, Heussi wrote that "historical thoughts are *Vertretungen* ('presentations') that purport to suggest meaning."[20] Each work of history is, according to Heussi, a compound of *Vertretungen* and *Vorstellungen*. In *Vertretungen* the past is presented; in *Vorstellungen* it is made sense of.

This lack of interest in the distinction between *Vertretungen* and *Vorstellungen* may well be due to a peculiarity of *verbal* pictures. In language it is even more difficult than in paint or in marble to denote something without at the same time releasing an uncontrollable flow of connotations. Consequently, it requires quite a bit of imagination to sense denotation in pictures that are cast in language—in, for example, the books of historians. Denotation is always bound up with meaning, but the fact that in language denotation doesn't exist in a pure form does not, of course, mean that metonymical denotation is reducible to metaphorical connotation, as representationalism implies.

Where does all this leave us? I have argued that presence resides in the denotative region of language, in what Heussi calls *Vertretungen*, in what story and text contain *in spite of* the intentions of its authors. To put it differently: presence does not reside in the storiness of stories, but in what a story inadvertently has to be—in, that is, the things a story has to present in order to present a story. In still other words: presence travels with our stories not as a paying passenger but, as I said in the previous chapter, as a *stowaway*.

This stowaway, however, is not hiding deep down in the recesses of our stories. It is rather a sunbather on the upper deck. In the form of "common knowledge"—or, as I have also called it, "public secrets"—it resides right in front of us, but in places that coincide with our blind spots. Presence succeeds in going unnoticed not because it is hidden from view, but because it coincides with our culture. In a sense it *is* our culture. Culture, after all, is the set of things we do not have to talk about, our private collection of public secrets. As common knowledge, presence is indestructible—and because it cannot be remembered it is also unforgettable. So like a scattering of Flying Dutchmen, presence floats through the here and now, manifesting itself—at convenient and not so convenient moments—in the form of *Sehnsucht*, in the form of Srebrenica historians reproducing their object, and in countless other forms. Floating through the here and now, this presence of the past also makes me *feel* things, *think* things, and *do* things that are at odds with who I think I am—and so forces me to rewrite my story about myself.

Because it is indestructible, this "common knowledge" *stays* present on the surface of the here and now. It is as presence, then, that the past is more dramatically present than naïve historical realists assume. And it is as presence, too, that the past is more radically absent than historical constructionists claim. For, as presence, the past is terribly close, though it can never be reached. As presence, the past is the exact opposite of what historians think it is. Historians—especially representationalist historians—assume that the past is "lost," that it is gone forever, but that it can be "represented" in "representations" that can be taken along in the hand luggage with which we traverse time. As presence, however, the past is the exact opposite, the cruel Proustian irony: indestructible, uncannily close, and—despite its closeness and its durability—utterly impossible to conserve in "representations."

The antinomy is caused by the fact that in presence "time" is traded for "place." In presence, the past is present in the here and now in much the same way as in transference the past of a psychoanalytic patient is present in the psychoanalytic situation. I think there is hardly anyone who sensed the way the here and now is charged with an uncanonical past as clearly as the poet William Wordsworth. In *The Prelude*, "a long poem," as the subtitle reads, "upon the formation of my own mind," Wordsworth tries to recreate his past from what he saw on his walks—from, that is, *places*. And that's what *The Prelude* is: Wordsworth's sublime effort to surprise himself with the truths about himself that could be gleaned from, as he called them, "spots of time."

The "Sudden Incursion of Unreality"

One of Wordsworth's themes in *The Prelude* is that we can only be moved by the "spots of time" we encounter insofar as we are first alienated by our past. How exactly we have to be alienated from the past in order to be overwhelmed by it is the theme of Roland Barthes's posthumous little masterpiece *La chambre claire*—translated into English as *Camera Lucida*.[21] Barthes's book—subtitled *Reflections on Photography*—was prompted by the death of his beloved mother. It is the record of something we all do once in a while: to wrest the reality of our own personal past out of the photographs we find in albums and old shoeboxes. Barthes's attempt to get in touch with his mother by questioning photographs had, however, an uncanny or, rather, downright disturbing result: when, eventually, he IS moved by the reality of his mother, the photograph that brings about the magic is not a photograph of his mother as he knew her, but a photograph of his mother as he *never* knew her: as a child.

Barthes's own explanation of this anomalous phenomenon revolves round the well-known concepts of *studium* and *punctum*. Our semiconscious ideas of what counts as nice themes and forms, of what "demands" to be photographed, may be referred to as *studium*. *Studium* is, in the words of Barthes, "of the order of *liking*, not of *loving* . . . it is the sort of vague, slippery, irresponsible interest one takes in the people, the entertainments, the books, the clothes one finds 'all right'" (27). Sound themes and artsy good taste can, however, be thwarted by a detail that is overlooked by the photographer. Such a detail Barthes calls a *punctum*—and, significantly, he bestows his *punctum* with an autonomous power, a power that exists independently of his own receptivity. A *punctum*, Barthes says, "rises from the scene, shoots out of it like an arrow, and pierces me" (26).

One of Barthes's examples of his being "pierced" by reality "shooting out" of a photograph is the rutted dirt road in André Kertész's image of a blind gypsy violinist somewhere in the Hungarian countryside. This road, with its textured surface, Barthes argues, has ended up in the photograph completely accidentally: Kertész, trying to take a picturesque picture of his *studium*, could not NOT have photographed it. This, according to Barthes, is the way reality may find its way into a photograph. It goes without saying that a photograph is the result of how something has been *seen* by the photographer, but the reality that—later on—may "touch" or "move" the spectator is not to be found in what has been seen, but in what succeeds in getting "on board" of the photograph unnoticed. The consequence of Barthes's train of thought is, of course, that it is not the talent, the professionalism, or the vision of the photographer that causes pictures to move us, but the simple fact of his being on the spot when he releases the shutter. And that indeed was his conclusion: "The Photographer's 'second sight,'" Barthes says, "does not consist in 'seeing' but in being there."

Barthes suggests that the reason he was touched by a picture of his mother as a child, rather than as the woman he had seen with his own eyes, is that as an adult, his mother was conscious of how she wanted to be represented. In portraits, not only the photographer aspires to "good taste"—to, that is, *studium*—but the subject as well. Portraits thus involve a kind of counterproductive conspiracy between the photographer and his subject that tends to exclude the accidental. In this sense, photography, as the pursuit of the picturesque, batters reality into silence *precisely* by trying to depict it eloquently. Barthes's mother is gone forever—that is: *dead*—to the extent she succeeded in controlling how she wanted to be remembered. But, happily, she survived in as far as she didn't care whether and how she lived on.

Barthes's ideas about the ability of the past to reach out and overwhelm us in the present were taken up, amplified, and radicalized by a writer I discussed in the previous chapter: W. G. Sebald. *Austerlitz*, the book Sebald had just finished when he died, explores the Barthesian theme of how the past may "move" us. The motive as well as theme of the book is, as Sebald calls it somewhere, to bring "remembered events back to life." This, however, is a very misleading designation—for the remarkable thing about *Austerlitz* is that it is the opposite of a hermeneutic enterprise. In Sebald's book "remembered events" are not typically brought "back to life" by the exertions of an interpreter but by the ability of the past to make its way to the present *completely on its own*. With Sebald, the events somehow bring *themselves* back to life.

Sebald introduces his outrageous claim rather inconspicuously. In the beginning of the book the eponymous hero lectures the nameless narrator about a small painting by the seventeenth-century master Lucas van Valckenborch. Somewhere in the middle ground of this painting, a view of Antwerp across the frozen river Scheldt, a woman with a canary yellow jacket can be seen—a woman who has just fallen on the ice. In this unsightly detail in an unsightly painting, the past lives on in a way that touches Austerlitz. "I feel," he says, "as if the moment depicted by Lucas van Valckenborch had never come to an end." The moments that "never end"—that travel through time in their full scope—are, according to Austerlitz, the moments in which something went wrong. The woman in the canary yellow jacket *falls* forever, and, as Austerlitz says, "nothing and no one could ever remedy it."

Sebald develops his theme by showing the peregrinations in which Austerlitz tries to uncover the fate of his parents. Like *Camera Lucida*, the book starts from a void in the present, but with Sebald, absence encompasses much more than with Barthes. Austerlitz doesn't possess photographs of his dead parents, has no idea what they looked like, doesn't even know that he *had* parents other than the ones that turn out to be his stepparents. Austerlitz doesn't *have* a void, he *is* a void. In Sebald's novel absence is not a *part* of life—it *is* life. The past Austerlitz doesn't know, the past that isn't present in the form of representations, is more real than the present in which he has to move around. When he finally hits upon snapshots from his childhood, he is impressed by their mysterious power. "One has the impression," Austerlitz reflects, "of something stirring in them, as if one caught small sighs of despair . . . as if the pictures had a memory of their own and remembered us, remembered the roles that we, the survivors, and those no longer among us had played in our former lives."

Strangely, the photograph that "has a memory of its own," and performs the extraordinary trick of "remembering him," is a photograph in which Austerlitz doesn't wear his normal, "representative," clothes but is dressed up for a very special occasion and wears the completely "unrepresentative" costume of a page. That, incidentally, seems to be a kind of pattern. Commenting on the fact that for Walter Benjamin reality was preserved much better in kitsch than in high art, Winfried Menninghaus has remarked that "life is present in secondary forms." Sebald's insistence that the past reaches Austerlitz by means of a thoroughly unrepresentative picture suggests that we should go a bit further than the observation that the reality of the past shies away from traveling in "primary" forms, in, that is, representations that go to great lengths to be mimetic or realist. Curiously often we are hit by the reality of the past when that reality wears the mask of *un*reality. Marcel Proust was touched by the past when he saw the whitened faces at the ball of the Duc de Guermantes. R. G. Collingwood was, in, I think, 1916, moved by the past by the blackened Albert Memorial—blackened because the glittering gold would have attracted German zeppelins.

Apparently it is not the faithful representation of a representative slice of reality that has the best chances of touching us, but the "sudden incursion of unreality in the real world."[22] On the face of it, this looks like the opposite of Barthes's *punctum* (which may be defined as "the incursion of reality in the stylized, unreal world of the *studium*"). It may, however, have the same effect: it releases the stowaway, it liberates reality from the medium in which that reality appears. Not just in "real time"—as military men nowadays call the here and now—but also ex post facto, when we are gazing at the specific way in which an "incursion of unreality in the real world" has been represented by an observer, an artist, or a photographer, when, that is, we are studying what historians call a "source." But, according to Sebald, it is not just photographs that "can remember us." Physical remains and objects that are handed down to us from the past can accomplish the same feat. When, on his quest for his lost past, Austerlitz returns from Prague, he is somehow struck by the capital of a cast-iron column. Sebald then writes: "What made me uneasy at the sight of it was not the question of whether the capital . . . had really impressed itself on my mind when I passed through Pilsen with the children's transport in the summer of 1939, but the idea, ridiculous in itself, that this cast-iron column, which with its scaly surface seemed almost to approach the nature of a living being, might remember *me*, and was, if I may so put it, a witness to what I could no longer recollect for myself."

By using words like "scaly surface," Sebald evokes primordial reptiles and as such the cast-iron column is similar to the photograph that shows Austerlitz dressed up as a page. Both picture and column are "incursions of unreality in the real world" of the kind in which, as I have argued, the past may break loose. Neither column nor photograph "*represents*" the past—they do not in any way describe or evoke what the past "looked like" and they throw no light whatsoever on Austerlitz's "roots." What they succeed in doing is much more difficult: they telescope something that has *no meaning*, something like the sand on the photo by Kertész, into the here and now. They are, as Wordsworth would have said, "spots of time."

What Sebald says about things "remembering us" is really the same as what I have called being moved by the presence of the past. Now, we have seen that to steer clear from the domain of meaning is very hard—not because we wouldn't want to, but because the structure of our system of representation forbids it. Presence, I have argued, resides not in meaningful representations but in the denotative region of language, in what Heussi calls *Vertretungen*, in what story and text contain *in spite of* the intentions of its authors. Friedrich Schlegel sums up the difficulty of getting into contact with this denotative region exceptionally well: "Mann kann nicht sagen *dasz* etwas ist, ohne zu sagen *was* es ist" ("one cannot say THAT something is, without saying WHAT it is"). Remarkably, Austerlitz's cast-iron column, as well as the photograph he comes across, somehow succeeds in what Schlegel deemed impossible: each projects a "that" without at the same time imposing a "what." And it is as a "that," not as a "what," as "presence," not as meaning, that the past may pierce us like an arrow and "remembers us."

Sebald thus teaches us that presence owes its existence to the tragic fact that representations of reality necessarily create *un*reality. To refer to Schlegel again: with every representation we come forward with, we not only create a manifest "what" but also a subterranean "that"—and it is the absence of "that's" on the surface level of representation that generates a sense of *un*reality. We passionately try to catch the real in our representations, but, unfortunately our sense of reality always convinces us that reality is where representation is not.[23] But stowed away in these representations, in these exercises in what Barthes called *studium,* the past is very much present. Not however as "a part of us"—something that is ontologically inferior than that of which it is a part: we ourselves. Instead, the past is, in a very real sense, *bigger* than us, an attribute of the field we are in. The past is not in any way "behind" us, but is, as a huge collection of "spots of time," a part of the reality in which we operate. We can discover it by doing the things that lie on our path. Or rather: by doing the things that, after we have done them, appear to have been on our path. We find ourselves, according to Hugo von Hofmannstal, not *within* but *without* ourselves: "Wollen wir uns finden, so dürfen wir nicht in unser Inneres hinabsteigen: draußen sind wir zu finden, draußen. Wie der wesenlose Regenbogen spannt sich unsere Seele über den unaufhalt-samen Sturz des Daseins. Wir besitzen unser Selbst nicht: von außen weht es uns an, es flieht uns für lange und kehrt uns in einem Hauch zurück."[24]

5

Thirsting for Deeds

Schiller and the Historical Sublime

I think he was just normal. Isn't it always the case, though? It's always the normal ones that you don't really think they're going to do something like this.[1]

As a Dutchman I may not have quite the right credentials to comment on Friedrich Schiller's vision of the historical sublime. Schiller writes: "Who doesn't prefer to marvel at the great contest between fertility and destruction in Sicily's farmlands, doesn't prefer to feast his eye on Scotland's wild waterfalls and hazy mountains, than gaping, in rectilinear Holland, at the unsavoury victory of perseverance over the most stubborn of elements?"[2] And Schiller is indubitably right. Tourists looking for the sublime shouldn't visit Holland—though with the murder of Pim Fortuyn in 2002 and Theo van Gogh in 2004 and with the sublime "no" (a bit spoiled, I must confess, by the French also saying "no") against the EU constitution, Dutch society recently made some headway in making up politically for what it lacks geologically.

But, of course, Schiller was referring exclusively to the fact that in Holland even "nature" is "culture"—or, as he called it, "a market garden pure and simple" ("einem regulären Wirtschaftsgarten"). From a rational point of view, Schiller went on, such a well-raked plot of land is much to be preferred above Ossian's wild nature. But, Schiller says, "men have not only the need to live and to submerge themselves in comfort, and they have other vocations than just to understand the phenomena around them."[3] With the last part of this sentence we are in the middle of Schiller's ideas about the sublime, or—as it is called in German—"das Erhabene." That people have needs other than to live through the one day to the next with their stomachs filled with the fruits of their "regulären Wirtschaftsgarten" most of us can easily accept, but what can Schiller mean by these "other vocations" he mentions? What more can humans—and especially the phlegmatic individuals like you, reader, who love to read books—pursue than to "understand the phenomena around them"?

Rather surprisingly, for Schiller the most important "other vocation" was the disruptive force with which societies every now and then break out from the cosiness of a settled life—or as he calls it, "Erschlaffung" ("slackening"). History is, Schiller says, "the awesomely magnificent drama of change: destruction, followed by creation, followed by destruction again."[4] Schiller thus stands in a line of thinkers who only half believe in tradition. His conviction that history is primarily "metamorphosis"—that things change not just marginally but fundamentally, yes, more fundamentally than we can even imagine—puts him in the same league as thinkers like Vico and Burckhardt. Like them, Schiller is not hampered—as most historians are—by the impulse to look for what *connects* us to our past. In the previous chapter I have argued that the presence of the past does not reside in the storiness of stories and one may well say, I think, that for unhistorical historians like Vico, Schiller, and Burckhardt history is not a more-or-less continuous "story" but, as Burckhardt said, "ein wundersames Prozess von Verpuppungen" ("a marvelous succession of metamorphoses").

It isn't that easy, though, to ascertain what Schiller's ideas about this "awe-inspiring drama of history" entail. One of the main reasons is, rather paradoxically, that Schiller loves to theorize so much. This, so it seems to me, is especially true with regard to his insights about the sublime in history. In his irrepressible urge to expound his views discursively he resembles Tolstoy. And as with Tolstoy, his verbosity doesn't suit him very well. In *War and Peace* Tolstoy devotes page after page, even whole chapters, to his theories about history, but these rather shrill theoretical passages—interesting as they might be—do not contain his most penetrating insights. On the contrary: Tolstoy's

most disturbing views on "how history comes about," and how historiography *distorts* "how history comes about," lie hidden in the way he
himself represented, in his novel, a past reality.[5] With Schiller too the
ideas he *professes* to have tend to obscure the ideas he in fact embodies
in his work.

The view of history, for example, that is implicit in his early play *Die
Räuber* ("The Robbers," first staged in 1782) is, I think, more profound,
more radical, and more unsettling than the ideas he jotted down in
"Vom Erhabenen" (which was written in 1793). I do not know any
writer who has improved upon an encounter with Kant—and Schiller
is no exception. In fact, "Vom Erhabenen" (subtitled "Zur weitern Aus-
führung einiger Kantische Ideen" ["Toward the further elaboration of
some Kantian ideas"]) is a dark and impenetrable forest—or rather,
because it's quite short, an inextricable knot of tumbleweed. Personally, I find it hard to understand why so many studies about what
Schiller has to say about the sublime focus on *this* work. If one insists
on having Schiller's ideas dished up discursively, a later essay, "Über
das Erhabene" (published in 1801), is much to be preferred. In "Über
das Erhabene," Schiller has freed himself from Kant and partially recu-
perates the views he expressed intuitively, or, as he himself would say,
"naïvely," in *Die Räuber* and—somewhat less spectacularly—in his second play, *Fiesko*.

So, in this chapter I will not enmesh myself in the intricacies of what
Schiller has to *say* about the sublime, but attempt something that, perhaps, is more rewarding: to try to fathom what conception of the "historical sublime" is *actually operative* in an early work like *Die Räuber*.
Apart from having the advantage of being less "sentimental" and more
"naïve" than the essays, *Die Räuber* also has the benefit of treating the
sublime *from the inside*. For this is another feature of the theoretical
essays. As soon as Schiller starts to philosophize, history stops being *in
us*, and becomes something that is *out there*. In his theoretical writings
the sublime is seen as something with which we humans may be *confronted*, as "a power" outside us. In his theoretical writings "history"
is—in short—what it is to historians: a foreign country, something of
the past. In his plays however history is what historians don't want history to be: something of the present, something operative in the here
and now, in themselves, in *us*.

Committing History

The difference between history as experienced from the inside and history as experienced from the outside may be reconceptualized in terms of what dominates what. In Schiller's theoretical essays the historical sublime dominates *us*: in the sublime historical events Schiller meditates upon in his essays a way of life is "overtaken" by what's new. In Schiller's plays, however, the sublime is not primarily something that "overtakes us," but first and foremost *we*—or at least some of his heroes—"overtake" the things we take for granted. In many of Schiller's plays the drama springs from the urge to make, or even to *commit*, history. Once followed, this urge irrevocably changes things—and it is the loss of contact between what *was* and what *has been brought about* that lends such heartbreaking "tragedy" to what happens between his characters. The end of *Die Räuber* is a case in point. The highly charged reunion of robber Karl Moor and his love, Amalia, ends in Karl murdering her. This much-criticized murder may have a melodramatic ring, but is in fact quite logical. Moor exclaims, "For can a great sinner ever retrace his steps? A great sinner never can never retrace his steps, I should have known that all along."[6] To understand the tension of what happens between Karl and Amalia one should realize that Karl is not just an ordinary "sinner"—but a "sublime" one.

The exact status of the robbers is, in fact, an ambiguity of the play that has given rise to many misunderstandings. In my opinion one can only understand the play, and the sensation it provokes, when one accepts that Schiller's robbers are not just "parasitic" on the existing order, but follow a revolutionary trajectory. They are more like modern al Qaida terrorists or, perhaps better, the *Comité du Salut Public* than latter-day Robin Hoods. In the opening scene Karl's brother Franz senses what Karl is up to when he reminds his father that Karl "much preferred reading about the adventures of Julius Caesar, Alexander the Great, and other pitch-dark heroes, than the story of the repentant Tobias."[7] And Karl himself remembers that when he was a boy he wanted to rise and go down like the sun: "When I was a naughty boy it was my favorite thought: to live like the sun, to go under like the sun. It was a naughty boy's thought."[8]

At the end of the play Karl has followed a trajectory that has transported him beyond the bounds of the status quo, a trajectory that has—in a sense—*changed* the status quo and that has transformed him into a man other than the man he was destined to be: the husband of Amalia. As soon as Amalia senses that she loves someone who doesn't exist anymore, she asks him to kill her. At first he refuses, but then Amalia cries, "You can only kill those who are happy, but you spare those who are through with life"[9]—which, indeed, is what sublime historical actors like terrorists of all persuasions do. Finally Karl concedes: "Moor's love should only be killed by Moor." This is followed by the laconic stage direction: "he murders her."[10]

The thesis of *Die Räuber* is that the loss of contact between what *was* and what *has been brought about* cannot be mended. "Rather will a bullet return to the barrel" ("Eh soll die Kugel in ihren Lauf zurück-kehren") than what is done can be undone. This incommensurability also explains why, in the play, persons from the opposing sides of the divide are "dead" for each other: up till the last act, Amalia and Karl's father cannot but believe that Karl is dead, while Karl, for his part, is convinced for some time that his father is dead. It might be remarked that, structurally, Schiller's vision is the exact opposite of what Walter Scott did in his novels. As I said in chapter 3, Scott typically places the male hero of his novels on the near side of a chasm brought about by a historical mutation and the heroine at the far side. The novel then recounts how the hero descends into what has become historically obsolete. At the end of the novel the bride is transported to the near side, to *our* side of history and "the old" is taken up in "the new." With Schiller, however, such a reconciliation is utterly impossible. There can be no marriage between what was before and after a metamorphosis, just as there can be, to put it somewhat unromantically, no interbreeding between a chimpanzee and a Homo sapiens. Scott's novels are prototypical Restauration novels, while Schiller's *Räuber* could only be written *before* a major revolution.

Because he exploits—and to a certain extent *revels* in—the fact that in history things cannot be "undone," Schiller is the quintessential *historical* playwright. As far as I know, he is one of the very few writers for whom the drama, the tragedy, doesn't spring from some moral conflict, but from the urge to "commit" history. Schiller makes it quite clear that one cannot dismiss the urge to commit history as just a criminal aberration. In *Fiesko* the hero thinks: "Virtuousness?—the sublime fellow is tempted by other things than the man in the street— how would he share virtuousness with him?" And a little later: "It is despicable to empty a wallet—it is insolent to embezzle a million, but it is unspeakably great to steal a crown."[11]

Schiller firmly believes that doing unimaginable, awesome, terri- ble—in short, *sublime*—things is, whether we like it or not, ingrained in how we humans progress through time. That's why he speaks about— as we have seen—a vocation, a destination, a "Bestimmung." Like Vico before him, Schiller has a conception of human history that is far more profound than that of the average historian: for him human history is just the last stage of human *evolution*—and it is by doing brutal, unimag- inable, *sublime* things that we have changed ourselves from prehistoric *orribile bestioni*, as Vico calls them, into civilized human beings.

This evolutionary point of view, which sets him apart from the profes- sional historian, surfaces perhaps most straightforwardly in his "Etwas über die erste Menschengesellschaft nach dem Leitfaden der mosaischen Urkunde" ("Some remarks about the first human society, as suggested by Moses's record")—which he ostensibly wrote in 1792. I do not know whether Schiller knew or read Vico's *Scienza Nuova*, but in this essay he puts forward the very Vico-like proposition that Adam—in his disobe- dience against God's commandments—wrested himself free from his instincts, and that this "sublime" disobedience may count as "the first mark of his self-motivation, the first gamble of his reason, the first sign of his moral existence." It's true, Schiller maintains, that Adam's "fall" introduced "evil" in the world, but, he says, precisely because of that it also cleared the way for moral goodness. Adam's successful attempt to supersede his instincts is, according to Schiller, "without doubt the hap- piest and greatest event in human history." And, he concludes, "from this moment the story of his freedom unfolds."[12]

The Brink of Time

In bringing about a new evolutionary level, the initial step, the step beyond the status quo or, to put it in evolutionary terms, the *mutation*, is crucial—and it is precisely *this* that makes *Die Räuber* such a reward-ing work. In later plays—like *Wallenstein*—Schiller concentrates on exploring the amalgamation of the new and the old—but one can very well maintain that *Die Räuber* is the vintage text about *how "the new" actually comes about.* It is this initial move, or "original sin," that I want to comment upon in the remainder of this chapter.

But before I go on, I will pause for a moment and say a few words about the effect *Die Räuber* has on a contemporary public—or, rather, on an outsider like me who was not obliged to read the play at school and for whom the text is new and fresh. I must say that I found it an astonishing piece. This text, more than two hundred and twenty years old—written halfway between Milton's *Paradise Lost* and Dostoyevs-ki's *The Devils*—still has the ability to shock. Of course there are dull passages, and much of the action depends on things that are hard to believe or even downright ridiculous, but especially in the monologues of Karl, his brother Franz, and the evil genius Spiegelberg, Schiller's lyrical style transports him to depths that only very great writers can hope to reach. Even to modern ears, these monologues strike home as viciously as contemporary novels by Michel Houellebecq or Elfriede Jelinek. Just listen to Franz as he reflects in his first great monologue on the Christian imperative that he honor his father: "*why* did he make me? Not out of love for me I guess—I still had to become an 'I' . . . What then is so holy about the whole thing? Does it have anything to do with the act itself by means of which I was created? As if that was something else than a bestial process to satisfy a bestial desire!"[13]

But the subversive effect of the play does not reside only in what characters like Franz, Karl, and Spiegelberg actually *say*. It is not even dependent on the relish with which—to name just one example—a raid on a convent is described, with graphic details about the gang-banging of nuns and the way the robbers force the ugly abbess to dance nakedly for them—a description, by the way, that ends with Schiller mentioning that Karl's men have left a nice little souvenir: the nuns "will have to drag their nine months along with them."[14]

The main reason *Die Räuber* still makes such an impression is what I would like to call Schiller's "thematic perversity." I will skip minor perversities like the fact that in *Die Räuber* medicine is prac-ticed to kill rather than to heal, and the fact that to deliver oneself to the authorities is the most cruel punishment that can be imagined, and go straightaway to Schiller's main themes. In *Die Räuber*, the two most conspicuous perversities are that it is not the younger, intellectual "Jacob-like" Franz, but the older, outgoing "Esau-like" Karl, who has our sympathy, and, second, the twisted relation between fathers and sons. With regard to the latter: it is not merely that the old count Moor is so appallingly weak, but Schiller's insistence that fathers are accountable to their sons instead of the other way around. In the final act, the old Moor blubbers that he wants to impart to his son "my tears, my sleepless nights, my agonizing dreams, I want to clinch his knee, and cry, cry loudly: I have sinned in heaven and for you. I do not deserve being called father by you."[15]

This, I suspect, was heavy stuff when the play was first performed in 1782. At the end of the play Schiller makes Karl exclaim "that two people like myself would destroy the whole structure of moral society"[16]—and because there is, apart from Karl, also Franz, there really *are* two people "like him." The effect is what Karl predicts it to be. The play demolishes the foundational myth of society. By what he makes the two antagonistic brothers say and do, Schiller demonstrates that society is held together by arbitrary conventions—and that conventions can be overthrown by anyone who dares to think for himself, has an appetite for power, and doesn't care about personal happiness.

For antagonistic as they might be, the brothers agree about the spuriousness of the foundations of society. Here is Franz: "Justice resides in the man who prevails, and the limits of our power designate the end of our laws."[17] A remark that becomes even more poignant in the light of what he says somewhat later: "I will exterminate everything around me that encroaches upon my being master."[18] And this, a few pages later, is Karl: "The law has degraded into a snail's pace what could have become the flight of an eagle. The law has never brought forward a great man, but freedom breeds giants and extremes."[19]

Hans-Jürgen Schings and, later, Rüdiger Safranski have argued that in the relations between the brothers and their father the "Great Chain of Being" has been broken.[20] I think that's true—but I also think that it isn't the whole truth. There can be little doubt that in *Die Räuber* the past has been left behind, but, according to Schiller, the past *has* to be left behind in order to add a new and vital link to the "Great

Chain of Being." This surely doesn't mean that the new link is already available—or has even been envisaged. On the contrary: the link can only be "valid" when it is made in a state of blindness with regard to the future. Schiller, in short, is interested in what is so beautifully epitomized in the German word *Selbsthervorbringung*. What *Die Räuber* makes so hallucinatorily clear is what it feels like "to stand on the brink of time." Karl and Franz, each in his own peculiar way, do not in the least know where they are heading to; they only know—or think they know—what they want to leave behind.

This, I think, is the veritable *sublime* moment. So, my contention is that the sublime in history is not what one retrospectively designates as "terrible" and "unimaginable" events—as most theorists about the sublime do, as even Schiller himself tends to do when he is in a professorial mood—but the prospect of the awesome void before you at the moment you have burnt the ships *behind* you. I want to stress that this conception of the sublime has nothing to do with the cliché that "one never knows what the future holds in store." As we all know only too well, life almost always stays within the beaten track. Of course we do not know what will happen tomorrow, but we trust that what will happen tomorrow will somehow fit in the stories we bring over from today. We are—in short—definitely not in the habit of "burning ships behind us"—not as individuals, and even less so as societies. Only very seldom—in 1789, in 1914—is there a widespread readiness to put a whole *way of life,* a culture, on the line. And the horrible truth is that at such moments people behave in accordance with the fourth thesis I proposed in chapter 1: they start to make history not *although* it is at odds with—yes, destroys—the stories they live by, but *because* it destroys the stories they live by.

In the next chapter I will argue that this condition of "standing on the brink of time" might be called *vertigo*[21]—"Akrophobie," "Schwindel." In one of the lyric monologues that are the hallmark of Schiller's genius he describes this "vertigo": "O, to stand on that terrible sublime height," he writes in *Fiesko,* "and to revel from above in the tempestuous human maelstrom . . . to direct, by just playing with the reins, the unruly passions of the people like so many fiery steeds, to quench the flaring pride of the vassals with *one*—one breath!"[22] In this position of "vertigo" it is almost impossible not to *do* something. The void *has*

to be filled—if need be by jumping into it. It should be remarked that
vertigo may feel like "the fear of falling," but in reality it is—according to psychoanalysis—a *wish to jump*, covered by a fear of falling. In a
position of vertigo, the sense that the void *has* to be filled may mushroom into something so overwhelming, so oppressive, that "the wish
to jump" breaks through "the fear of falling." Vertigo thus predisposes
to making—nay, *committing*—history. Once in a state of vertigo, it may
seem utterly impossible for one *not* to step down from the brink of
time, *not* to jump into the unknown, *not* to start to make history.

Of course, this condition of vertigo is a state of mind, of consciousness. In reality the future always has the same blank and implacable
face; in reality everything ultimately has its way if just left alone. But
although the void, the abyss of what lies ahead, is a reified metaphor,
a figment of the imagination, the desire to jump can be so oppressive as to become a veritable compulsion: something, something radical, something unheard of, something *sublime* has to be done. This, I
think, was more-or-less what happened in Germany in August 1914.
Schiller sensed this urge to fill the void by *doing* something, by action,
as scarcely any writer before or after him. It is one of the themes of
Fiesko—as when he makes Fiesko decide: "I have to expand myself in
the [public] space."[23]

It also pervades his dramatic and historical work. It has always
struck me that in his *Geschichte des Abfalls der Vereinigten Niederlände
von der Spanischen Regierung* ("History of the Secession of the United
Netherlands from the Spanish Government") Schiller doesn't speak—
as a historian would do—of "Aufstand," "Aufruhr," or "Erhebung" but
of "Abfall" (lit. "falling down"). By using this word, Schiller indicates
that what the Dutch did was more a "falling *from* something" than
an "aspiring *to* something." The word *Abfall* testifies that for Schiller
making history is not a matter of rationality and chance, of choice
and necessity, of balances upset and redressed, but of making the best
of the situations we find ourselves in after doing unimaginable and
unimagined things. For Schiller, then, what the Dutch did to Philip
the Second is perhaps quantitatively but not *essentially* different from
what Adam did to God. In both cases he speaks of *Abfall*, and both
cases may be regarded as mutations in the evolution of humanity, an
evolution Schiller always describes in terms of "freedom."

It might be remarked that freedom, with Schiller, is thoroughly paradoxical. For Schiller, freedom is not just the opportunity, but the *obligation* to do unheard of, terrible things, things that are not determined by what came before. The paradox is that these terrible things somehow *have* to be done—not because some individual "freely" decides to do them, but because it is the way humankind, as *Gattung*, has to produce the metamorphoses by which it progresses through time and brings about its own *Selbsthervorbringung*. A "free" action, with Schiller, does not so much mean one that is freely chosen as one that is not determined by the context from which it springs. Schiller does not consider the specific course of human evolution as preordained: the terrible, "sublime" things that are the outcome of men's "höhe dämonische Freiheit" are determined neither by what came before nor by what they led up to.

In the Beginning Was the Deed

It would be utterly wrong to equate this evolution with "progress." Like Vico, Schiller has a clear eye for the fact that historical mutations cause loss, that in a very real sense the new situation is poorer than the one it replaces. In the little work I mentioned earlier—"Etwas über die erste Menschengesellschaft nach dem Leitfaden der mosaischen Urkunde"—Schiller writes that Adam's *Abfall* really is a *fall*, "because man changed from an innocent into a guilty creature, from a perfect apprentice of nature into an imperfect moral being, from a happy instrument into an unhappy artist."[24]

Though the view that "making history" is filling up the void by doing unimaginable things pops up in many of Schiller's works, it is in *Die Räuber* that it is embodied most vigorously. When in the second scene of the first act, Karl Moor burns his ships behind him, and embarks upon his career as chief of a band of robbers, he exclaims: "My mind thirsts for deeds."[25] And that in fact is what he does: he starts to *do things*. In his "inauguration address" (when he has been chosen as the robbers' leader) he subsequently makes clear—both to himself and to his brothers in arms—that only by doing things that are incompatible with what is left behind can the new supersede the old.

Knowingly contradicting the facts, Karl cries: "I do not have a father anymore, I do not have a love anymore, and blood and death shall teach me to forget that I ever cared for things."[26]

Where his deeds will lead him, Karl doesn't know. Interrogating a starry-eyed new recruit, Karl speaks the admonishing words, "First get acquainted with the depth of the abyss before you jump into it."[27] But he knows full well that the depth of the abyss can only by fathomed by giving in to "vertigo"—by, that is, jumping into the void. After the robbers have sworn to follow him he tells them all there is to know about their destiny: "Come on, let's go! Do not be afraid of death and danger—we are ruled by an imperturbable destiny! What will happen to you will happen to you: on the soft, plush cushion of power, in the brutal turbulence of combat, or on a public gallows! One of these is our destiny!"[28]

In fact—and this, I think, is an important point—from the moment he has embarked upon his career, Karl is determined by his deeds, instead of the other way around. His deeds are not made by him, but he is made by his deeds. The fact that he doesn't know where his "sublime" fall will take him means that he will end up where his deeds will bring him. In his insistence that the sublime kind of acting that results from jumping into the unknown—or, perhaps better, *embodies* the jump into the unknown—is essentially unpremeditated, Schiller again parts company with how common historians used to think. Historians are very resistant to the idea that deeds may precede words, that, as Goethe said in his *Faust*, "Im Anfang war die Tat" ("In the beginning was the deed"). Historians are inclined to connect deeds, however unpremeditated they look, with what came before—and always manage to come forward with evidence that, "after all," these seemingly unpremeditated deeds are not as unpremeditated as they look.

Yet it may well be that the *really* important events in history, the events that do not just build upon what already exists but really inaugurate the new, come about in the manner Schiller describes. Just look at the war in Iraq. We have been led to believe, and—perhaps more important—we very much *like* to believe, that the decision to go to war was the result of an "inductive" process, by which I mean that first there were reasons and then, second, a decision. Thanks to the publication, in the London *Sunday Times*, of a secret memorandum that records the minutes of a meeting of Tony Blair's senior foreign policy and security advisors, we now know that the decision to attack Saddam Hussein was a *deductive* decision. First there was the decision to go to war and then, secondly, reasons had to be found that would support the decision. Or, in the words of the memorandum: "intelligence and facts" had to be "fixed around the policy." I like to think that here, in this memorandum, the "Im Anfang war die Tat" principle is caught in the act. In fact the principle was operative on an even deeper level, a level from which, when you come to think of it, the decision would have been funny if its results weren't so distressing: Bush and Blair invaded Iraq in order to find the reason why it had to be invaded.

Schiller, of course, would have said that Bush and Blair "nach Thaten gedürstet hätten," and I, for my part, would have added, in terms of what I have said just now, that they had given in to vertigo, that they had not been able to resist the temptation to commit a "sublime" act of history. The "deductivity" of the decision to oust Saddam Hussein — and also some of the other points I have touched upon in this chapter — is rather crassly illustrated by what a senior advisor to President Bush said in an interview with the *New York Times*. This anonymous person told the *New York Times* reporter that people looking at events from the outside — as, for example journalists, commentators, and historians — are (as he said) in "the reality-based community" — which he defined as the group of people who "believe that solutions emerge from [a] judicious study of discernible reality."

According to this official, then, people in the "reality-based community" think and work according to the principle of "inductivity." They believe that "in the beginning is the word." But, this senior advisor said, "that's not the way the world really works anymore . . . we're an empire now, and when we act, we create our own reality. And while you're studying that reality — judiciously as you will — we'll act again, creating other new realities, which you can study too. . . . We're history's actors . . . and you, all of you, will be left to just study what we do."[29] Though this advisor, senior as he might be, seems to believe that creating new realities by sublime historical acts is a recent American invention, he is, I think, quite right in distinguishing how events *look* from the outside and how these events actually come about.

To put it somewhat differently: sublimity only has the aspect of sublimity when one looks at it from the outside, from, that is, the perspective of inductivity. From the inside, there is just *acting*. Consciousness—if ever it comes—lags behind. This, in fact is my conclusion: Schiller's *Räuber* achieves something a theoretical, or a historical, work could not even aspire to. It shows *both* faces of sublime acting, the inside as well as the outside of "das furchtbar herrliche Schauspiel der alles zerstörenden und wieder erschaffenden, und wieder zerstörenden Veranderung." The two faces of sublime acting come together in a single sentence. In the third edition of *Die Räuber*, which prints the text of the play as it was actually performed in Mannheim in 1782, Schiller makes Karl say—just before he kills Amalia—"You only think about deeds like these when they are done."[30] Then he drives his dagger right into the heart of his love.

6

Into Cleanness Leaping

The Vertiginous Urge to Commit History

You imbeciles, braggarts, idiots, you think that history is made in
drawing-rooms where upstart democrats fraternize with titled liber-
als. . . . Imbeciles, braggarts, idiots! History is made in the trenches where the soldier, possessed by the nightmare of war-madness,
plunges his bayonet into the officer's stomach and then, clinging like
grim death to the buffers of a train carriage, escapes to his native
village there to set on fire his landlord's manor.

—Lenin[1]

I n one of the many memorable scenes in Robert Musil's *Der Mann
ohne Eigenschaften* General Stumm is looking for the one idea that
will bring his country redemption. He plans to lay this "great redeeming idea" at the feet of his beloved Diotima, confident that his trophy
will make an indelible impression on her. In order to find his prize,
Stumm visits the place where it surely can be found: the Viennese Court
Library. For the general, who is not very comfortable with books, the
library is "enemy territory" and consequently, for him, locating the
"great redeeming idea," capturing it, and then bringing it home is a
kind of military operation. When, after a long, long visit, Stumm is
finally outside again he is dumbfounded: he hasn't captured, or even
discovered, the "great redeeming idea," but he is very impressed with
the orderliness of the library, and especially with the orderliness of
the library catalogues. They embody, he ponders, "an all compassing
universal order." General Stumm (whose name translates as "dumb" or
"mute," but who, ironically, may well serve as a spokesman for Musil
himself) also draws a conclusion that is rather atypical for the regu-
lar visitor to libraries: "Only now I understand," the general reflects,
"why we soldiers, who are accustomed to the greatest order, must

be prepared to give our lives at each and every moment." And then Stumm speaks the ominous words "Irgendwie geht Ordnung in das Bedürfnis nach Totschlag über"—"Somehow or other, order, once it reaches a certain stage, calls for bloodshed."[2]

This may not be the kind of idea that visitors to libraries and readers of journals would call "redeeming," and, to be sure, it doesn't occur to the general to lay this particular thought—the one thought that he has thought up all by himself—at the feet of Diotima. Yet the quantum leap between order and bloodshed is Musil's grand theme in *Der Mann ohne Eigenschaften*. Musil's book is a unique attempt to clarify how the "perfect civil order"—as he calls it elsewhere—of late nineteenth-, early twentieth-century Europe could mutate into the carnage of the First World War. Musil's thesis is that war is "die Revolution der Seele gegen die Ordnung"[3]—"the soul's revolution against order." With his claim that *Ordnung* "somehow" transmutes into *Totschlag*, Musil in fact addresses one of the key issues of historiography: how to account for those mind-boggling and sometimes extremely bloody events in which we enter something really, sublimely new. This question, of course, is the question I already hinted at in chapter 3: the question about *discontinuity*. It is one of the big puzzles of history: how to understand events that surprised the participants themselves—even if they themselves had enthusiastically participated in bringing them about.

This is not just an epistemological question. The question of why and how humankind every now and then surprises itself with events it couldn't even dream of is first and foremost a metahistorical question into the mechanics—or perhaps better, the dynamics—of history. Historians have two good reasons to shy away from it. The first is that addressing metahistorical questions necessarily involves "speculation," and ever since Popper intimidated historians into the belief that their questions should be falsifiable, speculation is essentially taboo. An even better reason to stay on the sidelines is the fact that historians are much better at establishing continuity than at explaining discontinuity. Historians come out best when they can show how even the Thirty Years' War, the French Revolution, the First World War, or the Holocaust are somehow intended in more-or-less conscious desires, thoughts, notions, plans, opinions, decisions, and/or feelings in the period *before* the fact. Now, the belief that events are rooted in what came before is just one more version of the idea that, ultimately, people do things because it is in their interest to do so, because some way or other they think it serves them in their struggle for life. The fact of the matter is, as I indicated in the previous chapter, that "sublime" historical events derive their energy from the willingness of a significant number of people to "burn their bridges behind them" and to embark upon the unknown—no matter the consequences.

By sidestepping the question "What is the force that moves nations?" (as Tolstoy phrased it), historians do not just dodge the phenomenon of discontinuity. They also help to dissimulate agency. The historians' abstinence suppresses the fact that though in sublime historical events the yeast vanishes in the baking, the yeast is essential for the result. "Dissimulation of agency" does not mean that the participants in a sublime historical event completely disown their participation—or even their responsibility—but that retrospectively it is almost impossible *even for themselves* to access both the contingent, irrational, "sacrilegious" aspect of what they did and the fact that it was precisely this contingent, irrational, sacrilegious aspect that made the event happen. It might be recalled that in my introductory chapter I showed that dissimulation of agency can be beautifully illustrated by the wording of the American Declaration of Independence. The famous phrase "we hold these truths to be self-evident" suggests that these "truths," though perhaps unrecognized and unfulfilled, had always been there—and that the revolutionists only gave them their due. But that, of course, is a typical ex post facto account. The decision to throw off the British yoke was not the result of "self-evidencies." On the contrary: only after the irreversible step had been taken and, even more importantly, only when the step had turned out to be successful, did it occur to Thomas Jefferson that the reasons for taking the step were not contingencies but "truths," and not just truths but "self-evident truths." It is a supremely common, and supremely sly, operation: the one thing without which the American Revolution could not have taken place—the willingness to do something unheard of—evaporates in the process of coming to terms with it. The net effect of this operation is as spectacular as it is unpalatable. It is the fifth thesis of chapter 1: the more we accustom ourselves to ascribing what we did to the supposed reasons for our doing it, the more we transform ourselves into people who did not do it.

In this chapter I will resist ex post facto thinking and attempt to make the most of the experiential validity of discontinuity. To do so requires bringing to a head, instead of leveling down, the tension that characterizes all historical (and biographical) discontinuities: the tension between the fact that discontinuities are *made* by the participants, yet come as a surprise, even, or perhaps especially, *to themselves*. These two poles—the unmitigated "doing" as well as the unhypocritical "wondering"—tend to obliterate each other. They cannot fully inhabit the same consciousness and mutually start to nibble into each other as soon as the event is over. This mutual cannibalism—also known, among historians, as "revisionism"—has the form of doubting whether, after all, the discontinuous event was really "made" by the participants, and/or whether it wasn't, after all, rather less surprising than initially experienced. In what follows I will propose a perspective that gives both poles their due—a perspective from which, I think, one may say sensible things about "discontinuity" without dissolving its disturbing essence in the medium needed to come to terms with it.[4]

"Im Anfang war die Tat"

Of old, the primary strategy to account for discontinuity, for how *Ordnung* "somehow" transmutes into *Totschlag*, is to explain it away—to transform it into some form of continuity. I will come back to that. Apart from explaining it away, there have been two perspectives on how what's really new comes into being. The first is that we stumble upon the new by pursuing something else—that the new is the *unintended by-product* of the continuation of "old" projects, of projects, that is, that fall within the "horizon of possibilities" of what they unintentionally wipe away. The idea that by aiming for the *gradual* we sometimes become saddled with the *radical* is the solution of the eighteenth-century Scottish philosopher Adam Ferguson. Many of the ablest and most sensitive historians take this approach. Another solution to the problem of discontinuity is to trace the "new" to *dissatisfaction* with the old. This is the revolutionary frame of reference that Marx and Lenin brought to perfection: when the old has "had its day" something that is not just quantitatively but qualitatively different will take its place.

Both perspectives have their merits, but they fail to explain something that, though pretty obvious, is not spelled out in Musil's operationalization of discontinuity: the simple fact that discontinuity is disturbing, unpleasant, risky, and/or dangerous. To put it differently: discontinuity doesn't square well with received ideas about the supremacy of self-interest. And it doesn't matter, I hasten to add, whether self-interest is defined, as in the good old days, in terms of liberalism or historical materialism, or in terms of the paradigm that has for a long time taken their place, that of evolutionary biology. The fact of the matter is that discontinuity does not contribute to the well-being of the participants: trading *Ordnung* for *Totschlag* means trading "the better" for the worse. Given the fact that discontinuity doesn't seem to have economic or evolutionary "survival value," the two perspectives have complementary lacunae: Ferguson's "unintended by-product" hypothesis doesn't explain why sometimes we *knowingly* throw ourselves headlong into the new; Marx's "dissatisfaction" hypothesis doesn't consider that what we are willingly and eagerly heading for may be against (what we take to be) our best interests.

As a hygienic countermeasure against these ways of accounting for discontinuity, I would like to propose the counterintuitive thesis that discontinuities, mutations, and historical landslides—for example, the French Revolution, the First World War, and the Holocaust—are not "rooted" in what came before, but are the result of an irresistible urge to cut ourselves loose from our moorings. From this perspective, discontinuity is not a regrettable side effect of our ambition to attain some desirable goals. No, from this perspective discontinuity is in a very real sense precisely *what we are after*. It is, for short, my fourth thesis from chapter 1: we may start to make history not despite the fact that it is at odds with—yes, destroys—the stories we live by, but *because* it destroys the stories we live by.

The thesis that discontinuity is not the unintended by-product of something else, and not the instrumentally rational answer to dissatisfaction with the old, is nicely encapsulated in what Goethe says in his *Faust*: "Im Anfang war die Tat"—"In the beginning was the deed."

By replacing the primacy of "words" with the primacy of "deeds" I do not mean to imply that things tend to start with actual *actions*. From the work of J. L. Austin and Gilbert Ryle, we know that most "deeds" have the form of words. So a "deed," in my definition, is any instance in which we simply do, say, or decide something without proper premeditation. And by "proper premeditation" I mean the amount of weighing, deliberation, or simply conscious attention that according to the myth we live by is apposite for the "deed" in question. One could say that whereas stories, especially good stories, are *over*-determined, "deeds" are *under*-determined: they "contain less" than they suggest, and they are not as solidly grounded as would be required by their effect, their consequences, or their magnitude. If my definition of "deeds" makes you think of George W. Bush's decision to invade Iraq, I cannot help it.

Why is my thesis that "in the beginning is the deed" counterintuitive? It's counterintuitive because human beings are instinctively inclined to produce explanations for why things that surprised everyone, including themselves, "had to happen." Nobody who is "in his right mind" could imagine that the Berlin Wall would come down, or that fully fueled passenger planes could be used as missiles targeting the World Trade Center. Yet, as soon as these things happened, our narrative instinct began to spit out reasons why they *had* to happen. Humans seem to be subject to a kind of "narrative gravity": events tend to storytelling like objects tend to fall.

Devising post-hoc explanations that satisfy our lust for a good story is the specialty of historians. Historians are just as creative, just as brilliant, and just as ruthless in establishing historical continuity as each of us is in creating biographical continuity. I will give just one example—an example I borrow from the quintessential historian, Leopold von Ranke. In the second volume of his *History of England* Ranke discusses one of the most radical episodes of the English Revolution, the purge of the members of Parliament who were hostile to the plan of trying the king for high treason. This purge created what has become known as the "Rump Parliament" and was a major step in the creation of a republic. Ranke reflects: "The Republic in England did not arise from old Parliamentary claims that were gradually raised higher and higher, but from a different group of ideas, ideas to which the Parliament was just as decidedly opposed as the monarchy itself."[5] Now if ever there were a historical discontinuity, it was the revolutionary decision to have the king convicted—and the way Ranke tackles it is typical. The moment he realizes that he will not be able to explain the discontinuity away by referring to "old Parliamentary claims," he migrates to a deeper level—a level at which the fact that the events surprised even the parliamentarians themselves can remain intact, without his having to abandon the axiom that some way or other the "deed" must be rooted in "words"—in, as Ranke says, "eine Reihe von Gedanken." The more brilliant the historian is, the better he or she is at suggesting that, after all, there *is* a level at which "words" can be shown to precede deeds. Master historians such as Tocqueville and, more recently, Sebastian Haffner succeed in convincing us that deep down, traumatic discontinuities like wars and revolutions are not *that* discontinuous.

Establishing continuity is a very strong urge—and for a good reason. It may well be (as I have argued in my book *Waterloo, Verdun, Auschwitz*)[6] that it is the degree of discontinuity rather than the amount of death and destruction that makes an event traumatic. On an experiential level discontinuity is the extent to which a particular event wasn't supposed to happen, the extent, that is, to which the event was at odds with the worldview from which it emerged. Consequently, to come to terms with a traumatic event means to establish a worldview from which the traumatic event stops being "impossible." This, I think, was precisely what the great early nineteenth-century historians did: they devised a worldview from which the French Revolution stopped being impossible. In the stories they told, the events were "liquidated"—in both meanings of the term: the revolution was both taken up in cultural circulation and "strangled."

The classic formulation of this rather ambivalent mission was provided by Ranke. Ranke said that the important thing for the historian is "die letzte und nächste Vergangenheit mit der früheren in Einklang zu bringen." That is to say: it is the task of the historian "to bring the most recent events [by which Ranke meant the French Revolution] into harmony with the things that went before." The task Ranke has in mind for the historian suppresses, I think, its origin: the fact that the revolution was a deeply disturbing instance of "im Anfang ist die

Tat." The suppression of its origin goes a long way toward explaining its success. It might be argued that Ranke's conception of history derives its appeal, its innovativeness, and its energy from the subliminal ambition to come to terms with the monstrous "deed" that the French had been capable of doing. But, though the *origin* of the work of Ranke and his colleagues lies in the primacy of deeds, it *celebrates* the primacy of words. Ranke and his colleagues left no stone unturned in their attempts to show that "deeds," however unexpected, are really *secondary*—and "in harmony" with what came before. It doesn't even matter with *what* exactly these deeds were in harmony, as long as it antedated the deeds in question. Ever since Ranke, the historian is a high priest who has the magical ability to transform the primacy of the deed into the primacy of the word.

Yet—although our urge to forge discontinuities into continuities is irrepressible, and we very much like to succumb to "narrative gravity"—the belief that if you go down far enough, "deeds" can always be shown to be preceded by "words" is untenable. In actual life, the appetite very often comes with the eating. It may even be maintained, as Joseph Conrad said more than a century ago, that action is "the first thought, or perhaps the first impulse, on earth."[7] And in *Der Mann ohne Eigenschaften* Musil shows in a way that is not only very humorous but also in accordance with experience that when it *really* matters, premeditation, deliberation, and just plain thinking are overtaken by, and *want* to be overtaken by, "events." Decisions that are really, and literally, *vital* are not determined by conscious thought processes but by what Musil, playing on Schopenhauer, calls "the principle of insufficient ground." In the chapter that is aptly called "Dethroning the Ideocracy" Musil claims that "in the last analysis, all thoughts come out of the joints, muscles, glands, eyes, and ears, and from the shadowy general impressions that the bag of skin to which they belong has of itself as a whole."[8]

Musil and Conrad refer to what one might call "the myth of thinking": there is much talk about thinking, but in actual practice thinking, as a sustained effort to ascend from premises to conclusions, is extremely rare. What we call "thinking" often is a kind of *pathos*, interrupted by involuntary bouts of association and an occasional flash of inspiration. When we say "I'll think about it" what we really mean is

"I'll wait until something occurs to me." Most of the time, what we call "thinking" just "happens" to us, or, as Musil said, "it is life that does the thinking all around us."[9]

The thesis that deeds often antedate reasons is backed up by psycho-neurological research. There is an ever-growing corpus of studies indicating that many of our actions and reactions are not in any way announced by what goes on in our brains. That in many instances Goethe is much more right than Saint John is also suggested by contemporary psychology. In many, sometimes very ingenious, experiments, psychologists have corroborated an observation of the eighteenth-century philosopher Friedrich Heinrich Jacobi: "Die Handlungen bilden die Meinungen, nicht umgekehrt" ("Deeds determine opinions, not the other way around"). In decisional theory—a branch of psychology—Jacobi's dictum goes under the awe-inspiring name of "post-decisional dissonance reduction." "Post-decisional dissonance reduction" refers to the phenomenon that we humans are very much inclined to align our beliefs, our opinions, and our values with the choices we have made. It is an effect that has been demonstrated in countless experiments, of which one of the most straightforward was done at a racetrack (by Robert Knox and James Inkster). People who had just put money on a horse were asked to assess the chance that that particular horse would win. The conclusion was that betting on a horse very much increases the belief that that particular horse will prevail. This belief is, to say the least, not very rational, but it is thoroughly human: instead of gathering all the information we can about the chance that a particular horse will finish first, we put our money rather impulsively on a horse and start to believe that the horse of our choice has quite a good chance to win.[10]

Remarkably, and contrary to what you might expect, impulsive decision making and "post-decisional dissonance reduction" are more pervasive in situations where *more* is at stake. Recent research findings do not exactly confirm Diotima's remark, in *Der Mann ohne Eigenschaften*—"Where the really great things in life are concerned, it doesn't so much matter what one does"[11]—but they clearly indicate that the tendency toward impulsive decision making is stronger the more important the decisions are. In the supermarket we vacillate between brand A and brand B, but a car is bought at an odd moment and in an offhand way, and a partner just falls into our lap. In fact, in spite of all our romantic ideas about love, it is quite common—and entirely in line with the theory of "post-decisional dissonance reduction"—that people *fall* in love after having *made* it. The English language is in this respect one of the most logical languages in the world: first, love is "made," and when that is done satisfactorily, we may "fall" into it. Writers, more closely in touch with experience than are academicians, discovered the phenomenon much earlier than psychologists. In *Père Goriot* Balzac describes how Eugène Rastignac successfully storms Mme. de Nucingen, after which Balzac remarks laconically that "at the time Rastignac was at his boarding house again he had fallen in love with Mme. de Nucingen."[12]

That especially in what we call "matters of the heart" the appetite comes with the eating is a central motif of Stendhal's *Le rouge et le noir*. In fact I know of no other book that describes the politically, and morally, incorrect inversion of sex and love in such an exemplary way. The hero of *Le rouge et le noir*, Julien Sorel, does not conquer the women he has fallen in love with, but falls in love with the women he has conquered. I will give just one example. The very first time Julien meets Mme. de Rênal—the wife of the man who has employed him as a tutor—he has, as Stendhal says, "the bold notion of kissing her hand." Stendhal emphasizes that this impulse has nothing to do with "love at first sight." Julien's shockingly preposterous impulse is no better motivated than by the realization that he "owes it to himself." The impulse frightens Julien but—and this is vintage Stendhal—he quenches his fear with the realization that there are very good reasons to follow his impulse.

Stendhal makes it abundantly clear that none of these reasons has to do with the emergence of love. In fact, it is only *after* Julien has kissed the hand of Mme. de Rênal that he notes her beauty, and, remarkably, he doesn't at all like what he sees: Julien "hated her because of her beauty," Stendhal says. "It was the first block on the road to fortune." As in an Alfred Hitchcock movie, the trajectory of Julien's feelings mocks the foundationalist that hides in every one of us: with Julien, reality follows appearances. Infatuation sprouts from hand-grabbing instead of the other way around. Stendhal even goes so far as to suggest that not only in the beginning is not the word, but that words would have been the end of it. In Paris, he remarks, Julien's relations with Mme. de Rênal would quickly have been "simplified" because "the young tutor and his shy mistress would have found the explanation of their situation in three or four novels. . . . The novels would have outlined for them the parts to play, showed them the model to imitate; and sooner or later, although with no pleasure, perhaps reluctantly, vanity would have forced Julien to follow the model."[13] And indeed, in matters of the heart, things begin with deeds and end with good reasons.

Why Not?

If the tendency to impulsive decision making is stronger the more there is at stake, then the phenomenon "Im Anfang war die Tat" must also be operative in situations where *societies as a whole* set out a new course and start to do things for which the consequences are incalculable. And when the deeds are huge, "post-decisional dissonance reduction" must grow to monstrous proportions. It might be regarded as the central thesis of this book: in gross, traumatic, historical landslides, enthusiasm doesn't need propaganda; in such events, atrocities *precede* ideologies; in historical catastrophes, people start to hate *after* having been cruel. In anomalous situations, "war" is not the continuation of politics by other means, as Clausewitz asserted war to be. Instead, an anomalous war creates a new reality, a reality that completely determines the political arena.

The idea that *Im Anfang* could very well be *die Tat* didn't fare very well (to say the least) in the continuity-obsessed nineteenth century, but was toyed with in late eighteenth-century Germany. As far as I know it was a contemporary and friend of Goethe and Jacobi who first explored the theme: Friedrich Schiller. Schiller, who is to the French Revolution as Marinetti and the Italian Futurists are to the First World War, was obsessed with how we "fall" into the unprecedented. It is the theme of many of his plays, but—as I showed in the previous chapter— it is in his early works—like *Die Räuber* and *Fiesko*—that he explores the theme of how "the new" actually comes about most thoroughly. It might be recalled that I have said that Schiller was not particularly interested in bringing to a head the moral tensions *within* a particular world—as the typical eighteenth-century playwright would do—but focuses on the tension between *two different* moral worlds, an old one and a new, separated by an "original sin" that makes them fundamentally incompatible. We have seen that original sins are Schiller's primary fascination, not only in his historical works (for example, *Die Abfall der Niederlände*), but also in his plays.

Because he exploits—and to a certain extent *revels* in—the fact that "in the beginning is the deed," and in the concomitant fact that deeds cannot be "undone," Schiller is the quintessential *historical* playwright. He is one of the very few writers with whom the drama, the tragedy, springs from the urge to "commit" history. In his "Etwas über die erste Menschengesellschaft nach dem Leitfaden der mosaischen Urkunde" Schiller traces this urge to commit history all the way down to the first man: Adam.[14] Eating from the apple was the first sublime "deed." In his disobedience against God's commandments, Adam wrested himself free from his instincts, and, as Schiller says, from this moment of "sublime" disobedience "the story of [man's] freedom unfolds."[15]

Schiller makes it quite clear that one cannot dismiss the urge to commit an "original sin" as just a criminal aberration. He firmly believes that doing unimaginable, awe-inspiring, terrible—in short, *sublime*—things is, whether we like it or not, the essence of history. In bringing about a new evolutionary level, the initial step, the step beyond the status quo—or, as I will explain in chapter 9, the mutation-inducing catastrophe—is crucial. This is the subject of Schiller's *Raüber*. In the previous chapter we've seen that in the second scene of the first act, the hero, Karl Moor, burns his ships behind him and embarks upon his career as chief of a band of robbers, exclaiming, "My mind thirsts for deeds" ("Mein Geist dürstet nach Thaten"). This in fact is what he does: he starts to do things. Indeed, from the moment he embarks upon his career as a robber, Karl is determined by his deeds instead of the other way around. The fact that he doesn't know where his "sublime" fall will take him means that he will end up where his deeds will bring him.

It is not just in the domain of fiction that *Im Anfang* very often is *die Tat*. Without what Musil called the "principle of insufficient ground," the abysses of history cannot really be fathomed. Joseph Conrad noted that in history as well as in our own private lives this principle often has the form of giving in to the question "Why not?" That he may be right was suggested by a letter in the *New York Review of Books* in 2007. In that letter the renowned Stanford historian Robert Conquest confessed that his somewhat less renowned colleague Tibor Szamuely understood Stalinism better than he did. "I remember saying to him," Conquest writes, "that I could see why Stalin had Marshal Tukhashevski shot, but why did he do the same to his old friend Marshal Yegorov? Tibor's answer was 'Why not?'"[16] Conquest's letter is remarkable: it doesn't happen *that* often that a historian acknowledges that far-reaching things can be done "just like that," that monstrous historical deeds sometimes are no better motivated than as a giving in to the question "Why not?"

History as Dissonance Reduction

It is, of course, a rather disquieting thought: the principle that in the beginning was the deed implies that we engage upon war and revolution because every now and then we are tempted to flee forward into a sublime "Why not?" It means that we call down historical catastrophes upon ourselves because we give in to an impulse to put a way of life on the line and want to "commit some nice little history." But apart from being disquieting, the principle also begs some questions. I will address three of them briefly. The first question is how the concept of "In the beginning was the deed" squares with the fact that our consciousness tells us that we have control over what we do. The second is the phenomenological question of how to imagine this compulsion to commit deeds that are "underdetermined," to do things for which we have insufficient reasons and that are against our own best interests. How do we imagine deeds that make *us* instead of the other way around? How do we imagine decisions that make themselves instead of being made by us? The third question is whether these deeds by which we embark upon the unknown, these "original sins," are random or whether there is a kind of pattern underneath. What kind of unthought-of things do we tend to do when we start to do things that we cannot think of?

The first question is whether the thesis that "Im Anfang war die Tat" is not simply disproved by the fact that our consciousness tells us continuously that we have control over what we do. The answer to this question is "no": in many ways our consciousness deludes us. There is, in fact, quite a bit of empirical evidence for the thesis that "deeds" precede "words." It is the subject of one of my favorite psychological theories, the theory I already mentioned in the introductory chapter: Daryl Bem's "self-perception theory." This theory—originating in the 1970s—offers an intriguing psychological counterpart for the dialectics between impulsiveness and post-decisional dissonance reduction that is contained in the phrase "Im Anfang war die Tat." According to Bem, individuals do not have privileged access to themselves. They do not derive their identity somewhere from "within"—but by examining their own deeds, and by subconsciously answering the question, "What kind of person am I, considering that I do the things I most obviously do?"[17]

That there is quite a bit of truth in Bem's theory is affirmed again and again in psychological experiments. A very elegant experiment was done by the psychologist Robert Abelson. In the first phase of his experiment Abelson showed his subjects—heterosexual males—pictures of a variety of women, and told them that their heartbeat had accelerated when they viewed some of the pictures, whereas in reality this was not the case. In the second phase of the experiment the subjects had to judge the attractiveness of the women in the pictures. Remarkably, the subjects found the women whom they thought had made their hearts beat faster more attractive than the women whom they thought had *not* affected their heart rates. In other words, the men in Abelson's experiment had drawn conclusions about what they "felt inside" on the basis of information they had received from "outside." Self-perception—in this particular case induced by the experimenter—gave rise to evaluations and feelings that were experienced as real, personal, and authentic.

Bem's "self-perception" theory is also convincingly confirmed by Timothy Wilson in his classic *Strangers to Ourselves*. Wilson shows that, yes indeed, we have only limited access to ourselves. We derive much of our knowledge about who we are, what we like, and what we feel from what we "see ourselves doing."[18] Wilson coined the phrase "the adaptive unconscious"—a phrase with which he wants to highlight that most of our actions and reactions are taken care of without control of or interference from our consciousness. Yet, strangely, these autonomous actions and reactions are almost always very adequate and—stranger still—very much *feel* like our own. In psychology this is known as the Wilson/Nisbett thesis. It consists of two parts. The first part is hardly challenged anymore among psychologists: many of our judgments, feelings, thoughts, and actions are brought about by *the adaptive unconscious*. The second part, however, is still a bit controversial. In the words of Wilson, "Because people do not have conscious access to the adaptive unconscious, their conscious selves confabulate reasons for why they responded the way they did."[19] Put differently: though our consciousness may not be very good at controlling our actions, it is extremely good at inducing the belief that we do what we do because we have good reasons to do so.

That in many cases, and on different levels, "words" follow "deeds" instead of the other way round is also demonstrated by modern neurophysiological research. There is by now a lot of evidence that the relation among action, experience, meaning, and consciousness is far more complicated than common sense suggests. Time and again the conclusion has to be that what we experience of "the world" is not the raw data. The experiences we experience have been filtered, twisted, and tortured in a way our consciousness cannot even fathom. As Tor Norretranders puts it in his book *The User Illusion*: "What we experience has acquired meaning before we become conscious of it."[20] And again: "Our consciousness claims that it makes the decisions, that it is the cause of what we do. But our consciousness is not even there when the decision is made. It lags behind, but it does not tell us that."[21] This is what Norretranders calls the *user illusion*: we project our consciousness back onto decisions and actions that emerged before our consciousness joined the party. A crucial ingredient of the *user illusion* is that we habitually cheat with time: in order to be able to hold onto the belief that we are master of our deeds, we subconsciously engage in—as Norretranders calls it—"subjective relocations of time."[22]

Before I switch to my second question I cannot resist repeating what I already said in chapter 1: theories like those of Bem, Wilson, and Norretranders are, or rather should be, of special interest to historians.

Contrary to what they may want us to believe, historians also have no privileged access—access from "within"—to what they are interested in. Historians have to infer from the deeds that can be seen from the outside what the inside must look like. Bem's "self-perception" theory is especially apposite in situations where cultures have to come to terms with the historical catastrophes they have committed. Much of what happened in postrevolutionary France as well as in post-Holocaust Germany can be understood as attempts to find answers to the question "Who are we that this could happen?" In fact, in my book *Waterloo, Verdun, Auschwitz* I tried to show that societies strive toward "dissonance reduction" in much the same way that individuals do.

Vertigo

My second question is the phenomenological one, of how we can imagine this compulsion to go *va banque,* to put the things we used to value on the line and to flee forward in a sublime "why not?" How exactly does General Stumm's "order" transmute into "slaughter"? And if the decision to invade Iraq was made before the reasons for doing so were in place, what predisposed Bush and Blair in their resolve to commit history? Is it in any way possible to say sensible things about mutations when—by definition—they are not determined by the context from which they spring?

To answer these questions I would like to recall what I said in my Schiller chapter about "vertigo"—a concept that is, I think, a very good antidote to our irrepressible urge to create continuity. What I call "vertigo" has nothing to do with U2—though there is a consanguinity with Alfred Hitchcock's famous movie and with W. G. Sebald's novel *Schwindel, Gefühle,* which was translated into English as *Vertigo.* According to my dictionary, "vertigo" means "dizziness" or "giddiness," and the connotation is that these sensations are brought about by height. But neither "dizziness" nor "giddiness" does justice to what I want to express, so I will stick with "vertigo." As I understand it, vertigo is more than just dizziness because it involves an inclination to surrender to that sensation and to fall accidentally and/or unaccidentally. Vertigo is also not identical with a "fear of heights" because, in my conception, fear is secondary. Vertigo may feel like "fear of fall-ing," but in my discussion of Schiller I have already indicated that in reality it is—according to psychoanalysis—a *wish to jump,* covered by a fear of falling. In a position of vertigo, the sense that the void before you *has* to be filled may mushroom into something so overwhelming, so oppressive, that you start to fear that you will not be able to resist "the wish to jump."

According to the by now completely forgotten French writer Roger Caillois, "vertigo" can be an ingredient of games. In *Les jeux et les hom-mes* (translated as *Man, Play, and Games*), Caillois distinguishes four such ingredients: *agon* (competition), *alea* (chance), *mimicry* (make believe), and *ilinx* (the Greek word for whirlpool). According to Cail-lois, ilinx, or vertigo, entails the "destruction of the stability of percep-tion" and creates "a kind of voluptuous panic in an otherwise lucid mind."[23] Vertigo is what we enjoy and seek in activities like the dance of dervishes and the Mexican *voladores,* in merry-go-rounds, and in racing downhill. Vertigo, Caillois says, is "linked to the desire for dis-order and destruction, a drive which is normally repressed." In adults, Caillois adds rather tamely, "nothing is more revealing of vertigo than . . . the intoxication that is experienced in military barracks—for example, in noisily banging garbage cans."[24] Apart from Caillois, the concept of vertigo was employed by Søren Kierkegaard, and later by Jean Paul Sartre in *L'être et le néant.* The most hallucinatory and per-ceptive evocation of what I mean by vertigo can, however, be found in Henrik Ibsen's play *The Master Builder,* but to do justice even remotely to the way Ibsen lets his master builder build towers, climb towers, talk towers, flee towers, and eventually fall from an impossible tower he himself has erected would require a separate chapter.

In order to give at least a faint idea of what I mean by vertigo I will give four short examples: three from literary writers and one from a clinical case study. First, vertigo is, as we've already seen, a major theme in some of Schiller's early work—in, for example, *Die Räuber* and *Fiesko.* In these plays Schiller evokes the sensation of how it feels "to stand on the brink of time." His heroes typically have taken leave of the present, and Schiller explores the prospect of the awe-inspiring void that opens up before them the moment they have burnt their ships behind them. The sensation of vertigo that this void induces is evoked in the passage from *Fiesko* I already quoted in chapter 5: "O, to stand on that terrible sublime height," Schiller writes, "and to revel from above in the tempestuous human maelstrom . . . to direct, by just playing with the reins, the unruly passions of the people like so many fiery steeds, to quench the flaring pride of the vassals with *one*—one breath!"[25] Schiller makes us feel that in this position of "vertigo" it is almost impossible not to *do* something: his heroes struggle with the wish, and with the concomitant fear, to step down from the brink of time, to jump into the unknown, and to start to make history.

The second evocation of vertigo is provided by Marcel Proust. At the very end of *À la recherche du temps perdu* Proust's hero Marcel is looking back at the enormous amount of time, of *personal* time, behind him. He reflects:

> I felt a sense of tiredness and fear at the thought that all this length
> of time had not only uninterruptedly been lived, thought, secreted
> by me, that it was my life, that it was myself, but also that I had to
> keep it attached to me at every moment, that it supported me, that
> I was perched on its vertiginous summit, and that I was unable to
> move without its collaboration, without taking it with me.[26]

A few sentences later Proust describes this sensation of vertigo: "I felt giddy at the sight of so many years below me, yet within me, as if I were miles high." Proust then goes on to compare Marcel's sensation with being perched on the top of "living stilts"—"stilts which never stop growing, sometimes becoming taller than church steeples, until eventually they make walking difficult and dangerous, and down from which, all of a sudden, [we] fall." Proust does not go as far as to suggest that the depth *attracts* him, but it is quite clear, I think, that if Marcel's death instinct had been a little stronger, and his creative passion a little weaker, he might have succumbed to the depth beneath him and let himself fall from his stilts.

My third example is Ulrich—the incomparable *Mann ohne Eigenschaften*. Musil consistently presents Ulrich as a man who is on the verge of stepping over the brink. "Within reality," Ulrich observes, "there is a senseless craving for unreality";[27] and he is inclined to give in to that craving, to "abolish reality," and to *do* things, things that—because they do not spring from their environment—are by definition "unheard-of." By his readiness to break free from what we are enmeshed in, Ulrich is the antithesis of Paul Arnheim, whose specialty is the extrapolation of current projects. As Diotima notes, Arnheim is "an outstanding contemporary, which is why he is and needs to be in touch with present-day realities." Ulrich, on the other hand, is, according to Diotima, "always on the point of taking a leap into the impossible." Whereas Arnheim "has a feeling for everything that has taken a long time to become what it is," Ulrich is quite prepared to burn the bridges behind him. "And you?," Diotima snaps, "What about you? You act as though the world were about to begin tomorrow."[28] Diotima is right. Ulrich, Musil writes, "had run the gamut of experience . . . and felt that he might . . . at any time plunge into something that need not mean anything to him personally so long as it stimulated his urge to action."[29]

Vertigo is not just a theme in literature and philosophy; it is also a clinical phenomenon. That is to say, real people in the real world can actually *suffer* from vertigo. They may even seek help for it. Needless to say, as a clinical phenomenon vertigo occurs when some psychic balance is disturbed. The psychoanalyst Charles Rycroft describes a prototypical case. Rycroft's patient was a man whose father was without any ambition and who was satisfied with a lackluster job as a traveling salesman. The mother of the patient was a strong woman who was openly cynical about the capacities of the men in the family. After the death of his mother, when he was twenty-three years old, the patient, like his father, took on a job as a traveling salesman. He was so successful that within twenty years he had become one of the executive officers of the company. Six weeks after his appointment he had his first attack of vertigo. His patient, Rycroft remarks, felt that he had "climbed too high."[30] The moment he became an executive officer he was no longer able to maintain his psychic balance by making himself dependent on *others*. His success went to his head—to the extent that he literally got dizzy.

The dizziness, Rycroft says, covered an urge to do irreparable things. The patient, he discovered, had an almost irresistible impulse to put his success on the line and to court disaster—which in turn frightened him very much. One of his obsessive thoughts was, as Rycroft puts it, "to bring about a catastrophic explosion that would kill himself and everybody that happened to be around."[31] Rycroft compares his patient to the biblical Samson. "The elation that preceded each attack of vertigo," he says, "was analogous to Samson's final access of strength; it was the courage that comes of despair."[32]

It is my contention that the phenomenon described by Schiller, Proust, Musil, and Rycroft is not just a literary theme or a psychiatric syndrome, but is, or can be, experienced by each and every one of us. It is a phenomenon that has to be distinguished from the fear of heights—as Hitchcock clearly shows in *Vertigo*. The fear of heights is experienced when you are standing safely on the ground. Fear of heights is resistance to going *up*. Vertigo, on the other hand, has to do with not quite trusting yourself when you have a depth beneath you. One of its characteristics is that it only manifests itself when you have a certain freedom of action. In an airplane, in a hang glider, or dangling from a parachute, you won't suffer from vertigo. Height, in other words, is a necessary but not a sufficient condition. Vertigo is the result of the fear that you won't be able to resist something. Therefore, as I said above, vertigo is not primarily a fear, but is in part a wish, a wish that is so threatening that it feels like a fear. Often there is a multiplier effect. First there is a wish, then there is a fear that we will not be able to resist that wish, then there is the wish to make short shrift of that fear, then there is the fear that our fear may not deter us enough, and so on. This multiplier effect may cause the sensation of a whirlpool, a maelstrom, a vortex that manifests itself as dizziness.

Ingrained in the sensation of vertigo is the inclination to give in to it. Vertigo predisposes one, as psychoanalysts say, to "counterphobic" behavior.[33] Giving in to vertigo is a strategy for escaping from an unbearable tension by *doing* something—by doing what is forbidden, by eating the apple, by committing an original sin. Vertigo thus is the condition in which we may jump into the unknown, in which we may start to do things that are at odds with what we regard as our identity, in which we put a way of life on the line, in which we start, as Musil said, "ein Revolution der Seele gegen die Ordnung." In this sense vertigo is not just a psychological but also a cultural phenomenon. And, consequently, cultures too can be susceptible to counterphobic behavior—not unlike Rycroft's patient. In history, vertigo has the form of the impulse to create accomplished facts, of the determination to leave the beaten track, to stop stumbling along, and to flee forward— straight into the unknown.

Revolutions are perhaps the prime examples of fleeing forward. Or, to be more precise, revolutions are cascades of episodes of flee- ing forward. The French Revolution was, from the moment the États généraux was convened until Napoleon's invasion of Russia, a jumble of more and less successful attempts to create accomplished facts. An irrepressible urge to flee forward and create accomplished facts was also one of the prime features of Adolf Hitler. It is in this connec- tion not without significance that Hitler seems to have cherished his own personal version of the adage that "Im Anfang ist die Tat." Otto Wagener, who accompanied Hitler on some of his speaking tours in the early 1930s, recalled that Hitler applauded Goethe's revision of Saint John's line, but thought it could be improved upon. Hitler said to Wagener that he felt it should be: "In the beginning was the urge." Hitler believed, Wagener writes, that "the urge" was "the spark of life, which resides in us as well," and that "the urge existed from eternity! And the urge was a creation of God, and God himself was this urge."[34] It may well be that it was Hitler's ability to leave the beaten track behind, and to plunge into an orgy of "counterphobic" behavior, that made his "flight into power" so terribly and somnam- bulistically effective.

A more sympathetic—but no less straightforward and perhaps even more spectacular—example of fleeing forward is how, in 1989, in the German Democratic Republic people started out with shouting "Wir sind das Volk"—"We are the people"—but then took a quantum leap to the new by altering just one word: "Wir sind EIN Volk"—"We are ONE people." "Wir sind das Volk" was a courageous twist within an old frame of reference; in "Wir sind ein Volk" a real historical mutation was brought about.

Moved by the Past

Finally, our third question: are these deeds by which we embark upon the unknown, these "original sins," completely random, or is there a kind of pattern underneath? It is not a coincidence, I think, that the authors who wrote most perceptively about the primacy of deeds did so in the years just before and just after major historical catastrophes. On the eve of the First World War the poet Rupert Brooke wrote a poem that epitomizes the vertiginous state of mind of the turn of the century:

> Now, God be thanked Who has matched us with His hour,
> And caught our youth, and wakened us from sleeping,
> With hand made sure, clear eye, and sharpened power,
> To turn, as swimmers into cleanness leaping.[35]

The third question is "When, how, and in which direction do we tend to leap?" It is a tough question—it asks, in effect, how and when we can transcend our frame of reference. And indeed, ultimately the question of discontinuity is the question of how we can do things that we couldn't imagine doing—the question, that is, of the mystery of human creativity. It eludes the medium in which we have to answer it. As I quoted Henri Bergson in chapter 1: "The intellect lets what is *new* in each moment of history escape. It does not admit the unforeseeable. It rejects all creation."[36] But I think we can at least try to say whether there is anything definite about how and when we manage to come forward with things that are beyond our "horizon of expectations," with deeds that are at odds with the stories we live by.

First, I would like to recall what I said in chapter 1: we seem to experience cultural vertigo only when our previous "original sin" has lost its capacity to weigh us down. Ultimately what weighs us down is trauma. When there is no trauma to weigh us down, we may begin to experience a vertiginous dizziness that is not unlike the dizziness Rycroft's patient felt when he was no longer weighed down by his past. Put differently: we may start to commit history at moments in which we no longer have "a history before us," or, perhaps better, in which we have "consumed" the future that a former sublime historical event has given us. I will, in this respect, venture a hypothesis that may be a bit contentious but that explains some of the phenomena that are otherwise hard to account for. This hypothesis is that we may start to experience cultural vertigo when we are in danger of getting to know ourselves. A state in which we are in danger of getting to know ourselves may lead to what Heidegger called *Seinsvergessenheit*. In order to regain the blessed state in which we once more, though on a different level, do not know who we are, we have to do something that is truly at odds with what we regard as our identity. Then we have to destroy the things we feel at home in.

My second remark is that the horrendous, sublime—in short, historical—"deeds" in which we flee forward can be conceptualized as instances of what in chapter 3 I called *inventio*. In rhetoric *inventio* has less to do with creation *ex nihilo* than with something quite different but no less radical: *metamorphosis*. *Inventio* is what in German is called *Selbsthervorbringung*—"transforming yourself ever more into what you are."[37] It is born in praxis, in, that is, *deeds*. The idea is beautifully epitomized in what the English writer E. M. Forster once said: "How do I know what I think, until I've read what I wrote?" *Inventio* is surprising yourself with things from beyond your frame of reference, and—at least as important—immediately and without reservation embracing your discovery as more in line with who you are than what it replaces. These surprises come in the form of deeds—as in the case of Forster, the deed of writing. The metamorphoses Forster alludes to need not be the result of long hours behind a desk. They may well be the result of inventions made in the heat of an argument—as in Saint-Just and Robespierre bringing about modern France in their improvised speeches in the Assemblée nationale, Slobodan Milosevic inventing post-Yugoslav Serb nationalism (and himself) in his infamous impromptus at Kosovo Polje in 1989, and George W. Bush inventing himself on the ruins of the World Trade Center.

One of the attractions of the notion of *inventio* understood as *metamorphosis* is that it offers a conception of how the old may suddenly become cliché, be discarded, and be traded in for something new—even though neither the value nor validity of this new is established. I think one can very well identify this rhetorical *kairos* with the "event" (as Alain Badiou would say) of discontinuity. The *inventio* perspective is especially relevant for history because it implies that the "new"—that which is literally unimaginable—is invented out of "what has been superseded." It would mean, as I will show in the next chapter, that *Selbsthervorbringung*—the way humanity has leapfrogged through time—is a process of "going forward by going backward." The role the past plays in the birth of discontinuities is, however, radically different from the role we usually assign to history. The new does not "build upon the past" and is not "rooted" in the past, but bursts forth when what we have forgotten "takes possession" of us. We will see in the next chapter that to "commit" history is to "invent the new" out of knowledge that is too common to be recognized as knowledge.[38] Saint Just and Robespierre invented the idea of popular sovereignty out of "common knowledge" about the derelict États généraux. Alfred von Schlieffen invented (at the end of the nineteenth century) the German military predicament (as well as the solution to it) out of the myth of the Battle of Cannae. And one might hypothesize that George W. Bush leapt into the "cleanness" of the Middle East because a concoction of high school knowledge about Richard the Lionheart, Abraham Lincoln, and Douglas MacArthur suddenly took possession of him.

7

Inventing the New from the Old

At the very time when men appear engaged in revolutionizing things and themselves, in bringing about what never was before, at such very epochs of revolutionary crisis do they anxiously conjure up into their service the spirits of the past, assume their names, their battle cries, their costumes to enact a new historic scene in such time-honored disguise and with such borrowed language.

—Karl Marx[1]

Right now, in the twenty-first century, our involvement with our past much more resembles the way history figured in the eighteenth century than how it functioned in the nineteenth and the first half of the twentieth century. Today's equivalents of the eighteenth-century antiquarians—the professional *eruditi* that swarm in and around the history departments—are diligently bringing chunks of the past to light, while historians who are less than professional—yes, downright amateurs—make off with all the loot and write the books that sell. The task of trying to say sensible and timely things about the process of history is taken up by outsiders, by political scientists like Samuel Huntington, economists like Robert Reich, sociologists like Anthony Giddens, and physiologists like Jared Diamond. And again, like in the eighteenth century, the past is a commodity, a huge collection of *idées reçus* from which anybody who has an axe to grind can take the things she needs to make the points she wants to make. Historians like to raise hell over the postmodern commodification of history—but by looking down their nose at thinking about the process of history, they *themselves* have been instrumental in bringing about what they say they deplore.

For thinking about the process of history seems to be a psychological necessity. Or rather, reflection about *how we have become what we are* is a psychological necessity. Thinking about how we have become what we are doesn't necessarily have the *historical* form it acquired with the French Revolution. For a long time it had a religious form, and in this epoch of globalization, in which each of us is more than ever before "a party of one" as well as an interchangeable member of a species, thinking about how we have become what we are seems to wear the guise of evolutionary biology. It may well be that the historical mode of making sense of life was just an interlude—and that by now, as Hans Ulrich Gumbrecht has remarked, "the legitimizing discourses about the functions of history have degenerated into ossified rituals."[2] By answering the question of how we have become what we are in an up-to-date way, books like Richard Dawkins's *The Ancestor's Tale* and Chris Stringer's *The Origin of Our Species* may well be the modern counterparts of the works written by Michelet, Ranke, and Macaulay in the nineteenth century.

To the extent, however, that humans are animals who have taken their evolution in their own hands, reflection on how we have become what we are is and remains reflection on the process of history. And if history, as a discipline, wants to be relevant again—in the sense of offering fresh answers to the perennial question of our descent—historians had better put aside their misgivings about substantive philosophy of history and start to "speculate" again—to come forward with questionable hypotheses about how we actually *make* history, how the new erupts from the old, how we mutate and evolve by acting in ways that somehow we recognize as *historical*. I am not, to be sure, propagating an ideologically inspired "anthropogony" along the lines of Marx, Spengler, or Reinhold Niebuhr. What I *do* propose, however, is to attempt to *re*connect critical and substantive philosophy of history. Such a reconnection does not, in my view, imply that we have to elevate ourselves above the things that came to pass, but, rather, that we take the low road and try to get into contact with what one may call "the bowels" of history, with, that is, the things from which the self-styled down-to-earth historian has learned to abstract. Now, rather counterintuitively, getting in touch with the bowels, the reality, or, as I have called it in chapter 3, the "presence" of history is much more difficult than taking the long view. The reason is, as I've already indicated, that as soon as we start to think about the process of history we seem to be damned to a discourse of meaning. Up till some decades ago, this damned excellence in attributing meaning had the form of being able to make sense (in either an utopian or a dystopian way) of whatever presented itself to the historical eye, whereas since we discovered the pleasures of "trauma" we rather like to revel in how things do *not* make sense.

In both cases however, we talk meaning. In fact, escaping from this discourse of meaning became virtually impossible the moment we took a linguistic turn and ended up in the mirror palace of representation—the mirror palace from which not even Derrida could escape. I will not here attempt to outline the assumptions, perspectives, and programmes that add up to the paradigm of representationalism. Let me just say that at bottom representationalism is a histrionic defeatism about the ability to know the world, coupled to a dissimulated determination to turn the medium into the message. Accordingly, "truth"—in the sense of a valid fit between "the world" and "what we may say about the world"—is, in representationalism, a will-o'-the-wisp that one shouldn't pursue. Instead, to establish some sense of stability and coherence, we practise hermeneutics: we tickle what is said about the world with what we remember about what others—or we ourselves—have earlier said about the world. And we tickle what we remember about what has earlier been said about the world with what is said about the world right *now*. This flirtatious interaction may bring about a pleasurable "breakthrough" between text and reader, new and old, outside and inside, "object" and "subject"—and this pleasurable breakthrough we call "meaning."

By opening up interpretative spaces hermeneutics *connects* things— or rather, it connects not things but *representations* of things. In the final analysis hermeneutics is, as Quentin Skinner has repeatedly insisted, intertextuality—and as such, I would like to add, it is essentially metaphoric. According to Lakoff and Johnson, as we have discussed earlier, "The essence of metaphor is understanding and experiencing one kind of thing in terms of another"[3]—and that is exactly what hermeneutics does: it induces the sensation of meaning by interpreting one thing in terms of another. And because hermeneutics is the primary—or, arguably, the *sole*—tool of representationalism, representationalism is also essentially metaphoric. By being bound up with metaphor, representationalism is irremediably *horizontal*: it may suggest illuminating, surprising, and inspiring ways to see one thing in terms of another, but precisely because of this it doesn't bring us any closer to the inexorable—and ultimately meaningless—numinosity of reality.

In chapter 3 I argued that in order to reestablish contact with the reality of history, we should forget about the things that came to pass and had better focus on the living on of the past in the here and now. I have called this subconscious persistence of an unacknowledged past "presence"—and I have defined it as "the unrepresented way the past is present in the here and now." Presence is what is not included in our story about ourselves—it is what makes us do things that are at odds with our identity, and, as such, it is less about "figuration" than about *pre*figuration. If "culture" is—as I think it is—the set of things we do not have to talk about, the set of things, that is, that need not, that *cannot* be represented, then our culture is made up of "presences"—of common knowledge that is so common that it isn't knowledge anymore, of things that are so subtle that they cannot be forced through the throats of immigrants who want a residence permit, of, in a word, the surreptitious and omnipresent *myths* that distinguish us from the barbarians.

The study of three-thousand-odd pages in which a group of Dutch historians described the Dutch role in the massacre in Srebrenica in 1995 is—as I showed in my second chapter—quite a good example of the way the past may prefigure our conceptions instead of the other way around. The mission of these professional and competent historians was to explain how a battalion of Dutch peacekeepers didn't so much as lift a finger when Bosnian Serbs invaded the Srebrenica enclave, separated the Muslim men from the women, and—as it turned out afterwards—massacred some eight thousand of them. We have seen that the Dutch historians, while conscientiously trying to elucidate what happened, unwittingly replicated some of the most salient characteristics of the events they studied. They copied the strange "impartiality" that had made Dutch authorities blind toward reality, they copied the ambivalent style of leadership that had prevented Dutchbat from drawing a line in the sand, they copied the dependency on rules that had made it impossible to go along with the unexpected, they copied the preference for "attainable" rather than vital goals, they copied the silent, obliging live-and-let-live system that made it difficult to handle conflict, and so on. The things the historians copied were precisely the things that are not included in the stories the Dutch like to tell about themselves. The replications referred flawlessly to the un- or under-represented dispositions, the *myths*, that distinguish the Dutch from the "barbarians."

My point here, in this chapter, is that the Srebrenica example shows that one of the interesting things about presence is that it is operative *both* on the level of history *and* on the level of the historians who write history. Because of this dual sphere of action, studying the way the past is unwittingly replicated in how we conceive of the past is—so at least it seems to me—a promising way to reconnect critical and substantive philosophy of history. Ever since White's *Metahistory* historians have talked themselves into the belief that there is not a non-naïve way to practise substantive philosophy of history—and Whitean tropology is a creative and alluring strategy to make the most of what was left. If, however, the past is somehow present in the way historians write about it, then there *is* such a way: we could practice substantive philosophy of history by practicing critical philosophy of history. Goethe said in the introduction to his *Farbenlehre*: "Wär nicht das Auge sonnenhaft, Wie könnten wir das Licht erblicken?" ("If the eye was not like the sun, how could we see light?")[4]—and indeed what I propose is to try to discover, in history, whether we can say something about "the past" by studying how it has formed, and keeps forming, our "eye."

Vico and Metonymy

This is not by any means a *new* project. Answering the question of how we have become what we are—not by frantically digging up and solemnly preserving the dead remains of the past, but by fathoming time in things that are *alive*—was the passion of Giambattista Vico. These things that are alive, the myths that subconsciously prefigure our representations, Vico called "institutions." In a sense, Vico's institutions resemble what Richard Dawkins has called "memes"—the cultural assets that are so "self-evident" that they are handed down through the generations without them being taught by the one generation to the next. For Vico, the prime institutions, the cultural achievements that distinguish humans from other primates, are religion, matrimony and, most importantly, the custom of burying the dead. On this foundation a superstructure of other, less basic, but still very "self-evident" institutions has come into being. According to Vico these institutions not only determine the way we live but also constitute the sphere in which we communicate about the way we live.

Congruence between these two—between, that is, the level of history and the level of thought—was Vico's main heuristic, or, if one can use the word in this connection, methodological principle. One of the axioms of the *Scienza Nuova* is, in the translation of Bergin and Fisch, "The order of ideas must follow the order of institutions."[5] This, in fact, is a much discussed statement. Mark Lilla has complained that, in the *Scienza Nuova*, the connection between the two orders is "simply taken for granted"[6] and it is true that Vico never expounds how exactly this "following" is to be envisioned. Yet Vico definitely doesn't take the connection between the two orders "for granted." In his *Autobiography* he designates his "new science" as "a metaphysics of the human race,"[7] by which he means that it is his ambition to understand the outrageous fact that all nations have arrived at more-or-less the same point. One of the "institutions" the nations have in common is what Vico calls "the natural law of the gentes"—something like the form and substance of their legal instinct. Vico devotes dozens of pages to demonstrating that this natural law was not masterminded by dead white male philosophers, is not the shared heritage of some "primeval people," and is certainly not an abstract, timeless principle—as Grotius, Selden, and Pufendorf imply.

Against these misguided views Vico puts forward his own thesis, a thesis that consists of two parts. First of all Vico maintains that all "nations" (with the exception of the Jews) "metamorphose" along the same lines, and—secondly—he posits that these lines are stored in—yes, are completely available in—our "institutions." Rather like the way, one might add today, our evolutionary descent is integrally stored in our DNA. As Donald Verene has rightly observed, Vico asserts that the natural law of the gentes is "present as the actual life of any society."[8] Now Vico, a professor of rhetoric, had the brilliant idea of conceiving of these institutions as the "places" in the branch of rhetoric that is traditionally known as "topics." I hasten to add that "topics," with Vico, encompasses rather more than the collection of set pieces that can be used in a speech or an argument. For Vico, topics is the antithesis of Cartesian criticism. Whereas Cartesian criticism cuts things down to size, topics has the function of making the most of them, to "find" all we possibly can in what we come across. As Vico himself says: "topics has the function of making minds inventive."[9]

As we've seen in chapter 3, Vico practices a kind of radicalized "topics" in which the answer to the question of how we have become what we are is regarded as being completely available in "places" that can be "visited" on the plane of the present. Topics thus is instrumental *both* in how we have become what we are *and* in our ability to *fathom* how we have become what we are. By "making minds inventive," topics is the motor of history as well as the vehicle of understanding. How, according to Vico, topics actually generate history becomes apparent in one of his gnomic utterances on the origin of language. "The first founders of humanity," Vico says, "applied themselves to a sensory topics, by which they brought together those properties or qualities or relations of individuals and species which were, so to speak, concrete, and from these created their poetic genera."[10] In other words: first the world had to be "found full" with what was within reach of the senses, then the "first founders of humanity" had to invent more out of it than this sensory universe would allow by creating a nonsensory, poetic language.

Vico arrives at his intimations about our origins by making the most of what he finds in the "places" he visits in the here and now. One of these places—in fact a veritable treasure-house of topical knowledge—is language—and Vico indeed instils a lot of his insights from the etymology of words and phrases. To the modern reader, this Heideggerian penchant for etymology isn't consistently convincing, but one of the interesting things about it is that it makes Vico a decidedly unmetaphoric, yes, staunchly *metonymic* thinker. Vico doesn't use words and things to illuminate other words and things—instead he isolates them, descends into them, and "finds" in them everything he possibly can. He is particularly fond of *names*. Names "make his mind inventive" like nothing else. For Vico, names are beyond meaning. His idea is that in names we can descend to the point were things are taken up in language, to the point, that is, where their reality, their nature, their sublime individuality still stood out. Characteristically, Vico couldn't resist applying his insight to the word "name" itself. The creators of language, he says, "were rightly regarded as sages in all subsequent times because they gave natural and proper names to things, so that among the Greeks and Latins 'name' and 'nature' meant the same thing."[11]

Names are the primordial metonymies. Strictly speaking, a metonymy is a substitution of one word or phrase by another word or another phrase. The common example is "a fleet of 20 sails," but personally I prefer instances in which somebody is addressed with his diagnosis: "the ulcer in room 20 has a temperature," "the leg fracture has visitors," "the appendix is a bore." These examples highlight two features of metonymy. In the first place: they show that metonymy involves not a "horizontal" leap—like metaphor—but a "vertical" one—a leap, that is, from what I clumsily describe as one "level of being" to another. A sail can be said to have "less being" than a sailing ship, an ulcer has "less being" than the patient suffering from it, and a patient has "less being" than the person who used to be healthy but now has to stay in bed. Of course, "level of being" is quite a problematic concept. I do not in any way mean to say that a boat is less *real* than a sail, but it is quite clear, I think, that the idea of a sail was unthinkable without there being boats already in existence. Likewise, ulcers presuppose persons, but, happily, you can very well be a person without having an ulcer.

It is routinely said that metonymy is reductionist—but that's clearly wrong: one could also go *up* one or more levels and leap from *less* to *more* "being": "The mortal in room 20 has a temperature," or "The Greeks have left port." The examples, and the fact that the trope turns out to have an "ascending" as well as a "descending" mode, suggest that metonymy has an evolutionary aspect: metonymy seems to entail substitution of words and phrases from one phylogenetic level by words and phrases from an older or later, but in any case *different* phylogenetic level. Apparently, some metonymies juggle evolutionary priority per se: boats were invented before sails. In most instances however, metonymy doesn't exchange things from different stages of the evolution of humanity, but instead capitalizes upon the evolutionary structure of language.[12] The ability to name body parts is a later acquisition than the ability to name persons, and the ability to diagnose ailments is so recent as to be an ongoing project. But the distinction between these two subspecies of metonymy needn't concern us here. The important thing is that in metonymy a word or a phrase from one "level of being" is substituted with a word or a phrase from another "level of being," And because in giving a name a preverbal reality makes way for a sound and a sign, name-giving is (as Vico intuited) the starting shot for the metonymy game.

The second feature of metonymy is that by substituting one word for another, the omitted word is not wiped out and evicted from consciousness, but is conspicuous by its absence. In the phrase "the appendix is a bore," the patient, or the person, who is substituted for by his troublesome organ, is present precisely because he is so conspicuously absent. Metonymy thus has the curious property of making things present by *not* presenting them. Now, if the capacity "to make things present by not presenting them" is combined with the first feature of metonymy—the ability to bring about the transposition of different levels of being—we arrive at the exciting conclusion that in metonymy a supra-, or, if you like, an *infra-*, textual level of being is actually present in the text. Or, to put it somewhat less ceremonially, in metonymy we can make contact with a different level of reality than is vouchsafed by the words of which the text consists. This, I think, is the wonder of metonymy: whereas metaphor procures "transfer of meaning," metonymy brings about "transfer of presence." Transfer of presence is not an esoteric phenomenon. On the contrary: it is the ability of names to establish some kind of contact with a reality beyond words that explains the popularity of the commemorative practice of naming, or reciting, the names of the dead.[13]

Because of this ability to "present" a *different* level of reality than is warranted by the actual *meaning* of the word, and because metonymic substitutions go all the way down to the point where, by giving names, preverbal reality is taken up in the world of words, the linguistic phenomenon of metonymy can help us escape from our linguistic predicament. And, of course, if metonymy does indeed induce transfer of presence, there is no reason why it shouldn't do so in historical texts as well. The presence of the past isn't easily discernible though, not even, or perhaps especially not, in historical texts. It isn't helpful that metonymies *themselves* tend to go unnoticed—they have the annoying property of losing their conspicuousness over time. Initially they stand out, but in the course of time we grow so used to them that we don't notice their initial strangeness anymore. The language of historians is pervaded with such faded metonymies: in the sentence "after Trafalgar Britannia ruled the waves" half of the words are metonymies. It was the upshot of chapter 3: the omnipresence of innocently used metonymies makes historical knowledge thoroughly metonymical—and explains why historical texts may bring us into contact with the reality of the past *despite* their being written with the intention of making sense of it. Presence succeeds in getting "on board" unnoticed in as far as texts tap living culture, draw off the things we do not have to talk about, and unwittingly employ common knowledge. This, in any case, was what happened with the Srebrenica historians.

Inventio

Vico's topics may be regarded as a strategy to make the most of the living-on of the past in the here and now, to "invent" presence out of metonymical "places" that look perfectly inconspicuous. Vico's conception of history thus hinges on the idea of *inventio*—it is the key principle in both his critical and his substantive philosophy of history. With Vico, *inventio* is not just the primary tool when it comes to *fathoming* how we "have become what we are," but it is also by means of *inventio* that the process of history has taken the course it most evidently took. It is by means of *inventio* that time and again the "new" is invented out of "old" metonymical places. It is by means of *inventio* that "the nations" have mutated from one "level of being" to another and actually have reached the point they have today. I would like to add that Vico's thesis that it is by means of *inventio* that "we have become what we are" is thoroughly at odds with nineteenth-century historicist answers to that troublesome question. Historicism may be regarded as a sustained attempt to transcend the discontinuities that trouble us in the present by making sense of history. Vico on the other hand awakens dogs that lie sleeping and—by making "non-sense" of the here and now—*reinvents* the discontinuities that are stored in what we take for granted.

As far as I know, Vico does not explain the role *inventio* plays in his topics anywhere in his published works. How he conceives of *inventio* can, however, be inferred from what he has to say (in book 3 of the *New Science*) about the "Homeric question"—the question, that is, whether Homer was a kind of lonely comet or a name for a repository of poetic knowledge about our ancestry. Vico's main thesis is that Homeric poetry did not spring from "the matchless wisdom" of some ancient genius, but was the inventive way humanity overcame "poverty of language and need of expression."[14] Now, the idea that poetry has to be "invented" may sound quite unremarkable. Nevertheless, according to Vico, in practice nobody believes in it. In everyday life, he says, we always confuse "imagination" and "invention." The subtext of Vico's remarks about the Homeric question is that when we approach poetry from the outside—from, that is, later evolutionary stages—we inevitably get the impression that it was written from a surplus, but, Vico argues, it was precisely *that poetry* that elevated us to the level from which it now looks that way. According to Vico the poetry has made us into the persons we are—or rather, the poetic texts created the "common knowledge" out of which our culture consists. Ex post facto, poetry (art in general) may look like mimesis, as something brought about by "imagination," but for Vico poetry never is (as Giuseppe Mazzotta has said) "a mere allegorical cipher produced by a reflexive, ironic act of the will."[15]

Art that is really renewing is not brought about by imagination but by *inventio*. How can we envision this process by which something that is literally unimaginable is invented out of an old "place"? In order to answer this question we first have to realize that Vico, as a teacher of rhetoric, was immersed in the Greek and Roman rhetorical tradition. The prime authority on rhetoric was, of course, Aristotle. Now, Aristotle's conception of *inventio* is quite different from how even today we tend to conceive of it. For Aristotle, *inventio* takes place not only on the level of the text, but also—and more importantly—on the level of reality, where in fact the true nature of *inventio* shows. On the plane of reality *inventio* refers to the transformation that a really persuasive text procures in the public. Such a text, Aristotle argues, does not just *crush* opposing views: it does not stun, manipulate, or hypnotize the public, but *educates* it to new and more truthful positions. As Walter

Watson says: "Since the speech, if effective, persuades [the listener] of something new, a belief he did not hold before or not in the same way, the whole process is one in which the mind of the hearer invents itself."[16] In other words: true invention produces what the Germans call *Selbsthervorbringung* and what in biology is called *autopoiesis*.

In ancient rhetoric it was, as far as I know, exclusively *the public* that could have itself metamorphosed by an inventive text. But there is no reason, so at least it seems to me, why it shouldn't apply to *speakers themselves* as well. In a truly inventive text a speaker doesn't just imaginatively conjure up the arguments that he thinks will serve him best, but discovers what he "really" thinks about the issues at stake. For speakers too *inventio* is *Selbsthervorbringung*—if it isn't, it's just imagination. In the previous chapter I quoted E.M. Forster's remark: "How do I know what I think, until I've read what I wrote?" The metamorphoses Forster alludes to need not be the result of long hours behind a desk. They may well be the result of inventions made in the heat of an argument—like how Saint-Just and Robespierre brought about modern France in their improvised speeches in the Assemblée nationale, and how Slobodan Milosevic invented post-Yugoslav Serb nationalism (and himself) in his infamous impromptus at Kosovo Polje in 1989. But if even the speakers themselves are invented by the inventiveness of their speeches, what is the stuff inventions are made of? If it isn't from an authorial "surplus," where does *inventio* come from?

Again, Aristotle gives a clue. Because a really good invention operates as a catalyst rather than as a form of intimidation, it has to build upon things already in the mind of the listener. Aristotle calls this discontinuous progression in the direction of ever more "truthful" positions "dialectics." It is the subject of his *Topics*. Dialectics, according to Aristotle, is not—like logic—doing magic with what is beyond doubt, but making the most of *endoxa*—of beliefs that are—though questionable—"held universally."[17] With the help of *inventio*, such universally held, but doubtful, beliefs can be transcended into positions that are qualitatively different from those out of which they are invented. According to Aristotle, dialectical reasoning "is a discussion in which, certain things having been laid down, something other than these things necessarily results through them."[18] Aristotle's idea of dialectics presupposes something that at first sight may seem paradoxical, but is, on consideration, quite logical: to arrive at something that *really* is radically new, we have to go back. To persuade a listener, and to make him invent himself into somebody with a more "progressive" opinion, one has to kindle the convictions he forgot he had, to appeal to things that are too obvious to talk about, to awaken what I have called "common knowledge." Because these are precisely the things that have been superseded by earlier inventions, "dialectics," as expounded in Aristotle's *Topics*, really is the art of inventing the new out of the old.

Vico may be said to have transposed Aristotle's idea to the sphere of culture to, as he himself would have said, "the life of nations." The *Scienza Nuova* is the science of the series of inventions by which the nations invented themselves, of how time and again "mind" was "made inventive" and found more in what was left behind than it *itself* could have imagined, of, in short, the *Selbsthervorbringung* of humanity. Vico shows how in history as well as in thinking about history (and I would like to add, in philosophy as well) we go forward by going backward. *Inventio* therefore is closely related to memory. "Memory," Vico observes perceptively, "has three different aspects: memory when it remembers things, imagination when it alters or imitates them, and invention when it gives them a new turn or puts them into proper arrangement and relationship. This is the reason that memory is called 'the mother of the muses.' "[19] For Vico, this "going forward by going backward" is not a continuous progression but rather a series of mutations. If we just go forward, we stay where we are. It is only by reclaiming what we have forgotten, by allowing the presence of the past to take possession of us, that we start to go forward in an unimaginable way.

Although Vico himself was mainly interested in the early stages of how we have become what we are—in, that is, Homeric and pre-Homeric times—his topics, in which we "go forward by going backward," may well suggest an up-to-date substantive philosophy of history. The notion of *inventio* offers a perspective from which we can comprehend how, every now and then, people break apart from the stories they live by and start to commit deeds they hadn't even dreamt of. In such a topical view of history, to "commit" history is to "invent the new" out of old metonymical places. It is the tenor of what I said in the previous chapter: the revolutionaries of 1789 *invented* the idea of popular sovereignty out of "common knowledge" about the derelict États généraux, Alfred von Schlieffen *invented* (in the late nineteenth century) the German military predicament as well as the solution to it out of the myth of the Battle of Cannae, and George W. Bush *invented* his "crusade" to bring freedom and democracy to the Middle East out of a concoction of things everybody knows about Richard the Lionheart, Abraham Lincoln, and Douglas MacArthur. In all these cases the actors allowed themselves to be overwhelmed by the "presence" of what they had "invented"—to the extent that they enthusiastically sacrificed the (metaphorical) stories they lived by in order to "realize" this presence in the here and now.

The wonderful thing about Vico's topics is that it shows how all the stages we have left behind can be recovered by reinventing them out of our common knowledge. If civilization advances, as Alfred North Whitehead has remarked, "by extending the number of important operations we can perform without thinking about them," then Vico's topics is a way to get access again to all these submerged "operations." As a way to recover the reality of the past, topics may be regarded as the counterpart to the study of how it is "covered." One of Hayden White's brilliant insights was that it is important "to understand what is fictive in all putatively realistic representations of the world, and what is realistic in all manifestly fictive ones."[20] In the past decades only the first half of this project has been taken up: White's own "tropics" can be regarded as a research strategy to understand what is fictive in realistic representations of the world. If, however, "realistic" is taken to mean the way reality is present in the text, then Vico's topics indicates how we may come to understand what is realistic in fictive representations of the world. This, I think, is the road historians have to take when they want to recover some of the ground they have lost to all those outsiders who—whatever their historical qualifications are—allow themselves to be driven by the question of how we have become what we are.

8

Crossing the Wires in the Pleasure Machine

Jede Zeit ist eine Sphinx, die sich in den Abgrund stürzt, sobald man ihr Räthsel gelöst hat.

—Heinrich Heine[1]

Though history—*res gestae* as well as *historia rerum gestarum*—progresses by leaps and bounds, the mind of the historian is inclined, in the words of Henri Bergson, to "neglect the part of novelty or of creation inherent in the free act." Our intellect, Bergson goes on, "will always substitute for action itself an imitation artificial, approximative, obtained by compounding the old with the old and the same with the same."[2] If there is one single issue that deserves to shape discussions about the relation of history and theory in the upcoming years, it is, I think, how to circumvent the blind spot that makes it so difficult to say sensible things about how, in history as well as in historiography, the new—the exhilarating, frightening, sinful, sublimely new—comes about. Focusing on how we generate novelty means taking leave of the postmodern paradigm in which language is all. In the previous chapters I have argued that the leaps and bounds by which history progresses are manifestations of, as Goethe said, "Im Anfang ist die Tat." They spring from a *dehors texte*, from, that is, a domain that according to postmodernists like Derrida is not supposed to exist. Indeed, isn't "compounding the old with the old and the same with the same"—the strategy by which we threw out the baby of reality with the bathwater of realism—exactly what postmodernism was about? In this chapter, an exercise in what used to be called "substantive" reflection on the making of history,[3] I will try to connect the notion that "novelty"—or, perhaps better, *discontinuity*— springs from the *dehors texte* with Burckhardt's intuition that we have become, and continue to become, what we are in an endless series of *Verpuppungen* (metamorphoses). I will do so not by amassing material that supports my case—as I did in chapter 6—but by exploring one particular metamorphosis: the way Lenin succeeded in bringing off what came to be called the Russian Revolution.

Salting the Freshwater Pool

In his *Notes Towards a Biography*, Trotsky attributes Lenin's astonishing effectiveness as a revolutionary not to his strategic brilliance, his ruthlessness, or his ideological rectitude, but, surprisingly, to his *imagination*. Among the most valuable attributes of imagination is, according to Trotsky, the "ability to conceive of people, things, and phenomena as they really are, although one might never have had a chance to observe them."[4] Trotsky maintains that it was precisely this imaginative knowledge—if knowledge it may be called—in which Lenin excelled. Of course, Trotsky knew full well that his analysis put his hero in the same league as both Plato and Madame Blavatsky— but this, apparently, didn't prevent him from claiming that the quality of Lenin's judgments was quite independent of the amount of observation that went into them. Trotsky made things worse when he tried to specify what he meant. He attributed Lenin's "imagination" to "the ability to make use of one's experience and theoretical principles, to coordinate disparate hints and pieces of information that are, so to say, in the air, and assimilate them, to supplement them, unite them together according to some unformulated laws of harmony, and, in this way, to reconstitute in all its concrete reality a field of human existence."[5]

By representing Lenin as someone who had the gift of making right assessments about how situations would evolve, people would behave, and acts would work out, on the basis of information that was not "at hand" but "in the air," Trotsky portrays his brother-in-arms as a kind of sleepwalker, as a latter-day incarnation of what Victor Hugo called "the blind clairvoyance of the Revolution." Now, somnambulistic clairvoyance clearly doesn't belong to the stuff historical explanations are made of. It may make Lenin a suitable case study for what sociologists like Donald Schön have said about "how professionals think in action"[6] (if it is true, as Schön argues, that every good professional "knows more than he can say," then Lenin was a very good professional indeed), but it is hardly surprising that Trotsky's explanation for Lenin's success has not been taken up by historians of the Russian Revolution or biographers of Lenin.[7] As an explanation for Lenin's astonishing success "somnambulistic clairvoyance" looks like a dead-end street. Yet Trotsky's explanation for Lenin's success deserves to be taken as seriously as I think he wanted it to be taken. So what could he have had in mind when he attributes Lenin's success to his "imagination"? How to conceive of this uncanny but supremely useful ability to pick "disparate hints and pieces of information" from "the air"? Why did this ability give him such an enviable edge over his adversaries? And, last but not least, what does this metaphorical "air" stand for?

Obviously, Lenin's clairvoyant judgments cannot be put to the test. A valid test would require a context that is not contaminated by what is tested, and it was precisely in contaminating, or rather, changing, contexts in which Lenin excelled. Time and again he exasperated his friends, allies, and adversaries by brushing aside established opinions, by redefining situations, and by changing the rules of the game—most notably of course in the twelve months or so after his arrival at Finland Station in April 1917. Alexander Bogdanov, cofounder of the Bolshevik faction of the Communist Party, characterized Lenin's "April Theses" as "the delirium of a madman," and even Lenin's wife once said that she was afraid that "it looks as if Lenin has gone crazy."[8] Remarkably, Lenin not only got away with his outrageous *volte faces*, but nearly always succeeded in having his views prevail. It may well be that Lenin's extraordinary talent to beget the contexts that suited him best had less to do with charisma, skullduggery, or a "strong will" than with an amount of narcissism that even for a successful politician is quite exceptional. Narcissism, after all, is *not* "being in love with yourself" but is rather a disposition to see the "world"[9] as an extension of yourself coupled with the ability to get it to accept the image you project on it. But narcissistic or not, Lenin's capacity to recreate contexts

"in his image and likeness" seems to render the concept I just introduced—the concept of "somnambulistic clairvoyance"—completely
worthless: an epiphenomenon of Lenin's gift for creating self-fulfilling
prophecies. And that would be the end of it.

Instead, I propose to treat it as a beginning. Even Trotsky would
agree that what was at stake was not Lenin's ability to make the right
predictions about what was around the corner, but rather his knack for
creating the very corners from which his "predictions" were right. It's
a view that has been amplified by Slavoj Žižek. Referring to the discussions concerning whether 1917 was the right time, and Russia the
right country, for a revolution, Žižek writes that the Leninist strategy
was "to take a leap, throwing oneself into the paradox of the situation, seizing the opportunity and *intervening*, even if the situation was
'premature,' with the wager that this very 'premature' intervention
will radically change the 'objective' relationship of forces itself, within
which the initial situation appeared as 'premature.' "[10] For Žižek, Lenin
was unique because he sensed that what really weighs you down is not
the police, the law, or some moral code, but the fear of breaking with
received opinion, of bringing off what you really want, of succeed-
ing. And indeed, in a piece like "Letter to Comrades," written just a
few days before the coup, Lenin can be seen to convince himself that
there really isn't a good reason to stick to received wisdom about how
the revolution was to come about, a wisdom epitomized by a question
that even intimidated *him*: "Why should we stake everything?" In the
months just before the revolution Lenin repeats like a mantra what he
found in Marx: that insurrection is not a science—in which everything
depends on the right conditions—but an art—in which everything
depends on the freedom of the artist.

Žižek's view that Lenin created the situations in which his judgments were right squares remarkably well with the evolutionary perspective on history I sketched in chapter 6, a perspective in which
major, "sublime" discontinuities like the French and the Russian Revolutions provide the environments in which humanity mutates to a
new—though not necessarily higher or happier—level. I should say
straightaway that such an evolutionary perspective differs in at least
two respects from the passive gradualism we have come to associate
with the notion of evolution. The first difference is that in the domain

of history the concept of evolution makes more sense the more it focuses on the fact that humans influence, determine—yes, *create*—the context in which they have to survive. Though animals too engage in "niche construction," even our closest relatives—chimpanzees and bonobos—are incomparably more passively subjected to the interaction between their genes and their biotope than humans. Humans have capitalized on the discovery that survival need not be dependent on adaptability alone, that it can be achieved in a much more economical way by taming the environment and making it ever more "fitting" to the human phenotype. That adapting our environment to *us*, instead of the other way around, is so much more economical has a simple reason: this environment of our own making, usually called "culture," is *inheritable*, whereas the increases in adaptive fitness that individuals may attain are not, or are so only indirectly. We humans have, as biologists would say, superimposed a Lamarckian cultural evolution on a Darwinian substratum of genetic evolution.

The second difference has to do with the remarkable fact (discussed at length in the next chapter) that this gift for creating an environment in which we can thrive somehow didn't slow down our evolution—as one would expect with diminishing pressure from the environment. Nicholas Humphrey, Robin Dunbar, Matt Ridley, and many others have suggested that an explanation for the fact that human evolution kept going (and, if anything, even accelerated) can very well be that the more we disarmed our environment the more we became *our own* environment. We discovered, in short, that it was evolutionarily advantageous to become our own best enemy. In the next chapter I will show that being our own best enemy doesn't mean that we cannot stop fighting each other, but rather that we have replaced competitiveness *among* species with ever new forms of intraspecies competition. As a species we are obstinately creative in finding ways to give ourselves a hard time, or, perhaps better: to re-inject the selectiveness that we have taken away from nature into the culture we inhabit. Culture thus is not the success story we would very much like it to be. It is rather the result of what has been called the ratchet principle. Humans are incurably inventive, but our evolution is not solely, or even primarily, the result of inventions that "are in our best interest." It rather results from inventions from which there is no way back and that we have no choice but to live up to. And it is this having to live up to the things with which we have saddled ourselves that is ultimately in our best interest: in our best interest, that is, as a species, not as an individual member of that species. The idea that we may be "our own best enemy" is, in fact, but one remove from the thesis of chapter 6: retrospectively, the thesis that we "commit history" not *although*, but *because* it is at odds with our identity, starts to get explanatory power when it is rephrased in evolutionary terms: we become what we are by periodically being "our own best enemy" just long enough to bring about a new level of selectiveness from which there is no way back.

By combining the uncombinable—taming the environment while retaining the selectiveness that makes it such a potent evolutionary tool—humans have squared the circle of evolution. Humans have become the animals who have taken their evolution in their own hands—with the proviso, of course, that both aspects of the game, "preemptive adaptation" as well as "self-inflicted selectiveness," have acquired a dynamic of their own—to the extent that they have become quite independent from the individuals who take part in it. In any case, the culturally mediated evolution humans have stumbled upon is so much more efficient than genetically mediated evolution that it more than counteracts slow reproduction and the emasculation of the natural world. It should be clear by now that this culturally mediated evolution, efficient as it might be, is a mixed blessing. As a species we are unable to rest on our laurels indefinitely. As we've seen in chapter 1, this sublime restlessness was beautifully expressed by Wilhelm von Humboldt. Sooner or later, Humboldt says, we evict ourselves from our after all not too fancy and perhaps a little bit boring paradises and then we start to destroy "our homely huts" in order to build what we think will eventually be a castle.[11] Hegel somewhere remarks that the happy pages of humanity are blank—and indeed, history is the story of how as a species we compulsively keep taking away the ground from under our feet.

The key to how as a species we cater for selectiveness is the use we have come to make of mutations. In culturally mediated evolution we don't have to *wait* for mutations, we can bring them about by ourselves. Or perhaps more accurately: we can bring about the situations that put a premium on mutations. How mutations "work" in the genetically mediated evolution of the natural world is aptly described by Olivia Judson:

> Imagine you have a population of algae that have been living for generations in a comfy freshwater pool. Now suppose there's a ghastly accident and, all of a sudden, the pool becomes super-salty. Whether the algae will be able to survive depends on whether any individuals already have any capacity to survive and reproduce in salty water. If none of them do, they all die, and the population goes extinct. But if some do, then the survivors will reproduce, and over time, beneficial mutations will accumulate such that the algae get better and better at living in a high-salt environment.[12]

Now, human evolution, or at least the culturally mediated form of evolution we call history, differs from the evolution of algae in that humans create their own "ghastly accidents." It is precisely such ghastly accidents to which the Hungarian writer Sándor Márai referred when he asked himself "why . . . groups, classes, yes, whole societies every now and then decide to ditch the tranquil and well-organized idyll we call 'peace' in order to throw themselves vacantly in the adventure of their downfall."[13]

It seems patently paradoxical: is it by any means conceivable that evolution is propelled *forward* by events that are experienced as a *downfall*? It may not make the paradox less paradoxical, but it is, in this connection, important to note, first, that evolution is not a goal-directed process but only has direction and consistency when we look back, and second, that "ghastly accidents" of our own making have the curious property of changing their aspect radically the moment we pass the point of no return. What is afterwards experienced as trauma comes into being as the sublime "Why not?" I described in chapter 6. It is, when you come to think of it, a puzzling phenomenon: the fact of its taking place transforms the accident. As long as it hadn't taken place its traumatic painfulness was unimaginable, whereas afterwards it is its sublimity that eludes us. Ghastly accidents are ghastly because they cause what is the essence of trauma: the realization that we are irremediably cut off from what we took for granted (which, by the way, is not just a matter of the pain of nostalgia). Characteristically, it is only *after* a sublime historical event (as I would like to call the human equivalent for what befell the algae) that we may come to *know* what we have left behind. After their pool has become salty, bright, surviving algae may begin to understand what freshness is (the accident may even provide them with the brightness needed for their project). Be that as it may, the paradox that the mutations to which we owe our evolutionary success retrospectively *feel* like downfalls may not close our eyes to the fact that there is another side to Márai's words, the side of the daredevils who are not deterred by the sublimity of what they aspire to.

Fleeing Forward

Daredevils, that is, like Lenin. Unfortunately it is extremely difficult to get access to the forward-looking part of the Janus-faced events historical trailblazers bring about. We not only have to circumvent the fact that by definition we live under the aegis of the other, backward-looking part, but we are also hindered by a massive amount of what psychologists call "post-decisional dissonance reduction" (PDR), the tendency, mentioned earlier, to align our beliefs, our values, and our identity to what we actually turned out to be doing. Obviously, the more we surprise ourselves with our actions (and the less we are able or willing to dissimulate what we did) the more dissonance we have to reduce. It goes without saying that people involved in the making of history also engage in PDR. How this comes about is brilliantly shown in Tolstoy's *War and Peace*—a book that, by the way, also demonstrates that it might be evolutionarily advantageous to create a class of specialists, usually called "historians," to do the PDR that our historical actions have made necessary for us. Tolstoy's major theme is that one of the more fundamental issues that tends to get obliterated by PDR is the extent in which we did things "by guess and by God." For some reason we very much prefer to say (or have our historians say) that our calculations were wrong, that we made a mistake or that we were out-maneuvered, to admitting that we didn't know what we were doing. Unfortunately, the tendency to reduce dissonance is so strong that it is quite likely that it wipes out the phenomenon to which Trotsky drew our attention: Lenin, for example, would probably have insisted that he knew full well what he was doing *even if* the things he happened to do sprang from the "somnambulistic clairvoyance" that Trotsky describes.

Accessing sublime historical events isn't made any easier by the fact that the social sciences have little to say about the state of mind in which we sniff at just fine-tuning our "comfy freshwater pool" and contrive to make it salty instead. From Freud's "pleasure principle" onward, there have been quite a few theories that explain why and how we make things easier, safer, more gratifying for ourselves— theories, in short, that make us understand the mechanics of how we adapt our environment to us, instead of the other way around. But psychologists and sociologists alike stand empty-handed when they have to explain why we would give ourselves a hard time by drastically stepping up selectiveness. They do not really make us understand why we would overthrow the status quo, concoct plans to do things radically differently, or kill ourselves in some sublime terrorist attack.[14] Or rather, they try to squeeze these phenomena into what may broadly be called "the paradigm of complexity reduction." Even the most powerful theory in this respect, that of Niklas Luhmann, isn't up to the task of explaining the *creation* of complexity. Complexity-creation simply doesn't seem to fit the bill. As Jon Elster says: "Whereas dissonance reduction serves an obvious psychic function, it is not clear what need if any is served by dissonance creation. It could be that it serves no need at all, but simply reflects some kind of psychic malfunction, a 'crossing of the wires in the pleasure machine.' "[15]

It may well be, however, that the creation of complexity (or dissonance, or chaos, or increased entropy) is precisely the way in which we step up selectiveness. By this I do not intend to say that we start revolutions because we want to create complexity. As I will explain at length in the next chapter, I think that sublime historical events are cascades of fleeing forward brought about by people who sensed or thought that they could thrive in ever more uncertain, unpleasant, or downright dangerous circumstances. In his "Letters from Afar" Lenin writes: "There are no miracles in nature or history, but every abrupt turn in history, and this applies to every revolution, presents such a wealth of content, unfolds such unexpected and specific combinations of forms of struggle and alignments of forces of the contestants, that to the lay mind there is much that must appear miraculous."[16] To all appearances, Lenin discovered that he felt alive and flourishing in this environment that most evidently bewildered "lay minds." He may have sensed, like quite a few of his allies and adversaries, that letting things get out of hand and fleeing forward was actually benefiting him. From this perspective, the revolution was a bubble of complexity-creation—a bubble in which the participants drove each other to ever new heights of selectiveness. Needless to say, in this process of salting the freshwater pool the avant-garde didn't care about morality. People who are in the business of committing history have convinced themselves that, as Alain Badiou paraphrases Nietzsche, "morality is a residue of the old world."[17] And, perversely, from the perspective of the species, they are right. Lenin is the perfect embodiment of what Hugo Ribbert said at the beginning of the twentieth century: "The man who is thoroughly healthy in every respect simply cannot act badly or wickedly; his actions are necessarily good, that is to say, properly adapted to the evolution of the human race, in harmony with the cosmos."[18] Everything is permitted in the service of this "cosmic" task, right up to what is the *non plus ultra* of selectiveness: terror and indiscriminate shootings.

It would be wrong, however, to equate the circumstances that were the result of this bubble of complexity-creation with the complexity the revolution created at the level of the species. This isn't as complicated as it may sound. Let's return for a moment to what I said a few pages ago about the two features of culturally mediated evolution. The first feature is that humans have learned to devote themselves to creating an environment of their own making that frees them from having merely to adapt to the natural world. The second is that they discovered that it was evolutionarily advantageous "to become their own best enemy" and so to retain the selectiveness that makes adaptation such a potent evolutionary tool. I have called these features, for lack of better words, "preemptive adaptation" and "self-inflicted selectiveness." Now, insofar as Lenin was trying to create an environment in which *he* could thrive, he was engaging in preemptive adaptation. The peculiar thing is that the environment he could thrive in was an environment that was too uncertain, too dangerous—in short, too selective—for most others. Lenin sensed that salt water was his element, and consequently tried to make the pool as salty as he could. That he succeeded was the result of the fact that there were enough salt-liking and opportunistic algae like him to create the bubble that eventually made the pool salty indeed. But whereas for Lenin complexity-creation was a means to an end, on the level of the species it was just the other way around: the need for self-inflicted selectiveness made use of Lenin's determination to create an environment in which *he* could thrive.

In order to understand what complexity looks like at the level of the species, we'd best begin with what I take to be an axiom: that the best way to complicate a situation is to try to simplify it by throwing all considerations to the wind and fleeing forward. Fleeing forward is cutting oneself loose from the system of complexity reduction that is stored in conventions, received wisdom, and other things we take for granted. From the perspective of the species, then, complexity is contained in the clutter of accomplished facts with which we find ourselves when our fleeing forward has come to an end. In the evolutionary perspective on history that I propose, new evolutionary stages are not the result of what can be thought out beforehand (no matter how brilliant the mind of the thinker), but of the things we did without quite knowing what we did. It's the ratchet principle again: a sublime historical event is born in what on the level of the species is a fit of absentmindedness, in, as psychiatrists would say, a state of dissociation. This, I think, is what Vico had in mind when he said that "the wisdom of the ancients was the vulgar wisdom of the lawgivers, who founded the human race, not the esoteric wisdom of great and rare philosophers."[19] Because a sublime historical event adds complexity and is, by definition, a break with what we took for granted, one might say that it brings about a re-enchantment of the world—be it, of course, that the increased selectiveness makes it a re-enchantment of a rather prosaic or downright nightmarish kind. Insofar as it frees us from the insubstantiality of our comfy freshwater pool and launches us into the real again, each sublime historical event—or more accurately, every instance of stepping up selectiveness—is what Victor Hugo said of the French Revolution: "a return from the fictitious to the real."[20]

"The Inspired Frenzy of History"

Lenin was surely one of the all-time virtuosos in the art of fleeing forward, and we may pronounce ourselves lucky that Trotsky's account of him gives us an inside view of how sublime historical events are brought about. I might as well start with Trotsky's remarks, in his autobiography, about the improvised character of the revolution. Looking back on the tense and confused situation in Petrograd after the czar had abdicated (in March 1917), Trotsky writes: "On the decisions made and the orders given in those days depended the fate of the nation for an entire historical era." "And yet," Trotsky continues, "[our] decisions were made with very little discussion. I can hardly say that they were even properly weighed and considered; they were almost improvised on the moment."[21] Now, of course, it is not really surprising that decisions made in chaotic circumstances are improvisations. However, for two reasons Trotsky's observation stands out. The first is that if there is one ideology that abhors improvisation it is the Leninist brand of dialectical materialism. Ever since he had expounded the supremacy of theory—most notably perhaps in "What Is to Be Done?"—Lenin had reserved his most biting sarcasm for what he called "opportunists"—people, that is, who deviated from the line of march prescribed by theory, people who allowed themselves to be tempted by some contingency. As late as August 1917, after the Kornilov Putsch had failed, he had admonished his fellow Bolsheviks to stay on course: "The Kornilov revolt is a most unexpected . . . and downright unbelievable sharp turn in events. Like every sharp turn it calls for a revision and change in tactics. And as with every revision, we must be extra-cautious not to become unprincipled."[22]

In view of this insistence on the "principles" of revolution, the unabashed opportunism of the Bolshevik leaders right before, in, and after their successful coup d'état is quite remarkable—no matter that by then it was called "improvisation." One might say that for all the hullaballoo about the primacy of the word, the role of theory in what Lenin accomplished is deeply ironic: rather than guiding action, it guided nonaction. It helped Lenin, up until his coup d'état in October 1917, to *not* make revolution, to keep his powder dry, to give him good

reasons for postponing the cutting of the Gordian knot, to not having a go at taking command of the situation. Theory reappeared only
after the fact, after "the events intervened," after the Bolsheviks had
consolidated their power. By then, however, it still didn't guide action,
but mainly served as post hoc justification of what had been brought
about, as a Swiss army knife for post-decisional dissonance reduction.
In between these two periods—the period in which theory was a justification for postponing what had to be done, and the period in which
it was a justification for what already *had* been done—is a rather short
time span, maybe less than a year, in which deeds reigned supreme.
That in this vortex of events deeds had stopped being means to an end
is clearly shown in a letter in which Lenin announced that he was to
seize power the very next day. Instead of explaining what he wanted
to achieve with his coup, he said that "its political goal will be clarified
after the seizure."[23] And from the perspective I propose in this chapter,
Lenin was absolutely right: the coup—when successful—would clarify
the situation, and the clarification of the situation would be its "political goal." The goal would already have been attained (and would consequently no longer be a goal) the moment it became possible to state
what the goal was.

The seizure of power is as good an example of fleeing forward as one
might get. The "Why not?" that had taken shape in Lenin's mind had
mushroomed into such an irresistible compulsion to act that it made
him write that "delaying the action is akin to death."[24] In the sense
that this compulsion to act left no space whatsoever for the doubts,
feelings, and considerations in which we normally drift around, for
the conventions that connect us to ourselves, our culture, and our past,
for, in short, what keeps our feet to the ground, one could say that
the act, once performed, was born in a state of absentmindedness.
Insofar as the seizure of power was an attempt to simplify the situation, it aspired to reduce complexity, but because it necessitated further instances of fleeing forward it contributed to complexity creation.
It wouldn't be right, however, to say that what later became known
as "the October Revolution" was just one of the "improvisations"
Trotsky spoke about. In a very real sense the coup was the final turn
of the screw, the farthest stop to which the ratchet could be wound: it
became the focal point around which the complexity created in that

vortex of events could be reduced when things had quieted down. So, though the October Revolution was not the foundation of the house, but rather the ridge of its roof, Trotsky was quite right when he said that after the takeover the Bolsheviks were faced with the task of bringing "the consciousness of the masses into correspondence with the situation into which the historic process has driven them."[25]

The invocation of history brings me to the second remarkable feature of Trotsky's observation that the revolution was a cascade of improvisations: Trotsky blandly tells us that the decisions made in this maelstrom of events were "*none* the worse" for their improvised character.[26] In fact, it made them better. "The pressure of events was so terrific," he writes, "that the most important decisions came naturally, as matters of course, and were received in the same spirit."[27] Trotsky didn't for a moment doubt what made his and Lenin's improvisations so apposite. "Under the strain of circumstances [the] 'leaders' [Trotsky, one of those very leaders, placed the quotation marks] did no more than formulate what answered the requirements of the people and the demands of history." Retrospectively, it's one of the most striking aspects of the modus operandi of the Bolshevik leaders: they really believed that they knew what history "demanded." I don't think they believed that this was knowledge "on the shelf," knowledge, that is, that could be accessed at will. They rather were convinced that somehow they *embodied* history, that if they didn't compromise the "improvisations" that welled up in them with too many safeguards, too much soft-heartedness, or too much moderation they would perforce enact "the demands of history."[28]

Now, for us this is quite hard to understand: how can anyone in his or her right mind believe that he or she embodies history? That, however, might be posing the wrong question: it supposes that Lenin and Trotsky were just as "right-minded" as we are when we try to understand what they meant. But should we not consider the possibility that in order to believe that you are embodying history you'd better not be in "your right mind"? Or even that it was not just a belief or a delusion—but that in a certain state of mind you can do things that can be abbreviated as "embodying history"? Of course, this goes against the grain of what a right-minded historian is allowed to think, but the fact remains that hard-boiled revolutionaries like Lenin and Trotsky were adamant in their invocation of history—and, as Thomas Kuhn used to say: "When reading the works of an important thinker, look first for the apparent absurdities in the text and ask yourself how a sensible person could have written them."[29]

Trotsky, for that matter, was sensible enough to take it for granted that not *all* Bolshevik improvisations were "historical." He also was enough of a maverick to ask himself why some improvisations embody history whereas others do not. In answering this question, he initially comes forward with stock-in-trade Marxist rhetoric about the revolutionary vanguard being the "conscious expression of the unconscious historical process."[30] But having finished his Hail Marys, he adds that revolutions are made in moments in which "the highest theoretical consciousness of the epoch merges with the immediate action of those oppressed masses who are furthest away from theory. The creative union of the conscious with the unconscious is what one usually calls 'inspiration.' Revolution is the inspired frenzy of history."[31] Trotsky thus in effect says that an improvisation "embodies history" when it is "inspired," and unavoidable, opportunistic, or simply all too human when it is not.

Trotsky, who was not only a gifted writer, but also, by all accounts, the most "inspired" orator of the revolutionary era, had firsthand experience of what he was talking about. "Every real writer," he wrote,

knows creative moments, when something stronger than himself is guiding his hand; every real orator experiences moments when someone stronger than the self of his everyday existence speaks through him. This is "inspiration." It derives from the highest creative effort of all one's forces. The unconscious rises from its deep well and bends the conscious mind to its own will, merging it with itself in some greater synthesis.[32]

In a striking passage in his autobiography Trotsky caught this inspiration in the act. Looking back on the famous speeches he gave at the Cirque Moderne, he writes that he couldn't avoid falling under the spell of the "electric tension of the impassioned human throng." The crowd gave him the sensation, he writes, of "infants clinging with their dry lips to the nipples of the revolution." He felt, he remembers, an enormous pressure to live up to what the crowd expected and to deliver what was "in the air." And not being kept in check by a fixed text, let alone a teleprompter, he really *could* deliver: "Then all the arguments and words thought out in advance would break and recede under the imperative pressure of sympathy, and other words, other arguments, utterly unexpected by the orator but needed by these people, would emerge in full array from my subconsciousness." This is dissociated absentmindedness in *optima forma*. Trotsky writes that during his "inspired" speeches he was literally alienated from himself: "On such occasions I felt as if I were listening to the speaker from the outside, trying to keep pace with his ideas, afraid that like a somnambulist, he might fall off the edge of the roof at the sound of my conscious reasoning."[33] So in fact, Trotsky's speeches at the Cirque Moderne are a good example of what in rhetoric is called *inventio* and of what I have called (in the previous chapter) historical *autopoiesis*.

Lenin's "Intuition of Action"

It is this account of what inspiration is that inspires Trotsky's picture of Lenin. His point is really very simple: whereas he—Trotsky—rose to the occasion in his speeches, Lenin did so in his deeds. Lenin's "whole personality [was] centered on revolutionary action."[34] Trotsky's estimation that the inspired deed was a form of *inventio* that more than measured up to the inspired speech that was his own specialty made him write that "the collection of Soviet decrees forms in a certain sense a part, and not a negligible part, of the Complete Works of Vladimir Ilyich Lenin."[35] And just as Trotsky had "sleepwalked" his speeches, Lenin was so absorbed by his deeds that they left no room for himself. This is what I have called "absentmindedness": the state of mind in which what you do so completely "absorbs" you that there is no room anymore for the conventions that connect you to yourself, your culture, and your past, to what keeps your feet to the ground. In the most critical moments, Trotsky writes, Lenin "became as if deaf and blind to all that went beyond the cardinal problem which absorbed him."[36] Lenin was so occupied by his deeds that afterwards he couldn't always remember what he had done. When a "critical hurdle" was already "happily cleared," Trotsky notes, Lenin might complain that the problem wasn't solved yet. And when somebody would point out to him that he himself had done away with it, Lenin would exclaim: "Impossible! . . . and I don't remember a thing." In a piece he wrote on Lenin's fiftieth birthday, Trotsky gave a rather chilling description of what he called Lenin's "intuition of action": the ability "to strike a blow straightaway while the very idea of the blow was still shaping itself in one's mind."[37]

In these inspired deeds Lenin "somnambulistically" fled forwards. According to his fellow revolutionary Chernov, Lenin often muttered (in French) a remark that could also have been made by Schiller's robber Karl Moor: "Je ne sais pas où je vais, mais j'y vais résolument"[38] ("I don't know whither I'm going, but I'm going there resolutely"). And indeed, a determination to catch the moment, to fill it as completely with a deed as one possibly could, and to flee forward again to God knows where, is much more "Leninistic" than the farsightedness that was to become such a cherished part of the Lenin myth. Trotsky remembered that just a few months after the revolution Lenin had said that "for its success socialism in Russia needs a certain spell of time, *at least a few months.*"[39] These words, Trotsky says, "seem absolutely incomprehensible now: wasn't this a slip of the pen? Did he not mean 'a few years' or 'a few decades'?" But no, Trotsky went on, this was no slip. It was "his way of teaching people around him to consider all problems from the viewpoint of socialist construction—not in the long perspective of the 'final aim,' but in the immediate perspective of today and tomorrow."[40] Trotsky admired Lenin's intuition of action because it enabled him "at the sharp turns of history" to "cut corners and foreshorten distances." In fact, "cutting corners" is an illuminating metaphor—for insofar as the road before you can't be seen, "cutting corners" necessarily means *creating* corners. This "cutting corners" is, I think, not an epiphenomenon of a historical mutation, but its very essence. It is the ratchet principle at work. Trotsky gives quite a good example when he says that while Lenin was not at all impressed by "the magic of formality" he nevertheless clothed his decrees in formal language. This formal tone, Trotsky says, was needed: it was "the tone of a government which today is still suspended in a vacuum, but which tomorrow or the day after would become a force, and for this reason already today acts as a force."[41] The *tone* of power preceded power, as "playing government" preceded *being* the government.

Both Trotsky and Lenin interpreted the fact that the new "emerg[ed] in full array from [their] subconsciousness" (as Trotsky had phrased it) as evidence that they embodied history. Both emanated the belief that their embodying history entitled them to success, though this sense of entitlement certainly did not make them relax and wait until power would fall in their lap. On the contrary, it rather was an obligation to stake everything and to fling themselves without reserve into what Trotsky had called "the inspired frenzy of history." Like quite a few of their fellow revolutionaries they seem to have felt that only by *living* history, by being as absentmindedly present in the events of the day as was humanly possible, by *forgetting* about history, could history eventually be theirs. On consideration, Lenin's and Trotsky's belief that they embodied history can be factored in, on the one hand, the sense of embodiment per se, and, on the other hand, in the specific form this sense of embodiment took. Quite apart from what exactly they believed they embodied, a sense of embodiment was also present in Joan of Arc, Cromwell, Abbé Sieyès, Robespierre, Garibaldi, and Hitler—in, for short, everyone who more-or-less successfully salted his or her particular freshwater pool. The common denominator is that these figures had evacuated themselves: they had emptied themselves of what I have called the system of complexity-reduction that is stored in conventions, received wisdom, and other things we take for granted. This emptiness allowed them to become "appropriated" by what was latently present in their specific environment. As Trotsky wrote: "The latent powers of the organism, its deepest instincts, its flair, inherited from animal ancestors, all of this rose up, smashed through the doors of psychic routine and—together with the highest historico-philosophical generalizations—stood up in the service of the revolution."[42]

What "smashed through the doors" of Lenin's "psychic routine" was, I think, the repressed side of traditional nineteenth-century histories, the histories that had so effectively reduced the complexity created by the French Revolution. In those histories the primal scenes of the last decades of the eighteenth century were magisterially covered up by historicist historians, domesticated by gradual steps in the unfolding of a continuous historical process. But according to psycho-analysis, primal scenes have the annoying property that they do not stay where they belong: in the past. The Berlin psychoanalyst Udo Hock notes that primal scenes are "oblivious of *hic et nunc* and can-not be situated within the coordinates of time and space. Concealed, they keep their singularity."[43] They remain absently present on the surface of the here and now, and because they are not reproduced in remembering they retain their aura. When these primal scenes start to possess us we may flee forward in unpremeditated, "somnambulistic" acts, a process that might be likened to a kind of "remembering for-wards." As Kierkegaard says: "Repetition and recollection are the same movement, except in opposite directions, for what is recollected has been, is repeated backward, whereas genuine repetition is recollected forward."[44] In the sense that Lenin acted out, in history, what didn't have a place in historiography, the belief that he embodied history is the apotheosis as well as the nemesis of nineteenth-century histori-cism. It's quite ironic—and, as such, an illuminating example of how we intermittently engage in the self-inflicted selectiveness that makes us into who we are: by embodying history Lenin inaugurated a new complexity, a complexity that couldn't be reduced by the historicist system of complexity reduction from which it emerged.[45]

Imaginatio and Inventio

What does my analysis of Lenin and Trotsky add up to? Starting with Trotsky's remark that Lenin owed his success to his "imagina-tion," I have tried to sketch how in the arena of history novelty is brought about. As it turns out, what Trotsky called "imagination" isn't imagination at all. If this chapter had been just a little bit less about dissociation I would say now that Trotsky was of two minds about Lenin's imaginative knowledge. Insofar as he believed that history is a road into the future that perhaps cannot be foreseen but that really is already in place, his idea of "imagination" suggests that Lenin could make accurate predictions about what was around the corner. However, insofar as he followed his own unsurpassed insights into the somnambulistic way the new is brought about, he suggests that

Lenin *made* the corners—the corners from which his "predictions" were right. When Trotsky is in his "right mind" and defines imagination as the ability "to conceive of people, things, and phenomena as they really are, although one might never have had a chance to observe them," he is actually wrong. For what he shows us is that he and Lenin really *made* the Revolution. And this isn't *imaginatio* but *inventio*. It may be remembered that in the previous chapter I quoted Vico: "Memory has three different aspects: memory when it remembers things, imagination when it alters or imitates them, and invention when it gives them a new turn or puts them into proper arrangement and relationship."[46] Giving things a new turn and "putting them into proper arrangement and relationship" is precisely what Lenin did—and what Trotsky himself applauds when he attributes Lenin's imagination to the ability "to coordinate disparate hints and pieces of information which are, so to say, in the air" in order to bring about, "in all its concrete reality," a state of affairs that is qualitatively different from the one it swept away.

So it is only insofar as Trotsky was not "in his right mind" that he was able to fathom the revolution as the discontinuity it so evidently was. For giving things "a new turn" and "putting them into proper arrangement and relationship" was precisely what Lenin did—and what Trotsky himself applauds when he dares to be so eccentric as to attribute Lenin's imagination to the ability "to coordinate disparate hints and pieces of information which are, so to say, in the air" in order to bring about, "in all its concrete reality," a state of affairs that is qualitatively different from the one it swept away. Now, if even the eccentric Trotsky couldn't avoid sliding back into his "right mind" every now and then, how difficult will it be for civil, disciplined, and ironic historians like ourselves to ever get out of it? In fact, a prime ingredient of our being in our right minds is to refuse to believe in the possibility that the world might change radically. In his book about the recent meltdown of the financial system, Michael Lewis shows that "people, and markets [tend] to underestimate the probability of extreme change"[47] and that "the collapse of the subprime market was unlikely precisely because it would be such a catastrophe."[48] You had to be one of the weirdos Lewis portrays to see that though "the model used by Wall Street to price trillions of dollars' worth of derivatives

thought of the world as an orderly, continuous process" the world definitely "was *not* continuous, it changed discontinuously, and often by
accident"[49] (and, of course, Lewis's weirdos were weird enough to put
their money where their mouths were).

Yet, precisely because our mindset resists it, fathoming how the
exhilarating, frightening, sinful, sublimely new comes about should be
a question right up the alley of theorists of history. In recent decades
however, theorists of history stuck to being in their right minds rather
than venturing into the disposition from which the new emerges and
from which this emergence can be understood. It is, on consideration,
quite beyond the pale: in a century abounding in discontinuities, theorists of history have almost exclusively focused on what historians do
instead of on what happened in history.

9

Our Own Best Enemy

How Humans Energize Their Evolution

Homo homini homo.[1]

"As for me," Tocqueville sighs in his *Souvenirs*, "I don't know where this long voyage will end; I'm tired of repeatedly mistaking misleading vapors for the shore, and I often ask myself whether the terra firma that we have sought for so long really exists, or whether our destiny might not rather be to ply the seas eternally!"[2] Though Tocqueville's lament was prompted by a specific occasion—the fact that in 1848 he had once more to live through a revolution—the sentiment it expresses is a more general aftereffect of the French Revolution: the hesitant realization that the moment we started to make history we were doomed to keep making it forever. With Leo Tolstoy, a couple of years later, the sentiment has hardened into the conviction that peace-abiding citizens like himself are not the helpless victims of the groundswells of history but constitute them themselves. It is the question that inspires *War and Peace*: "What is the force that moves nations?"[3] Tolstoy, for his part, couldn't understand why historians squandered their energy on questions less relevant than the one he tried to answer himself, but it is really hardly surprising that the issue wasn't taken up by most of them. As long as the belief in human uniqueness reigned supreme, historians either took our compulsion to "ply the seas eternally" for granted or—but perhaps this amounts to the same thing—considered it to be a metaphysical issue way beyond their competence. In the last few decades, however, evolutionary biology has given the issue both a new urgency and a framework from which it can be addressed. From an evolutionary perspective the long, punctuated, but eventually always resumed and never completed "voyage" of our species is just as big a puzzle as it was for Tocqueville and Tolstoy—if only because of the sheer fact that *Homo sapiens* kept evolving with a speed, a drive, and a success outrageously disproportionate to the need to do so. Nature is as lazy as it can possibly be—so why would humans not relax and sit on their laurels the moment they had acquired a comfortable edge over their competitors? How to make evolutionary sense of the fact that humans, alone among species, "took off" on a kind of autonomous development that made it their destiny "to ply the seas eternally"?

One would suppose that big questions like these would be to the liking of the emerging discipline of "big history." That this happens not to be the case might at least partly be due to the fact that historians have long gotten out of the habit of taking big questions seriously. I've said it in previous chapters and I'll say it again: sometime in the 1960s—when Arnold Toynbee published the last volume of the epitome of speculative history and Karl Popper bullied historians to stick to their sources[4]—historians created a productive and cozy niche by settling down to empirical research and leaving the big questions alone. Since the days of Toynbee and Popper, however, things have changed considerably. Spectacular advances in archaeology, biology, anthropology, genetics, and evolutionary psychology have opened up the possibility of going beyond the documentary record in a completely new way. And indeed, recent attempts to give what David Christian terms "universal history"[5] a new try have capitalized on the torrent of recent (or not so recent) discoveries, insights, and theories in neighboring (or not so neighboring) disciplines. Yet as it is practiced right now, "big history" hasn't shed the theoretical prudishness that has characterized the discipline of history for so long. It is, by and large, just as theory-poor as the conventional, un-universal history it wants to replace.[6] Christian's own groundbreaking *Maps of Time*, for example, is emphatically descriptive, and the theory it contains (the idea that cultural change is the result of "collective learning") is so commonsensical that the best one can say of it is that it hardly hampers the pace of the narrative.[7] So though big history is a laudable attempt to chart not just the scenic passages or the last miles but the *whole* of the voyage we have come to travel, it does not as yet offer a theory about what launched it, what has kept us at sea, and what energizes our plying on.

In this final chapter I propose such a theory. I sketch a mechanism that explains how we metamorphosed from the *orribile bestione* that freed their hands by starting to walk on their hind legs to the modern *Homo google* who has exchanged the liberal proficiency to situate himself in time and space for the mediated immediacy of what he can summon on his computer screen. In order to arrive at such a theory we should, I think, home in not on the smooth transitions that are conjured up by the flowcharts in our biology textbooks but on the "revolutionary" episodes that troubled Tocqueville and Tolstoy so much: the instances in which we lightheartedly exchange hearth and home for a journey to we know not whence. Put differently: we are probably missing the essence of our long voyage when we forget that the process in which the earliest hominids became modern *Homo sapiens* is a process of *autopoiesis* (what, as we've seen, in German is called *Selbsthervorbringung*) in which each new modality emerges from a previous one from which it couldn't be foreseen.[8] I am well aware of the fact that many historians take the position that within the humanities employing an evolutionary framework can never be more than a metaphorical game—if it isn't just strutting along with plumes borrowed from the natural sciences.[9] This prejudice, parochial as it is, makes it all the more challenging to think up an evolutionary view of history in which "evolution" is not a crypto-Whiggish stopgap to unproblematize the convulsions by which we have become what we are, but the mechanism by means of which we—as a species—have ended up so breathtakingly far away from the rest of earthly nature.

The Revenge of the Plaice

In evolutionary science it is an axiom that *all* systems that feature both heritable variation and competitive selection evolve.[10] Heritable variation, the first ingredient of evolution, is the appearance of new characteristics that are somehow transferred to the next generation.

Biologists are primarily interested in the variation that is inscribed in changes in the genome, but heritable variation is, in itself, an empty category. Cultural renewal that is independent of the people who brought it about and that is passed on to the next generation also fits the bill. The second feature of evolution, competitive selection, refers to what Darwin called the "hostile forces of nature": an environment that on the one hand forces species to adaptive ingenuity and on the other weeds out newness that doesn't have survival value. At first sight it may come as a surprise that in evolutionary biology the second ingredient of evolution is hardly if ever treated as an *explanandum*. It is a kind of *given*, a part of the answer regarding how the other ingredient—heritable variation—comes about. On consideration this is not that strange: with humans "nature" may have shrunken to the weather forecast, the stroll in the park, and the turbulence in the plane, but for all other species nature (red in tooth and claw) remains an ineluctable and, at times, hostile presence. And of course, apart from the selective pressure exerted by the forces of nature, species embody—by living in the same biotope, by competing for the same resources, by eating and being eaten—quite parsimoniously *each others'* environment.

But though in genetically mediated evolution competitive selection may safely be treated as a kind of given, in culturally mediated evolution it is a problem. It is a problem because variation *needs* selectiveness—and one of the amazing evolutionary achievements of humans is that they have effectively done away with selective pressure from the environment (up to the one but latest virus). I already hinted at it in the previous chapter: humans have come to learn how to disarm the "hostile forces of nature"—they slowly began to realize that survival need not be dependent on fitness alone, that investing in "taming" the environment may pay off handsomely. It is true that to a certain extent other animals too engage in "niche construction," but humans have become so adept in it, and they came to dominate their environment to such an extent, that in a very real sense the whole planet became their "niche."[11] The ever more spacious and elaborate niche humans claimed from nature is commonly called "culture"—and it owes its success to the simple fact that it is *inheritable*. As Ernest Gellner has said: "Historical transformations are transmitted by culture, which is a form of transmission which, unlike genetic transmission, *does* perpetuate acquired characteristics. In fact, culture *consists* of sets of acquired characteristics."[12] Insofar as we live in this Lamarckian superstructure of our own making we have freed ourselves from the competitive selection other animals have to endure.

Theoretically, the disappearance—or, at least, the scaling down—of one of the two prerequisites for evolution should have brought our evolution to a halt. Circumventing competitive selection by taming our environment inevitably means that we are no longer incited to the adaptive ingenuity necessary for evolutionary change. Yet it is abundantly clear that not only did our evolution not stop, but that we started to ply the sea ever faster. As has been noted by (a.o.) Richard Alexander, human evolution accelerated the more it diverged from the ape line, with the result that we ended up stunningly far away from other primates.[13] The fact that humans evolved at such an extraordinary pace in an environment that came to lose its selectiveness leaves us with a pretty straightforward question: either we managed to keep evolution going without selectiveness (but how?), or we replaced the selectiveness furnished by the natural world with another, but at least as effective, form of selectiveness (but which?). Surprisingly, all recent attempts to write new "universal histories" dodge this question: they simply borrow the "givenness" of selectiveness from the natural sciences and tacitly assume that there is always enough competition (between groups, tribes, states, or whatever) to keep evolution going.

The answers evolutionary scientists have suggested all point in the same direction. The Cambridge psychologist Nicholas Humphrey has argued that the real challenge for humans was not climate, food shortages, parasites, or predators but their fellow human beings: human intellect grew so excessively because humans had to deal with the "uncertainties of social life."[14] The so called social-brain hypothesis was confirmed when Robin Dunbar found a correlation between the size of the fraction of the brain taken up by the neocortex (the brain region where much of the information processing needed for social life takes place) and the size of the group a species lives in.[15] But, as Alexander has argued, acceptance of the social-brain hypothesis raises a question that is at least as nasty: "If humans became potentially the most detrimental force with respect to the lives and success of their fellows, then why didn't humans evolve to live apart from one another so they wouldn't have to contend with competitive, aggressive, manipulative associates? After all, thousands of species do not live socially."[16] Alexander's own answer, though, isn't entirely satisfying either. He suggests that humans came to learn that living in groups enhanced their ability to compete with other groups (and that consequently the possibility of living nonsocially disappeared). But the hypothesis that intergroup competition was wedded to intragroup cooperation doesn't explain why groups would be willing to stay locked in competition with other groups. Put differently: Alexander may have solved the problem of why humans continue to live socially in the face of the demands that living socially makes, but the problem resurfaces on the level of the group: for why should groups compete with other groups—and expose their members to what he calls the "detrimental force" of competition—instead of retreating into some form of splendid isolation?

In the previous chapter I already suggested the answer I would like to propose. It concurs to a considerable extent with the theories of Humphrey, Dunbar, and Alexander: human evolution kept going (and, if anything, even accelerated) because the more we disarmed our environment the more we became *our own* environment. If this really is the case, as I think it is, then the question to be answered is: How did humans manage to maintain the high level of selectiveness needed for speedy evolution without falling apart as a species? The answer begins, I think, with realizing that selectiveness need not necessarily be a kind of steady state—as it is both in Dunbar's social-brain theory and in Alexander's alternative reading of it. In order to work, selectiveness can very well be intermittent and local. Indeed, Niles Eldredge and Stephen J. Gould argued quite a while ago that most of the time species display morphological stability and that this stability is only intermittently "punctuated" by rare bursts of evolutionary change.[17] But however helpful it may be in understanding speciation, Eldredge and Gould's theory of punctuated equilibria does not in itself explain the mechanism that enabled humans, as a species, to perform the stunning feat of "domesticating" one of the two very constituents of evolution: selectiveness.

Now, evolutionary change (whether speedy or slow) necessarily is the fruit of the other feature of evolution, the creation of variation. So before we go on with the question of how humans may have domesticated selectiveness, we should step back for a moment and consider the possibility that humans have—as a species—found an evolutionary shortcut: a way to create exactly the right kind of variation, the kind of variation that is so immediately and completely useful that it doesn't need selectiveness to weed out the junk. If, after all, humans could domesticate selectiveness, wouldn't it be just as likely that they discovered what, from an evolutionary point of view, is the *non plus ultra* of efficiency: the willful creation of handy new properties? In fact it is precisely this perspective that implicitly or explicitly informs quite a few accounts of how we have become what we are. In such accounts human ecological dominance is often attributed to a singular "moment of grace" in which—by a small but decisive quantum leap—humans acquired the key that enabled them to eventually create all the variation that went into man as he is right now, including language, art, ethics, agriculture, and a belief in the reality of credit. Perhaps the most straightforward is Richard Klein's hypothesis that around fifty thousand years ago a couple of fortuitous mutations enhanced the capacity of our brain in such a way that we were able in due course to acquire all the properties we now recognize as quintessentially human.[18] Other accounts assign the role of the evolutionary magic bullet to the ability to "imitate,"[19] a better memory, the emergence of abstract thinking, the benefits of "collective learning," a facility for symbols, or, as Matt Ridley suggests in *The Rational Optimist*, ideas that "began to meet and mate" and started "to have sex with each other."[20] The notion that we learned to create junk-free variation has the undeniable charm that it presents our evolution as something of our own making, but it flies in the face of one of the most basic tenets of Darwin's theory: the fact that things tend to stay as they are if there is no need for a change. The willful creation of variation cannot account for one of the most salient features of human evolution: the sheer energy with which it takes place, its speed, its nervous restlessness, the simple fact that we, to quote Tocqueville once more, keep plying the seas even when we don't have to.

Yet, because evolutionary change ultimately depends on the creation of variation, it is worthwhile to take a somewhat closer look at the mechanism by which variation is brought about. Darwin had no clue how variation emerged, but modern genetics has discovered that it is quite simply (to put matters much more briefly than we should) the result of mutations. Initially it is hard to see how selectiveness might influence the quality and/or quantity of mutations. Selectiveness is, after all, secondary: it has to work on the variation "delivered" by the mutations that pop up. However, the picture changes dramatically if it is noted that, contrary to received opinion, even at the level of the genes mutations need not be random accidents. There is by now ample evidence that sudden leaps in the selectiveness of the environment ("catastrophes") augment both the quantity and the adaptive potential of mutations, a phenomenon that is called "stress-induced mutation."[21]

A good example of "stress-induced mutation"—and of the extremely speedy evolutionary change it may bring about—is *Pleuronectes platessa*, the common North Sea plaice.[22] Since the beginning of the twentieth century the plaice has been intensively fished. Because consumers like their plaice big, fishermen are primarily interested in the big specimens, a predilection strongly reinforced by official policy: a plaice that doesn't have the required length has to be thrown back.[23] The result of the intensive fishing is that until quite recently there was a mere 10 percent chance that plaice would reach the age of five—a quite serious problem when you realize that plaice only starts to procreate at four. But the plaice has found a way out. You might call it the revenge of the plaice: in just a couple of decades he has become much smaller, so small in fact that he is becoming ever less attractive for consumers (whose eating preferences apparently evolve, if at all, markedly less quickly). The modern plaice is, on average, an impressive seven centimeters shorter than the plaice of a few decades ago, and, most importantly, starts to breed at a much earlier age.

For the plaice intensive fishing is a "stressful" state of emergency, a catastrophe that somehow "induces" the mutations needed to survive as a species.[24] Of course, the fact that decreasing in size and speeding up sexual maturity is a smart thing to do doesn't mean that individual plaices "know" what they are heading for: "stress-induced mutation" is not in any way the result of "experiences," let alone decisions, of individual members of the species. Strangely, however, the DNA involved *does* somehow "know" what it is doing: even a skeptic like Richard Lenski admits that under some conditions phenotypical changes are at least partly the result of an adaptive mechanism that promotes precisely the genetic changes that fit a new and stressful situation.[25] Clearly, not only does extreme, "catastrophic" change in the selectiveness of the environment stir up mutagenesis in general, but, as the authors of the groundbreaking *Nature*-paper remark, "cells may have mechanisms for choosing *which* mutations will occur."[26] So, apparently, stress-induced mutation fits the bill of a mechanism by means of which selectiveness might influence the quality and quantity of mutations.

Though stress-induced mutation is not in itself sufficient to explain how humans domesticated selectiveness, it does suggest in which direction the solution is to be found. For even though humans may not have been able to control mutagenesis *directly*, they may have learned to influence—or even to create—the circumstances that promote it. Put differently: whereas the North Sea plaice needs an external cause to enter an evolutionary rapid, humans may have learned that they don't have to *wait* for "mutation-inducing" catastrophes—they may have discovered that they can bring them about by themselves. This, in fact, is the first part of my thesis, a thesis I already suggested in the previous chapter: somehow humans have learned to re-inject the selectiveness that they have taken away from nature into the culture they inhabit—they have discovered that it is evolutionary advantageous to be their own best enemy. In as far as we are our own best enemy we habitually destabilize the status quo and create situations that put a premium on mutations—and, by doing so, we willy-nilly energize human evolution. This thesis implies that what I have called the "domestication of selectiveness" has a rather peculiar form: it does not mean that we have rendered selectiveness "harmless," but that as a species we have learned to unleash it once in a while upon ourselves.

To historians this may look thoroughly counterintuitive, in at least two respects. First: attempts to transfer the principles of evolution to history almost inevitably assign salient, "historic" events like the American Declaration of Independence, the Oath in the Tennis Court, the fall of the Berlin Wall, and the Treaty of Maastricht (in which Europe committed itself to the introduction of the euro) the role of mutations. According to this theory, however, it is not the events we call "historic" that constitute the mutations—they rather are the "catastrophes" that eventually *induce* mutations. So the Treaty of Maastricht is not a mutation but a catastrophe[27]—in the sense that the introduction of the euro generated levels of "stress" (manifested in, for example, the Greek debt crisis) that forced the European Community to mutate into an unprecedented and unforeseen polity, a polity that as yet lacks a proper name but can provisionally be designated as "supranationality." This brings me to the second counterintuitive aspect of my theory: it locates "stress" not before but *after* the event. Historians like to explain "historic" events by connecting them to the "tensions" that precede them. My thesis, however, implies that it is the other way around: that the event is not created by stress but *creates* it. Of course, this is not to say that stress is completely absent from the *status quo ante*. It simply means that the catastrophic kind of stress that induces mutations is a *result* of the event. Cultural renewal *begins* with a discontinuity, with, that is, the creation of a catastrophe: the catastrophe creates stress, and this stress induces mutations (in the form of cultural change).

The Ratchet Principle

If humans did indeed succeed in domesticating selectiveness—in, that is, taming the environment while retaining the selectiveness that makes it such a potent evolutionary tool—it would surely be a wonder of evolution, on a par with the build of the most exotic species and the architecture of the most complicated organ. It would not, however, imply that human evolution was (or is) energized by individuals who discovered the mechanism and brought it into practice—any more than the North Sea plaice owes the moving up of its sexual maturation to some clever specimens able to see beyond the end of their noses. In this respect the theory that humans have become what they are by domesticating selectiveness differs fundamentally from theories that explain human ascendancy by the willful creation of junk-free variation. In fact, one of its virtues is that it doesn't privilege humans over other species and conceives of human cultural evolution, including the particular brand of human cultural evolution we call history, as a blind process quite like the earlier maturation of the North Sea plaice.

So, according to my theory *Homo sapiens* owes its evolutionary success not to its being "sapiens" but to the birth, growth, and perfection of a blind urge to saddle itself with catastrophes to which it subsequently has to catch up. So when I said, a moment ago, that humans have "learned" that it might be advantageous to create mutation-inducing situations, and that they "discovered" the benefits of being their own best enemy, I did not in any way intend to say that this was a conscious acquisition. It may be true that the way we are our own best enemy has, over time, become ever less "brutal" and ever more "intelligent" (I will return to that), but that doesn't mean that the urge to do so became any less "blind." We do not create catastrophes with the intention of furthering our evolution and we haven't the slightest idea beforehand which mutations will be "induced" by the "stress" we create. Our being "sapiens" is, in short, not the motor but the *result* of our evolution: we have become what we are not *because of*, but *in spite of* our intelligence.

What form does "being our own best enemy" have in real life? How exactly do we create the "stress" we need to induce "mutations"? Or, in plain language, how do we bring off the "necessities" that make such wonderful mothers of inventions? Before suggesting how this question might be answered I would like to repeat what I said in the previous chapter: being our own best enemy doesn't mean that we cannot stop fighting each other. I do not doubt that habitually fighting our neighbors (and our neighbors fighting us), or, more broadly, a population-wide inclination to act upon the Hobbesian premise that life is a "war of all against all," does create quite a bit of stress, but because this stress would be a stable ingredient of life it would not speed up mutagenesis. Stress-induced mutation *only* occurs when the environment to which a population is exposed *suddenly* changes catastrophically. The thesis that humans have learned to promote mutagenesis entails that somehow they have learned to unleash such "catastrophes" themselves, and, most importantly, to target not just their neighbors but themselves as well. One might say that they have learned that from an evolutionary perspective *homo homini homo*[28] is to be preferred to *homo homini lupus*. Of course this does not mean that man cannot be a wolf to his fellows—it simply means that in order to become what he is he had to do something much more difficult and, in a sense, much more chilling: he had to be a "man" unto his own kin.

The way we bring about mutation-inducing situations can, I think, best be understood in terms of what in the previous chapter I called the "ratchet principle."[29] In its most elementary form the ratchet principle is nothing other than the creation of a state of affairs that cannot be undone—of, in short, an accomplished fact. Now, when you come to think of it, confronting *ourselves*—rather than someone else—with an accomplished fact is an interesting psychological phenomenon: it seems to imply that we do not quite trust our decision to create that fact. If we did, why shut the door at the possibility to go back on it? An accomplished fact is apparently an instance of "just doing it," without our being completely sure that the decision to create it stands up to scrutiny. From this perspective, the fact that the American Declaration of Independence was ceremoniously signed, the Tennis Court Oath formally pledged, and, for that matter, the Treaty of Maastricht solemnly ratified indicates *not* what the pomp and circumstance wants to graft in our minds, to wit that the participants[30] had an overwhelming confidence in what they did, but, on the contrary, that the signatories needed to bolster up their uncertainty by making sure that what they did was absolutely irrevocable.[31] That "Maastricht," for example, was not just *in fact* but also *intended* as a fait accompli is shown by Helmut Kohl's remark that "the most important thing is that it is clear that what we are doing is irrevocable, on the way to political union we are now crossing the Rubicon. There is no going back."[32]

This element of taking chances may be due to either the *process* of decision-making or the *nature of what is at stake*: in some cases we just snap our fingers at the rules of the game, in other—and much more interesting—cases even the most impeccable procedure still needs a leap of faith. In all instances, however, we break away from the status quo without the certainty that what we get is better than what we had. This willingness to take chances doesn't seem to square with one of the basic tenets of evolutionary science: that the members of a species—or, to be more precise: the "replicators"—aim at their own best interest. Indeed, the view that humans evolve by doing things that might not be in their own best interest is at odds with all other attempts to apply

an evolutionary framework to human history that I know of. A sophisticated author like W. G. Runciman, for example, builds his theory on
the assumption that "adaptive success is measured by the consciously
experienced psychological satisfaction that results from behavior that
advances [our] interests, values, and goals."[33] Put differently, theorists
like Runciman assume that "the biological reinforcement mechanism
of pain avoidance and pleasure attraction"[34] is fully applicable to the
sphere of human cultural evolution—all be it that they have the game
played with different players: instead of epicurean animals or selfish
genes, they posit rationally choosing individuals or selfish memes.[35]
But whereas conventional theories have their favorite replicators keep
evolution going by determining which one of the options open to them
promises maximum satisfaction or reproductive success, the notion of
the ratchet principle implies that our evolution may not be solely, or
even primarily, the result of inventions that "are in our best interest,"
but rather the result of inventions from which there is no way back
and concerning which we have no choice but to adjust.

This is the second part of my thesis: the catastrophes by which we
energize our evolution have the form of ratchetlike "leaps of faith,"
of, that is, accomplished facts.[36] The crucial feature of the ratchetlike
accomplished facts by means of which we energize our evolution is
that while the wager is that they will reconfigure the situation in a
beneficial way, their immediate effect is a marked deterioration of the
quality of life—which, of course, is just another way of saying that
they create the stress needed for cultural change. This deterioration
is the inevitable outcome of the fact that by creating an accomplished
fact we bring about a new playing field, a playing field that is incalcu-
lably more demanding than the one we left behind and because of that
steps up selectiveness. The ratchetlike way in which we are our own
best enemy is very well described by Adam Smith, who wrote (in a letter to his publisher) that while "infinite Good has been derived to this
country" from the union of Scotland and England (just before Smith's
birth, in 1707), "the Prospect of that good" was initially "very remote
and very uncertain":

The immediate effect of [the Union] was to hurt the interests of
every single order of men in the country. The dignity of the nobil-

ity was undone by it. The greater part of the gentry who had been accustomed to represent their own country in its own Parliament were cut out for ever from all hopes of representing it in a British Parliament. Even the merchants seemed to suffer at first. The trade to the Plantations was, indeed, opened to them. But that was a trade which they knew nothing about: the trade they were acquainted with, that to France, Holland, and the Baltic, was laid under new embarrassments which almost totally annihilated the two first and most important branches of it. The Clergy too, who were then far from insignificant, were alarmed about the Church. No wonder if at that time all orders of men conspired in cursing a measure so hurtful to their immediate interest.[37]

And indeed, though eventually ratchetlike faits accomplis like the union of Scotland and England open up new possibilities, in the short run (which can last decades, or even [as in the earliest catastrophes] millennia) they mainly confront us with demanding "embarrassments" that make life "catastrophically" more difficult.[38]

My contention is—as I already hinted at in the previous chapter—that many, perhaps all, major and minor discontinuities that have made us who we are—from the reckless and ill-considered "decision," millions of years ago, to start walking on our hind legs right up to the "shock therapy" with which Boris Yeltsin replaced (in, as he said, "one big leap") the old Soviet command economy with the unfettered discipline of the market, the introduction of the euro, and George Bush's decision to invade Iraq—can be interpreted as ratchetlike catastrophes to which we had no choice but to live up. I cannot hope, within the limits of this final chapter of my book, to prove my boisterous claim, but I can at least give some, necessarily rather sketchy, examples. The first is the introduction of agriculture. In fact the whole history of agriculture, from prehistoric times right up to the present, can be interpreted as a ratcheted process, in which time and again innovations were the forced response to accomplished facts. Matt Ridley writes that "one of the reasons that farming spread so rapidly once it starts is that the first few crops are both more productive and more easily grown than later crops. . . . If you burn down a forest, you are left with a soft, friable soil seasoned with fertilizing ash. . . . After a few years however, the soil is compacted and needs breaking up with a hoe, and weeds have prolif-erated."[39] And indeed agriculture may be said to only really have taken off when slash-and-burn techniques yielded less and less and muta-tions were needed to cope with an ever more catastrophic situation.

The story of agriculture is perhaps a special one because even — or, particularly — successful mutations sooner or later were the spring-boards for new catastrophes. In this sense the story of agriculture is the story of being driven ever further from paradise. Marshall Sahlins argued long ago that, on the whole, hunter-gatherers in the Stone Age may have been better off than most people were after the introduction of agriculture.[40] And indeed, where skeletal remains make it possible to compare human welfare before and after the introduction of agri-culture, bioarchaeologists link the transition to "a significant decline in nutrition and to increases in disease, mortality, overwork, and vio-lence."[41] So, the introduction of agriculture was not a station in the triumphal march of humanity, but a "disaster" that brought about a completely new level of stressful, "mutation-inducing" selectiveness. What ultimately made agriculture such an immense success were the inventions and discoveries ("cultural change") with which we tried to make the best of the situation in which we found ourselves. Until, that is, we couldn't resist to give the ratchet a further twist.

A second example is the way early modern Britain gave herself a hard time by embarking on a new (and ultimately very rewarding) mode of selectiveness: a capitalist market economy. From Marx and Weber up to Polanyi,[42] Wallerstein, and Wolf[43] the origins of a capital-ist market economy have been located in the groups, classes, or "core" nations that gained by it. All these explanations attribute the take-off of capitalism to an "un-ironic" relationship between what some indi-viduals or groups considered it to be in their best interest to do and what turned out to be the outcome of these actions. They all seek the answer in, as I have called it just a while ago, the "generation of varia-tion" — they explain the emergence of a market economy by pointing to the idea of making use of easily mineable coal, the creative activi-ties of merchants, the ability to overcome technological or economic "bottlenecks," or the determination of landlords to maximize rents. Yet, counterintuitive as it may seem, it might be argued that a ratch-etlike perspective, in which the new regime of selectiveness was a "catastrophe" for the groups and classes that eventually came out on top, fits the facts at least as well.[44]

The hodgepodge of decisions leading to enclosures, for example— according to Larry Patriquin, Robert Brenner, and others the true beginning of capitalism[45]—can be interpreted as a ratchetlike process of fleeing forward energized by the class that eventually lost out in the new, capitalist game—the petty subsistence farmers. Rosemary Hopcroft has drawn attention to the fact that "it was in regions were small peasant proprietors had the strongest hold over the land, and where the power of the local manorial officials over the peasantry was weakest, that commercial agriculture first developed and agrarian change first occurred."[46] Conversely, the groups and classes that ultimately benefited most—the big landlords, the tenants—initially had a hard time responding to it. But it was precisely these classes that generated the mutations that brought about what we now call capitalism. As Ellen Wood has remarked: "Landlords and tenants alike became preoccupied with what they called 'improvement,' the enhancement of the land's productivity for profit."[47] So it may well be that the takeoff of capitalism had more to do with the innovations with which people *responded* to the abolition of common rights and the accession of private property, than the other way around. Put differently: the enclosures may have been what intensive fishing was for the North Sea plaice: the catastrophe that created the stress that induced mutations. They induced Britain to mutate in the direction of a capitalist economy.

I have already referred in passing to my third example: the emergence, from the 1950s onward, of a supranational Europe. European integration is usually explained in terms of external influences, enlightened self-interest of the member states, or the "spillover effect"[48] (also designated as "integration by stealth"). But to all appearances, all the landmark events in which it was brought about[49] were not so much created *by* stress as *created* it. The current euro crisis may be a particularly stressful instance of the mechanism involved, but *each* of the major treaties was, as Stanley Henig has remarked, a *tabula rasa* that took enormous efforts to "fill."[50] The remarkable thing about European integration is that some of the politicians and civil servants who were most instrumental in bringing it about employed what I have called the ratchet principle quite consciously. As Walter Hallstein, the first president of the Commission of the European Economic Community, described the strategy: "Every step we take creates new situations, new problems, new needs which in turn demand yet another step, another solution to be worked out on a European basis."[51]

And indeed, European integration can very well be interpreted as a ratchetlike process of fleeing forward from the one accomplished fact to the other. In a remarkable article published in 1963, Jean Monnet, the Saint-Just of the European Union, candidly gave his recipe for integration: Europe, Monnet said, can and should be integrated by "a constant process of collective adaptation to new conditions, a chain reaction, a ferment where one change induces another."[52] The thing to do, Monnet said, is to create common problems, problems of such magnitude that they can only be solved on a European level. Profound change, he went on, "is being made possible essentially by the new method of common action. . . . To establish this new method of common action we adapted to our situation the method which had allowed individuals to live together in society: common rules which each Member is committed to respect, and common institutions to watch over the applications of these rules." Common actions—the introduction of the euro is but one of the latest—create an irrevocable commitment to a common interest.[53] The Monnet method,[54] a civil version of Napoleons "on s'engage, puis on voit," may well be designated as the strategy of the accomplished fact. The story of European integration up to the Greek crisis we are facing today is an endless alternation of accomplished facts and frantic efforts to solve the problems these facts create. So when you take the view that we energize our evolution by being our own best enemy, the spectacular restructuring of Europe we see today[55] is not an anomaly but exactly what you might expect. It is in having to live up to accomplished facts that we change not just marginally but fundamentally.

Fleeing Forward as an Adaptive Response

Why didn't humans sit on their laurels indefinitely, instead giving in sooner or later to the urge to flee forward in fresh accomplished facts and so ensuring that they "kept plying the seas"? In answering this question the first thing to bear in mind is that accomplished facts tend to generate one another. Even the most cursory glance at the major discontinuities of history shows that the accomplished facts in which we happen to be our own best enemy are not isolated, monolithic entities but trigger one another—and it is this cascade that constitutes the ratchet. As can clearly be seen in the American, French, and Russian revolutions, catastrophes are processes of fleeing forward, cascades of improvisations in which the key element is that for some reason the participants, when confronted by a problem or a threat, don't act "reasonably" (and retrace their steps) but flee forward to a next improvisation. As the Lenin case in the previous chapter clearly shows, these "next improvisations" generally don't solve the problem or defuse the threat but tend to create further problems and threats . . . that subsequently may provoke further accomplished facts. And so on.

The French Revolution, for example, consists of several of such "rapids." The first of these, the episode that goes by the name of the Tennis Court Oath (June 1789), shows the process in full swing: confronted with the closed doors of the Salle des Menus Plaisirs, the delegates of the Third Estate jumped to the conclusion that the Assemblée was being disbanded and moved their meeting to a nearby indoor tennis court. The bold decision to meet separately may already count as an accomplished fact, and the Third Estate immediately sped on to a much more momentous one when it embraced Jean-Joseph Mounier's improvised suggestion to swear "never to separate ourselves from the National Assembly, and to reassemble wherever circumstances require, until the constitution of the realm is drawn up and fixed upon solid foundations." From there on "France" fled forward ever further until it found itself back in a situation from which it was impossible to return and to which it had no choice but to live up. Please note that this cascade of fleeing forward was not *motivated* by a wish for "popular sovereignty." At the time they swore their oath the revolutionaries did not aspire to popular sovereignty. They didn't even have a programme. Until the Tennis Court Oath, William Doyle states, "almost all their deliberations . . . had been about the question of voting or the mounting problem of public order. The revolutionaries' programme only emerged finally in August, and its form could not have been entirely predicted in June, since much of it was deeply influenced by the events of the intervening weeks."[56]

The notion that the Third Estate had the right to claim "popular sovereignty" thus was not *input for*, but *outcome of* the revolution—or rather, it was invented along the way. In my reading of the revolution the cascade of accomplished facts that constitutes the episode of the Tennis Court Oath was a self-propelled process in which gradually it occurred to the delegates of the Third Estate that apparently it was popular sovereignty they wanted. And it was their discovery that they wanted it, that it was their "natural right," or even that popular sovereignty was "self-evident," that made the episode of the oath truly revolutionary, not the content of the constitution that eventually came out of it. So though the Tennis Court Oath is phrased as a commitment to bring something about (a "constitution" that is "fixed upon solid foundations"), the act of swearing had, in a very real sense, already done the trick. Peter Brooks has remarked that "many of the most suggestive analysts of narrative have shared [the] conviction that the end writes the beginning and shapes the middle"[57]—but my thesis entails that in an accomplished fact a *middle* is created and that starting from this middle both the end and the beginning are "written." In the case of the Tennis Court Oath "writing the end" means that the confederates began to interpret their world in terms of popular sovereignty, that they tried to come forward with a constitution that "lived up" to the accomplished fact of their oath, and that they began to act out the narrative they thought it presupposed. "Writing the beginning" works backward and meant (to use the words of the oath once more) that the delegates tried to "fix" the constitution on "solid foundations"—by, for example, harking back on Rousseau's theories about sovereignty. The fact that there are always utterances that both cover and antedate an accomplished fact doesn't mean that it is built on them. On the contrary, the peculiar thing about an accomplished fact is that its foundations have to be "fixed" when the building is already in place and has started to bristle with life.

In as far as creating an accomplished fact doesn't solve the problem or defuses the threat it is clearly maladaptive—and if it creates further problems and threats it's even worse than maladaptive. In the long run, however, fleeing forward in accomplished facts may be a very smart thing to do: if you flee forward far enough you may not "solve" the initial problem or, for that matter, the problems generated along the way, but you may succeed in making them completely irrelevant. This is the case if the cascade of fleeing forward creates what in the previous chapter I have called a new "regime of selectiveness." A regime of selectiveness is the technical term for what earlier in this chapter I called "playing field." It is what a "successful" accomplished fact brings about and constitutes—to borrow Koselleck's famous concepts—the *Erfahrungsraum* as well as the *Erwartungshorizont* of whoever lives under its aegis. A new regime of selectiveness makes the problems engendered by the earlier one completely redundant but also opens up an array of unforeseen new problems, problems that are more daunting, but also more challenging, than the ones that are left behind. A regime of selectiveness thus defines the direction of the adaptive mutations that are induced by the stress it engenders. It may be regarded as the cultural equivalent of what for other species is the environment in which they have to survive: it forces the population that lives under its aegis to adaptive ingenuity that is geared to the situation and weeds out newness that doesn't have survival value (that's why it's called a "regime of selectiveness"). It's the third part of my thesis: fleeing forward may be an adaptive response that brings about a new regime of selectiveness and, because of that, forces us to a new and higher level of adaptive ingenuity.

The regime of selectiveness created by the French Revolution, for example, did not so much *solve* the issues that had stirred up so much emotion when Louis XIV decided to convene the Estates General in 1789 but, rather, *swept them away*, replacing them with new issues, issues that induced everyone who had a stake in the matter to mutate in the direction the revolution defined. This new regime of selectiveness can, I think, be very well described in terms of "self-determination." Between 1789 and 1815 France "surprised itself" by "inventing," in a cascade of events, a regime of selectiveness that was aptly characterized by Jacob Burckhardt as *cogito ergo regnum*. The notion of "self-determination" is not limited to the (political) concept of popular sovereignty but refers to a much more general and quite pervasive climate in which custom and privilege were devalued and in which you had to be your own master in order to succeed.[58] To make the best of the new regime of selectiveness in which France had ended up you had to take your fate in your own hands—you had to become adept in self-determination, which, of course, was catastrophically more stressful and demanding (but also, in the long run, more rewarding) than the more confined life during the ancien régime of selectiveness. So whereas historians of all persuasions have called the French Revolution a "victory for the bourgeoisie," I propose to regard the revolution as the catastrophe that induced people to *become* bourgeois: the new regime of selectiveness put a premium on acquiring the characteristics that we came to designate as "bourgeois"—people "mutated" in the direction of an ever-greater ability to postpone gratification and to run their life as an enterprise to be managed by themselves.

The notion of regimes of selectiveness raises the question of whether the accomplished facts that have made us into what we are form a kind of fixed sequence, a sequence that constitutes *the* marching route of humanity. I don't think they do. I rather think that human evolution has thrived by a jumble, or a patchwork, of "catastrophes," some of them natural (like the Black Death),[59] and many local. That doesn't mean, however, that there isn't a problem. Although the routes may have differed, the fact remains that the present regime of selectiveness is indisputably global, which confronts us with a question not unlike the one that puzzled the historians of the Age of Enlightenment. How to explain, Edward Gibbon wondered, the fact that the major European countries, with their very different histories, have ended up at roughly the same point and have become "a great republic, whose various inhabitants have attained almost the same level of politeness and cultivation"?[60] And indeed, how to account for the absence of, as biologists would say, "species differentiation"? How to explain the curious fact that we have arrived at a truly global regime of selectiveness in which globalization is (at least a part of) *the* logical means to be our own best enemy?

The answer consists, I think, of two parts. First: there might be a kind of natural contagiousness: a group, population, or nation that creates a catastrophe for itself and adapts more-or-less successfully to it may, solely because of that fact, create so much stress for neighboring groups, populations, or nations that they too begin to mutate. Revolutionary France was the catastrophe that induced Prussia to discontinuous changes it wouldn't have considered when the ferment of change, and Napoleon's armies, hadn't reached Berlin. Britain became, in the nineteenth century, a catastrophe for other countries because of the competitiveness that was the result of the catastrophic industrial revolution it had unleashed upon itself. And so on. Put differently: whereas in the natural world species embody each other's selectiveness, human groups, populations, and nations may embody each other's stress. They do so not primarily by getting at their neighbors but by creating catastrophes for *themselves* and by more-or-less successfully living up to what they have brought about. The second part of the answer is even more intriguing. The willingness to create the kind of accomplished facts that force us to change may be one of the forms our penchant for competition takes. The sheer fear that neighboring groups, populations, or nations (or, as in the case of the Tennis Court Oath, a perceived adversary) are gaining the upper hand (by, for example, successfully adapting to a new and more competitive regime of selectiveness) may trigger a willingness to take chances. This is another manifestation of the third part of my thesis: we may have learned—as a species—that fleeing forward by creating accomplished facts can be an adaptive response to real or imagined threats.

The net result of these two mechanisms is that once in a while "bubbles of selectiveness" spring up in which clusters of groups, populations, or nations infect themselves and each other with the willingness to take chances needed to bring about discontinuous change.[61] These bubbles—coupled, of course, to the ability to imitate the mutations our neighbors engendered—ensure that the different groups, populations, and nations that live within each other's reach evolve along lines that are roughly similar.[62] But it's not just the *product* of the willingness to take chances that evolves: the *process itself* evolves as well. It stands to reason (and it would be in accordance with the principles of evolution) that the ability to be our own best enemy was not a once-and-for-all discovery but gradually acquired the form it has today. As Jablonka and Lamb say: "It would be very strange . . . to believe that everything in the living world is the product of evolution except one thing—the process of generating new variation."[63] In this chapter I have argued that it's much more plausible that we generate variation *indirectly* (by influencing the circumstances that promote it) than directly (by the creation of junk-free variation) but even then a mechanism that is so powerful that it can bring about the speedy and comprehensive evolutionary process exhibited by *Homo sapiens* cannot have been put in place overnight. The lack of empirical evidence means that the only way to chart the evolution of the tendency to be our own best enemy would be to do what the incomparable Giambattista Vico undertook in his *Scienza Nuova*: to "recreate" this itinerary in our mind. Even without attempting such a descent, however, one thing can safely be said: if it is true, as I have argued, that accomplished facts tend to multiply, and if it is also true that groups, populations, and nations may infect each other with the willingness to take chances, then the evolution of the capacity for "self-inflicted selectiveness" must have been a self-reinforcing process. In as far as the willingness to be your own best enemy became *both* an ever more salient part of the environment humans created for themselves *and* an ever more adaptive response to that environment, the evolution of the ability to flee forward in accomplished facts must have been fueled by its own success.

Eventually this adaptive response must have transmuted into what might be called "hyperadaptation." Whereas normal adaptation is a response to a real or imagined threat, hyperadaptation is a preemptive response to a threat that not only hasn't yet materialized but isn't even imagined. It is, for short, not a response at all but something we just can't resist doing once in a while—which is perhaps as good a definition of an "urge" you may get. In the short run hyperadaptation is worse than adaptive (because fleeing forward in accomplished facts *creates* stress instead of trying to respond to it) but in the long run it's supremely adaptive (if, that is, it's practiced intermittently and sparingly). In time, hyperadaptation—in the form of the proclivity to be our own best enemy—brought us further and further away from the natural environment and created the artificial environment we call culture in which we could thrive. It did so at a price, however, saddling us with the urge to bring about our own catastrophes once in a while, with the inability to sit on our laurels indefinitely, with the fate of having to ply the seas eternally. This is the fourth and final part of my thesis and the answer to the question I distilled from Tocqueville's sigh.

Conclusion

"What humans evolved," says evolutionary psychologist Merlin Donald, "was primarily a generalized capacity for cultural innovation."[64] I hope to have made clear in this chapter that this "generalized capacity" is not to be envisioned as a kind of Swiss army knife that we can take out whenever we see fit, but rather as the ability to make the most of the catastrophes we unleash upon ourselves once in a while. In the theory I have proposed, cultural innovation is the result of the mutations that are induced by the accomplished facts in which we practice the art of being our own best enemy.

I am well aware that this theory raises quite a few questions. I will mention just two. The first is the crucial question of *agency*: by what "cunning" mechanisms do groups, tribes, peoples, nations, cultures, and eventually even species "harness" individual acts in order to evolve? Or, looking from the other side: how do individual acts come to inaugurate—and sometimes even to embody—the sublime historical events by which societies end up in new regimes of selectiveness? The second brainteaser is the troubling psychological question how, why, and when we come to turn a deaf ear to the golden rule always to choose what it is in our best interest to do and instead throw rational calculation to the wind and take chances that normally we wouldn't even have considered? It's Tolstoy's old riddle, the question Ross and Nisbett identified as the raison d'être of social psychology: Why do people every now and then do things that are at odds not only with their interests, but with the views they held as well?[65] But I will not here, at the end of my book, enlarge on the qualifications and reservations I have so happily suppressed in the pages you've just read. I can only say that even if I have raised more questions than I've answered, I hope to have provoked a new interest in the curious duplicity with which we time and again "surprise ourselves" with accomplished facts—accomplished facts that chase us away from what we were and force us to become what we are.

Coda

There is a picture by Klee called *Angelus Novus*. It shows an angel who seems to move away from something he stares at. His eyes are wide, his mouth is open, his wings are spread. This is how the angel of history must look. His face is turned towards the past. Where a chain of events appears before *us, he* sees one single catastrophe, which keeps piling wreckage upon wreckage and hurls it at his feet. The angel would like to stay, awaken the dead, and make whole what has been smashed. But a storm is blowing from Paradise and has got caught in his wings; it is so strong that the angel can no longer close them. This storm drives him irresistibly into the future, to which his back is turned, while the pile of debris before him grows toward the sky. What we call progress is *this* storm.

—Walter Benjamin

Notes

Introduction

1. "Why does one study history? Without doubt in order to understand the life of humankind in its entirety" (Leopold von Ranke, *Tagebücher*, in *Aus Werk und Nachlass*, ed. Walther Peter Fuchs and Theodor Schieder, 3 vols. [Munich: Oldenbourg, 1964–1973], 1:238).

2. Drawing attention to prefiguration was one of the merits of Hayden White's *Metahistory: The Historical Imagination in Nineteenth-Century Europe* (Baltimore: Johns Hopkins University Press, 1973). It is, however, quite confusing that White illustrates the principle by giving accounts of the great nineteenth-century historians: it was precisely these historians who didn't succumb to ready-made prefigurations and tried to "figure" things out for themselves—and to the extent they succeeded they did *not* replicate their subject. Of course, their works have a form, but having a particular form does not necessarily mean that that form molds or prefigures what it contains. Things cannot *not* have a form.

3. "In truth: history doesn't belong to us, but we belong to history" (H.-G. Gadamer, *Wahrheit und Methode*, 2 vols. [Tübingen: J. C. B. Mohr, 1990], 1:281).

1. Burying the Dead, Creating the Past

1. R. G. Collingwood, *The Idea of History* (Oxford: Clarendon Press, 1946), 304.

2. Significantly, for the Tourist Board, being a museum is somehow more desirable than being the thing itself.
3. *De Volkskrant*, March 20, 2006, 2.
4. A few years ago Gadi Algazi wrote in his mission statement in *History and Memory* that the journal would focus on "interactions between official designs, lay appropriations, and academic discourse" ("The Past in the Present," *History and Memory* 13 [2001]: 1–2). I think the lay impulse to commemorate unimaginable events was appropriated by *academics*.
5. Pierra Nora, "The Era of Commemoration," in *Realms of Memory: Rethinking the French Past*, 3 vols. (New York: Columbia University Press, 1996–1997), 3:609.
6. Nora, "Between Memory and History," in *Realms of Memory*, 1:3. The phrasing of Nora's introduction to the English translation of the book is less bold than the original French introduction to the project, the translation of which was published in *Representations* in 1989. Originally Nora wrote that there appeared to be a "fundamental opposition" between history and memory.
7. It seems that Nora originally envisioned his project as a kind of commemoration along the lines sketched here: "The new history is a purely transferential history, and as in the art of war, everything is in the execution, a matter of tact in the historian's tenuous relations to his new object and of finding the right depth of immersion in the subject" ("Between Memory and History," 20).
8. Giambattista Vico, *The New Science of Giambattista Vico* [1744], trans. Thomas Bergin and Max Fisch (Ithaca: Cornell University Press, 1994), 331. There is also an affinity with Collingwood's logic of question and answer—but I will not go into that.
9. "Wenn wir anfangen außer uns zu wirken, dann zieht uns oft der Strom mit sich fort, wir gehen außer uns heraus, zerstören die heimische Hütte in uns, und in die Paläste die wir außer uns auftürmen, bleiben wir ewig Fremdlinge" (quoted in Arnold Labrie, *Het verlangen naar zuiverheid: Een essay over Duitsland* [Maastricht: Maastricht Uniprint, 1994], 16).
10. In this respect my views resemble those of Alain Badiou.
11. D. J. Bem, "Self-Perception Theory," in *Advances in Experimental Social Psychology*, ed. L. Berkowitz (New York: Academic Press, 1972), 6:1–62.
12. Eelco Runia, *Waterloo, Verdun, Auschwitz: De liquidatie van het verleden* (Waterloo, Verdun, Auschwitz: The liquidation of the past) (Amsterdam: Meulenhoff, 1999).
13. Henri Bergson, *Creative Evolution*, trans. Arthur Mitchell (London: Macmillan, 1920), 172.
14. See Jay Winter, *Remembering War: The Great War Between Memory and History in the Twentieth Century* (New Haven: Yale University Press, 2006).
15. Tony Judt, "The Courage of the Elementary," *New York Review of Books*, May 20, 1999, 31.

16. Reinhart Koselleck, "Kriegerdenkmale als Identitätstiftungen der Über-lebenden," in *Identität*, ed. O. Marquand and K. Stierle (Munich: W. Fink, 1979), 274.

17. Interestingly, both major crises in modern Western Europe (the French Revolution and its aftermath, and the great, dual twentieth-century world war in which Germany was cut to size, the *Ausnahmezustand*) also lasted about a generation: from 1789 till 1815, and from 1914 till 1945.

18. See Sergiusz Michalski, *Public Monuments: Art in Political Bondage, 1870–1997* (London: Reaktion Books, 1998).

19. See, for example, Henri Ellenberger, *The Discovery of the Unconscious: The History and Evolution of Dynamic Psychiatry* (New York: Basic Books, 1970).

20. Quoted in Michalski, *Public Monuments*, 44.

21. "The most remarkable thing about monuments is that you don't notice them" (Robert Musil, *Gesammelte Werke*, ed. Adolf Frisé, 2 vols. [Reinbek: Rowohlt, 1978], 2:506).

22. Quoted in Annette Wieviorka, "From Survivor to Witness: Voices from the Shoah," in *War and Remembrance in the Twentieth Century*, ed. Jay Winter and Emmanuel Sivan (Cambridge: Cambridge University Press, 1999), 140.

23. Geoff Dyer, *The Missing of the Somme* (London: Penguin, 1995), 85.

24. Quoted in Marita Sturken, "The Wall, the Screen, and the Image: The Vietnam Veterans Memorial," *Representations* 35 (1991): 120.

25. Wieviorka, "From Survivor to Witness," 138.

26. Nora, "Between Memory and History," 1.

27. Ibid., 7.

28. John Gillis, "Memory and Identity: The History of a Relationship," in Gillis, *Commemorations: The Politics of National Identity* (Princeton: Princeton University Press, 1994), 14.

29. *Phaedrus*, trans. R. Hackforth, in *The Collected Dialogues*, ed. Edith Hamilton and Huntingdon Cairns (Princeton: Princeton University Press, 1973), 520 (275a).

30. Vico, *New Science*, 537.

31. Ibid., 337.

2. "Forget About It"

1. *On the Art of Poetry*, trans. and ed. I. Bywater (Oxford: Clarendon Press, 1909), 71.

2. Nederlands Instituut voor Oorlogsdocumentatie, *Srebrenica, een "veilig" gebied: Reconstructie, achtergronden, gevolgen en analyses van de val van een Safe Area* (*Srebrenica, a "Safe" Area—Reconstruction, Background, Consequences, and Analyses of the Fall of a "Safe Area"*), 3 vols. (Amsterdam:

NIOD, 2002). Additional bibliographical information at http://www.sre-brenica.nl/Pages/OOR/23/379.bGFuZz1OTA.htm (accessed July 22, 2013).

3. As the instruction to the NIOD was worded. See the letter of Oct. 18, 1996, from the minister of education, culture, and science, the minister of defense, and the minister of foreign affairs to the Dutch Parliament (English translation at http://www.srebrenica.nl/Pages/OOR/23/375.bGFuZz1OTA.html [accessed July 22, 2013]).

4. The lectures held at the symposium are published in *Het drama Srebrenica: Geschiedtheoretische beschouwingen over het NIOD-rapport*. Special edition of *Tijdschrift voor Geschiedenis* 116 (2003): 185–328.

5. Eelco Runia, *Inkomend vuur* (Amsterdam: Augustus, 2003).

6. Later Blom made similar remarks in "Het NIOD-rapport onevenwichtig en intellectueel gemakzuchtig? Een kwestie van lezen," *Internationale Spectator* 56 (2002): 448–453; J. C. H. Blom, B. G. J. de Graaff, and D.C. L. Schoonoord, "Oordelen in uitersten," *Bijdragen en Mededelingen betreffende de Geschiedenis der Nederlanden* (BMGN) 118 (2003): 337–356; and J. C. H. Blom and B. G. J. de Graaff, "Het Srebrenica-onderzoek: Een extreem geval van eigentijdse geschiedschrijving," *Tijdschrift voor Geschiedenis* (TvG) 116 (2003): 300–322.

7. Dominick LaCapra, *Writing History, Writing Trauma* (Baltimore: Johns Hopkins University Press, 2001), 142.

8. Douglas Hofstadter, *Gödel, Escher, Bach: An Eternal Golden Braid* (New York: Basic Books, 1979), 59.

9. Eelco Runia, "The Parallel Process in the Training of General Practitioners," *Medical Teacher* 17 (1995): 399–408.

10. Sigmund Freud, "Erinnern, Wiederholen und Durcharbeiten," *Gesammelte Werke* 10 (London: Imago, 1914), 126–136.

11. H. F. Searles, "The Informational Value of the Supervisor's Emotional Experiences," *Psychiatry* 18 (1955): 135–146.

12. See, for example, D. M. Sachs and S. H. Shapiro, "On Parallel Processes in Therapy and Teaching," *Psychoanalytic Quarterly* 45 (1976): 319–415; H. K. Gediman and F. Wolkenfeld, "The Parallelism Phenomenon in Psychoanalysis and Supervision: Its Reconsideration as a Triadic System," *Psychoanalytic Quarterly* 49 (1980): 234–255; and L. Caligor, "Parallel and Reciprocal Processes in Psychoanalytic Supervision," in *Clinical Perspectives on the Supervision of Psychoanalysis and Psychotherapy*, ed. L. Caligor, P. M. Bromberg, and J. D. Meltzer (New York: Plenum Press, 1984), 1–28.

13. In the therapeutic setting there is transference from patient to therapist and countertransference from therapist to patient; in the supervision setting there is transference from therapist to supervisor and countertransference from supervisor to therapist.

14. See my *Waterloo, Verdun, Auschwitz*, 176–202.

15. Alain van der Horst, "Onmacht, onkunde en onwil," *Haagse Post*, Dec. 12, 2003, 26. The fact that 2002 was a very turbulent year in the Netherlands

(with the rise and murder of the charismatic populist Pim Fortuijn, two general elections—both ending in landslides—and the demise of a whole generation of politicians) does not, to my mind, sufficiently explain this apathy: it was not only the public media but, most conspicuously, the *professionals* (especially historians) who gave up.

16. *Herstructurering en verkleining. Defensienota 1991.* The third component of the plan was the abolishment of compulsory military service. The proposals were subsequently worked out in the *Prioriteitennota 1993.*

17. *Srebrenica, een "veilig" gebied,* 1:1041–1085. See also H. A. Couzy, *Mijn jaren als bevelhebber* (Amsterdam: L. J. Veen, 1996).

18. Quoted in *Srebrenica, een "veilig" gebied,* 1:1044. The Ossendrechtse Heide is a military training ground.

19. For the prehistory of the NIOD, see, for example, A. J. van der Leeuw, "Loe de Jong, het Koninkrijk en het Instituut," in *Een dure verplichting en een kostelijk voorrecht: Dr. L. de Jong en zijn geschiedwerk,* ed. M. de Keizer (The Hague: Sdu Uitgeverij Koninginnegracht, 1995), 21–58; and Max Pam, *De onderzoekers van de oorlog* (The Hague: SDU, 1989).

20. The future of the NIOD was finally settled when, in 1997, the minister of education, culture, and science endorsed the conclusions of the Kossmann committee (April 1997) that the NIOD was viable if it broadened its scope to twentieth-century warfare and genocide.

21. Y. Albrecht, "De waarheid in hoofdletters hebben we hier niet" (Interview with Professor Blom), *Vrij Nederland,* Nov. 2, 2002, 32–35.

22. Surprisingly, there were no restrictions as to the size and composition of the research group. Neither was there a budget: the NIOD could send its expense account to the minister. Unbelievably, there was not even a time limit. Only when the study was well on its way did the NIOD group promise that it would publish its results just after the general elections of 1998. When it proved to be impossible to live up to this promise, the NIOD agreed to be ready in the summer of 2001. This deadline couldn't be met either, and again the publication was postponed: first to November 2001, then to April 10, 2002—ironically, just *before* the *next* general elections.

23. See Blom, de Graaff, and Schoonoord, "Oordelen in uitersten," 339; and Blom and de Graaff, "Het Srebrenica-onderzoek," 300–322.

24. Lit. "to roll up one's sleeves."

25. Blom and de Graaff, "Het Srebrenica-onderzoek," 301.

26. See for the arrangement with the Dutch government Blom's "Proloog," *Srebrenica, een "veilig" gebied,* 1:9–31. For a critical assessment, see Van der Horst, "Onmacht, onkunde en onwil."

27. For example: Van der Horst, "Onmacht, onkunde en onwil."

28. Ultimately, the group consisted of eleven researchers. It might be remarked that in selecting these persons, the NIOD, like the Air Mobile Brigade, did not comply with standard recruitment procedures.

29. Van der Horst mentions that in 1997, because of major cooperation problems, a consultant was hired; Van der Horst, "Onmacht, onkunde en onwil." Blom himself has repeatedly called the fact that the group ultimately figured in toto on the title page of the report "a miracle"; quoted in Albrecht, "De waarheid in hoofdletters hebben we hier niet."

30. Dick Schoonoord, as quoted in Bas Blokker, "Knippen en plakken," *NRC Handelsblad*, Nov. 9, 2002, 23–24.

31. On this issue, see Frank Ankersmit, "Een schuld zonder schuldigen? Morele en politieke oordelen in het Srebrenica-rapport," *TvG* 116 (2003): 262–284.

32. "J. C. H. Blom (director), P. Romijn (head research)."

33. C. W. van der Pot, *Handboek van het Nederlandse Staatsrecht*, 13th ed. (Zwolle: Tjeenk Willink, 1995).

34. See Van der Horst, "Onmacht, onkunde en onwil" and Blokker, "Knippen en plakken." Several researchers are on record as having said that, after the completion of the report, they were advised not to speak to the press.

35. Quoted in Blokker, "Knippen en plakken."

36. This was said by at least two researchers. See Blokker, "Knippen en plakken." "We were tired," one of the researchers said. "I thought: suit yourself," another remarked.

37. In both instances the NIOD report itself is not quite clear, and because the minutes of the meetings of the cabinet are secret, and the ministers have as yet not disclosed anything, there is no way to ascertain what exactly happened in the cabinet. Blom, by the way, was the only researcher who had permission to see the minutes, albeit in a depersonalized version.

38. See for the evaluation of Kok: *Srebrenica, een "veilig" gebied*, 3:3141. About the cabinetlike mode of operation of the NIOD-team: ibid., 1:4.

39. The measures are described in Blokker, "Knippen en plakken."

40. Ibid.

41. Blom and de Graaff, "Het Srebrenica-onderzoek," 300–322.

42. One of the researchers said afterwards that in team meetings researchers sometimes talked like Dutchbat soldiers. "In Serbia you at least get a decent hotel and you don't have to sit on the floor when you are interviewing someone" (quoted in Blokker, "Knippen en plakken").

43. Their research object being, of course, the Dutch role in Srebrenica. Remarkably, when within a week after the publication of the report the Dutch cabinet resigned, the NIOD group was as completely overwhelmed by this "outside world of Dutch politics" as Dutchbat was overwhelmed in July 1995, when the Serbs attacked and within a week 7,500 Muslims were killed. And in fact, in this deluge, the research findings, the dozens of issues the report addressed, were as completely disregarded as the Muslims were in July 1995.

44. See below.

45. In a typical maneuver, the Dutch government had, back in 1993, promised the Dutch parliament that the Air Mobile Brigade would be at the disposal

of the UN for the Srebrenica mission for at most a year and a half, but this restriction was not communicated to the UN. The one-and-a-half-year deadline expired on July 1, 1995, but, not surprisingly, when that date approached, the UN did not experience the same sense of urgency as the Dutch government. Consequently, even in July, no replacement had been found. See *Srebrenica, een "veilig" gebied*, 2:1705.

46. See above, n. 22.

47. Quoted in Blokker, "Knippen en plakken."

48. I will not describe here the parallels in the sense of relief and in the way this relief manifested itself. Nor will I discuss the disturbing coincidence that not only an unknown, but probably large, number of Dutchbat soldiers but presumably also some of the NIOD researchers afterwards developed serious social, psychological, and/or relationship problems. For problems among soldiers, see my "De haat van de vredessoldaat," *NRC Handelsblad*, March 13, 2004; for the researchers, see Van der Horst, "Onmacht, onkunde en onwil."

49. Coincidence or not, the number of pages of the abridged version of the report (that appeared somewhat later) was approximately the same as the number of Muslims killed in the vicinity of the compound in Potocari—that is, within view of the Dutch.

50. Arthur Mitzman, *Michelet, Historian: Rebirth and Romanticism in Nineteenth-Century France* (New Haven: Yale University Press, 1990), 246. Mitzman designates "Michelet's secret wish to *be* suspended" "regression in the service of the ego." Likewise, Jakob Burckhardt could describe the Italian Renaissance as the discovery of the plasticity of matter (stone, paint, cities, states) because, as a writer, he *lived* on the hypothesis that in giving form to your conceptions you may create a reality that is at least as valid as the heritage you inherited. See my "Centauren aan de bosrand," in *Waterloo, Verdun, Auschwitz*, 52–82.

51. On the concept of "provocation" compare Freud's "Observations on Transference-Love" ("Bemerkungen über die Übertragungsliebe"): "One gets the impression that the resistance is acting as an *agent provocateur*" (*The Standard Edition of the Complete Psychological Works of Sigmund Freud*, ed. James Strachey et al. [London: Hogarth Press, 1953–1974], 12:163).

52. Freud, "Erinnern Wiederholen und Durcharbeiten," 127.

53. Though strictly speaking it is only one of the two kinds of acting out, in the following I will equate "acting out" with the transgression of *implicit* rules.

54. Consequently, "staying on the surface"—as a means of addressing transgression of implicit rules—is much more difficult than "deep" interpretation.

55. Quoted in *De Volkskrant*. See also *Srebrenica, een "veilig" gebied*, 1:30–31. Similar statements were reiterated on many occasions. Needless to say, in the following I am not criticizing a decision, but interpreting a phenomenon. I *do* think, however, that the confusion this decision provoked was caused by the gut feeling of many commentators that there was more to

it than the apparently tallying explanations Blom and his associates provided, that, in other words, something "uncanny" (in my view, a parallel
process) was going on.

56. See for example J. A. A. van Doorn, "NIOD-rapport: Te laat, te lang en slor-
dig bovendien," *Trouw*, April 17, 2002, 7.

57. One might even regard the fact that this pile of documentation was called
"information" as a provocation. In information theory, the informational
value of a message is an expression of what *could have been*—instead of
what *is*—communicated. As Charles Bennett says: "The value of a message is the amount of mathematical or other work plausibly done by its
originator, which its receiver is saved from having to repeat" (quoted in Tor
Norretranders, *The User Illusion: Cutting Consciousness Down to Size*, trans.
Jonathan Sydenham [1991] [New York: Viking, 1998], 78).

58. Albrecht, "De waarheid in hoofdletters hebben we hier niet," 34.

59. Blom et al., "Oordelen in uitersten," *BMGN*, 353. This point was also made
by Pieter Lagrou, "Het Srebrenica-rapport en de geschiedenis van het
heden," *BMGN* 118 (2003): 325–336. The NIOD report may be regarded as a
prime example of what Chris Lorenz calls "naive realism"; see his "Historical Knowledge and Historical Reality," *History and Theory* 33 (1994): 297–
328. Ironically, the immediate reactions of the politicians reinforced this
naïve realism. Many politicians professed to be "shocked" by the report—
which led to the fall of the cabinet. But insofar as they were really shocked,
they were belatedly shocked by what had happened in Srebrenica, not by
the findings or conclusions of the report. Nevertheless, the "shocked" reactions of the politicians (occasioned, not caused, by the report) was grist to
the mill of anyone who liked to believe that the way historians represent
historical reality offers—when done competently—a complete, unmedi-
ated, and unimpeded view of that reality.

60. This inexorability also permeates the discussion in the report's prologue
about what the Dutch *might* have done against the Serbs. Blom repeatedly
dismissed consideration of the options open to Dutchbat as "speculation."
See *Srebrenica, een "veilig" gebied*, 3:3143.

61. Ibid., 3:3133–3136.

62. Ibid., 3:3136; cf. 1:1076.

63. Cf. Blom's disparaging remarks about the "tragedy of Srebrenica" becoming
an "affair in the Netherlands"; *Srebrenica, een "veilig" gebied*, 3:3126.

64. Blom and de Graaff, "Het Srebrenica-onderzoek," 300; see also 310.

65. As was also the conclusion of the NIOD study. Cf. *Srebrenica, een "veilig"
gebied*, 1:1163.

66. In the case of the NIOD report, the distinction between "mission" and (relatively minor, but dirty, throbbing, abscesslike) "incidents" is, I think, a
more clarifying distinction than the distinction between "context" and "detail." See Blom and de Graaff, "Het Srebrenica-onderzoek," 310–311. But, of

course, the conspicuous frequency with which the researchers wrote about the importance of context makes it understandable that commentators regarded the context/detail dimension as a major clue in coming to grips with the report. See also n. 55.

67. I continue to treat the group as an undivided whole (though the articles written after the completion of the report are usually written by Blom and only one or two of his fellow researchers) because the researchers *themselves* kept insisting on their "unity of policy." Cf. "This article is also the fruit of consultations in the research group of the Srebrenica report. The authors who put it together thank the other researchers for their suggestions and contributions. When in the text there is talk of 'we,' most of the time the group as a whole is referred to" (these sentences, translated as faithfully as I could, indicate that not only the report as a whole, but even a relatively short article was "put together" from individual "contributions" rather than written) (Blom and de Graaff, "Het Srebrenica-onderzoek," 300n).

68. The (three) most important reactions are mentioned in n. 6.

69. All from Blom and de Graaff, "Het Srebrenica-onderzoek," 300–322. The display of modesty is similar to the display of modesty in Anglo-Saxon linguistic philosophy that is so brilliantly analyzed by Ernest Gellner in his *Words and Things* (Harmondsworth: Penguin, 1968).

70. For example: the group rather ostentatiously agreed with a reviewer who had pointed out "that *slivovitsj* is not brewed but distilled."

71. The embracing of the critique of the index is entirely comparable to the acceptance by the Dutch government: in both cases, an innocuous stricture is accepted to keep the substance (of the report/policy) intact while not creating the impression of being impervious to critique.

72. Of course, this intimidating bulkiness was a function of the way the researchers interpreted their "mandate." To deter attacks, they took care to demonstrate that they had maximally covered their object, that there weren't people they hadn't spoken to, documents they hadn't seen, sites they hadn't visited, sources they hadn't explored, clues they hadn't followed—that, in short, they had been, nay, *were* present "all over the place" and occupied every square inch of the "enclave" of their research object as completely as they possibly could.

73. In fact, Dutch society is based on mutual pacification between different religions. Mutual pacification by a silent, obliging, live-and-let-live system is so ingrained in Dutch culture that only when it is exported do its limitations become clear. The discovery in Srebrenica that, rather than a universal human value, this "obligingness" was a Dutch peculiarity that engendered contempt and hostility from Serbs as well as Muslims was/is rather difficult to come to terms with.

74. As was the title of their article in the *Tijdschrift voor Geschiedenis*.

75. See Blom and de Graaff, "Het Srebrenica-onderzoek," 127. The anger of the researchers when they couldn't recognize themselves in their colleagues' reactions to the report was not unlike the anger of the survivors of the Srebrenica bloodbath when they, for their part, didn't recognize themselves in the events as described in the report.

76. I will not discuss here how the mandate to "deter attacks by presence" functioned on the level of Dutch politics—but it is quite clear that the sheer "presence" of the NIOD research group "deterred" attacks on the Dutch government over the Srebrenica issue for more than five years.

77. As for example Jan Willem Honig and Norbert Both, *Srebrenica: Record of a War Crime* (Harmondsworth: Penguin, 1996); Frank Westerman and Bart Rijs, *Srebrenica: Het zwartste scenario* (Amsterdam: Atlas, 1997); and David Rohde, *Endgame: The Betrayal and Fall of Srebrenica, Europe's Worst Massacre Since World War II* (New York: Farrar, Strauss, and Giroux, 1997); as well as Schoonoord, "Oordelen in uitersten," 345.

78. *Srebrenica, een "veilig" gebied*, 3:3143.

79. To quote just one other such reiteration: "Anyway, in the light of the laws and customs of war, the separation of the able-bodied men in order to make sure whether there were soldiers among them who had to be taken into custody as prisoners of war was not uncommon or forbidden" (*Srebrenica, een "veilig" gebied*, 3:3158).

80. LaCapra, *Writing History, Writing Trauma*, 147.

3. Presence

1. J. G. Fichte, *Sämtliche Werke*, 11 vols. (Berlin: De Gruyter, 1971), 6:419.

2. The locus classicus of this dichotomy is perhaps William Dray, *Philosophy of History* (Englewood Cliffs, N.J.: Prentice-Hall, 1964). As Dray indicates, the critical/speculative dichotomy is equivalent to Maurice Mandelbaum's distinction between "formal" and "material" philosophy of history.

3. See my "Geheugencrisis," *Karakter* 2:7 (2004): 25–27.

4. Because in White's view different emplotments result in different—separate but coterminous—histories, in effect societies may be said to suffer just as much from *multiple personality disorder* as "Sybil."

5. Or, as it is nowadays usually called, "substantive" philosophy of history.

6. Saul Friedländer, *Probing the Limits of Representation: Nazism and the "Final Solution"* (Cambridge, Mass.: Harvard University Press, 1992), 1.

7. Aviezer Tucker, "The Future of the Philosophy of Historiography," *History and Theory* 40 (2001): 37–56.

8. Ibid.

9. In a discussion at the conference "Historical Studies: Disciplines and Discourses" (Budapest, Oct. 21–24, 2004).

10. Tucker, "The Future of the Philosophy of Historiography," 45.

11. See, for example, Donald Schön, *The Reflective Practitioner: How Professionals Think in Action* (New York: Basic Books, 1983).

12. Whether the ban on speculation was caused by the prohibition to strive for meaning or the other way around remains puzzling. Yet to be studied is how to understand this phenomenon.

13. http://www.lifegem.com (accessed May 4, 2005). I owe this reference to Ewa Domanska.

14. See Alain Badiou, *Petit manuel d'inesthétique* (Paris: Seuil, 1998).

15. Spinoza, *Ethica* [1677], ed. Nico van Suchtelen (Amsterdam: Wereldbibliotheek, 1979), 2.7.

16. See Enid Balint, "Surprisability," in *The Doctor, the Patient, and the Group: Balint Revisited*, ed. Enid Balint et al. (London: Routledge, 1993), 73–81.

17. Elucidating how discontinuity is brought about, and establishing a metahistorical perspective in which in the beginning was not the word but the deed, is precisely what I attempt to do in the "Committing History" project at Groningen University.

18. Frank Ankersmit, *Sublime Historical Experience* (Stanford: Stanford University Press, 2005).

19. Indeed, because it creates order, the continuity–discontinuity dichotomy *itself* is in the domain of continuity.

20. "Recommendations to Physicians Practising Psycho-analysis" [1912], in *Standard Edition*, 12:111. In the popular imagination Freud is seen as "deep," as obsessed with the past, an indefatigable miner. What "staying on the surface" entails for philosophy of history, I have tried to demonstrate in the previous chapter.

21. Quoted in John Gillis, "Memory and Identity: The History of a Relationship," in *Commemorations: The Politics of National Identity*, ed. John Gillis (Princeton: Princeton University Press, 1994), 6.

22. As in "Our journey is now finished, gentle reader" (Walter Scott, *Waverley* [1814] [London: Penguin, 1994], 471).

23. Ibid., 141.

24. Honoré de Balzac, *La comédie humaine*, 12 vols. (Paris: Gallimard, 1976–1981), 6:1044.

25. As Balzac designates himself in the *Avant-propos* of the *Comédie humaine*, 1:11.

26. "[U]ne espèce de fumier philosophique" (*Le peau de chagrin, Comédie humaine*, 10:63).

27. "Le cercle de vos jours, figuré par cette peau, se resserrera suivant la force et le nombre de vos souhaits" (*Comédie humaine*, 10:88).

28. Other examples are Claudio Magris's *Danube* (New York: Farrar, Straus, and Giroux, 1989) and Geert Mak's *In Europa: Reizen door de twintigste eeuw* (In Europe: Travels through the twentieth century) (Amsterdam: Atlas, 2004)—both written by literary, popular authors whose work is frowned upon by academics, but who address questions that are at least as valid, use methods that are at least as interesting, and have audiences that should be taken at least as seriously as those of academic historians.

29. W. G. Sebald, *On the Natural History of Destruction* (New York: Modern Library, 2004), 190.

30. W. G. Sebald, *Austerlitz*, trans. Anthea Bell (London: Hamish Hamilton, 2001), 192–193.

31. Compare what he says about "scruples of articulation" in *On the Natural History of Destruction*, 175.

32. Or, to be more precise: from (Cartesian) "critical philosophy" to (rhetorically inspired) "topical philosophy." See Ernesto Grassi, "Critical Philosophy or Topical Philosophy? Meditations on the *De nostri temporis studiorum ratione*," in *Giambattista Vico: An International Symposium*, ed. Giorgio Tagliacozzo and Hayden White (Baltimore: Johns Hopkins University Press, 1969), 39–50.

33. Donald Verene, *Vico's Science of Imagination* (Ithaca: Cornell University Press, 1981), 183.

34. Vico, *New Science*, 102.

35. On this issue my interpretation resembles Vittorio Mathieu's view that in Vico divine truth is revealed to man "in an upside-down form." See Vittorio Mathieu, "Truth as the Mother of History," in *Giambattista Vico's Science of Humanity*, ed. Giorgio Tagliacozzo and Donald Verene (Baltimore: Johns Hopkins University Press, 1976), 113–124.

36. *New Science*, 102. Vico doesn't use the term *istituzione*, but *cose* ("things"). See Fisch's discussion of the term in the introduction of *New Science*, xliii–xlv.

37. Ibid., 102.

38. *The Autobiography of Giambattista Vico* [1725, 1728, 1731], trans. Max Fisch and Thomas Bergin (Ithaca: Cornell University Press, 1944), 124. See also *New Science*, 166.

39. *The Autobiography*, 155.

40. Ibid., 153.

41. Vico, *New Science*, 262.

42. Ibid., 167. It is far too easy to say (as has repeatedly been done) that Vico teaches that things can be created *ex nihilo*.

43. I will not discuss here the unsettling fact that, for Vico, it is not the old places that are contained in (dialectically taken up in) the new ones, but the new ones that were contained in the old ones. In the sense that they contain less, new places are poorer than the places they replace. Culture is becoming not richer and richer but, rather, poorer and poorer. This may explain the sense of loss that comes with cultural change.

44. There is an ongoing debate whether "change" should be interpreted as "transference" or as "substitution." See the article about metonymy in *Historisches Wörterbuch der Rhetorik,* ed. Gert Ueding, 8 vols. (Darmstadt: Wissenschaftliche Buchgesellschaft, 1992–).

45. Heinrich Plett argues that all metonymical substitutions belong to one of four categories: (1) the general for the particular; (2) cause for effect; (3) substance for accident; (4) container for contained. See *Systematische Rhetorik: Konzepte und Analysen* (Munich: Fink, 2000), 192–196. Compare George Lakoff and Mark Johnson, *Metaphors We Live By* (Chicago: University of Chicago Press, 1980).

46. This makes metonymy related to what in rhetoric is called *catachresis,* the "improper use of words."

47. Marcus Tullius Cicero, *Ad Marcum Brutum orator,* ed. John Edwin Sandys (Hildesheim: Olms, 1973), 27, 92.

48. Heiner Boehncke, "Clair obscur: W. G. Sebalds Bilder," *Text + Kritik* 158 (April 2003): 55.

49. I borrow this phrase from *Disturbing Remains: Memory, History, and Crisis in the Twentieth Century,* ed. Michael Roth and Charles Salas (Los Angeles: Getty Research Institute, 2001).

50. "[D]ass wir uns ständig auf dünnem Eis bewegen, dass wir jeden Augenblick wegbrechen können" (quoted in Boehncke, "Clair obscur").

51. Boehncke, "Clair obscur."

52. In fact, the concept of "representation" obscures the fact that verbal, pictorial, and sculpted "pictures" are compounds of *both* metaphorical connotation *and* metonymical denotation.

53. Boehncke, "Clair obscur," 52.

54. Scott, *Waverley,* 148. On the face of it, Scott's is an atypical maneuver: in most metonymies something less civilized or abstract, something more corporeal or primeval, is placed into a higher-level context. In this sense most metonymies are like invasions of the barbarians. In terms of space, Waverley's journey is a visit *to* the barbarians instead of an invasion *of* the barbarians.

55. See, for example, Antonio Barcelona, "On the Plausibility of Claiming a Metonymic Motivation for Conceptual Metaphor," in *Metaphor and Metonymy at the Crossroads: A Cognitive Approach,* ed. Antonio Barcelona (Berlin: de Gruyter, 2000), 31–58.

56. Clement Greenberg, "Abstract, Representational, and So Forth," in *Art and Culture: Critical Essays* (Boston: Beacon, 1961), 133–138 (reprinted in *Theories of Modern Art: A Source Book by Artists and Critics,* ed. Herschel Chipp [Berkeley: University of California Press, 1968], 580).

57. "Die beiläufige Erwähnung eines Haar auf einer Nase wiegt mehr als der bedeutendste Gedanke" (Robert Musil, *Der Mann ohne Eigenschaften* [Reinbek: Rowohlt, 1978], 113).

58. Vico, *New Science*, 130. Unfortunately, in the English language the word "imagination" is used for both *fantasia* and *immaginazione*.

59. Ibid., 150. This is, in fact, a very intriguing maneuver: a part of nature—thunder—is taken out of it and transposed to another level (that of language) in the form of Jupiter, of whom it subsequently becomes just an attribute.

60. Ibid., 119 (emphasis added).

61. Verene, *Vico's Science of Imagination*, 175.

62. Vico, *New Science*, 129.

63. Ibid., 130.

64. In fact, this is one of two reasons. The other one is the "genetic" reason: that the domain from which the metonymy is taken supposedly *borders on* the domain to which it is transposed. See, for this view, David Lodge, *The Modes of Modern Writing: Metaphor, Metonymy, and the Typology of Modern Literature* (London: Arnold, 1977).

65. Therefore, all definitions (as the one in the *Shorter Oxford English Dictionary*) that point to single words ("scepter," "keels") cannot convey the essence of metonymy, namely, that it is a transposition involving two contexts.

66. The concept of "making things strange" is, of course, Shklovsky's. See Victor Shklovsky, "Art as Technique" [1917], in *Russian Formalist Criticism: Four Essays*, ed. Lee Lemon and Marion Reis (Lincoln: University of Nebraska Press, 1965), 3–24.

67. This capacity is, of course, strongest with "living" metonymies. In dormant metonymies like "Bush invaded Iraq" it is present as a potentiality. I will return to this later.

68. Genesis 2:19.

69. See Chris Lorenz, "Historical Knowledge and Historical Reality," *History and Theory* 33 (1994): 297–328. In fairness it should be added that Ranke, often regarded as the father of historical realism, at least was not a naïve realist. He was saved from that by his *Ideenlehre*.

70. The objection that the historian's text is a kind of précis of what the sources contain cannot be maintained. The phrases, clauses, and words the historian selects are metonymical because their representativity cannot be proved. It is their being selected that *makes* them representative—just as in politics being elected *confers* legitimacy. Compare, for the question of representativity, Lodge, *The Modes of Modern Writing*.

71. R. R. Palmer and Joel Colton, *A History of the Modern World* (New York: Knopf, 1971), 425. Because it took me no more than one minute to select this passage, it is, I think, rather improbable that my example is very unrepresentative.

72. I will not comment here on the possibility that many of its key concepts—the concepts that make Palmer and Colton's a distinctly *historical* text—

may be regarded as metonymies: "coalition," "freedom of the seas," "sea power," "reuniting," while "buffer state," "ascendancy," and "arbiter" are metaphors turned into metonymies. In fact, historians seem to have a preference for metaphors turned into metonymies. To name but a few: "Renaissance," "depression," "decline," and "revolution."

73. This is the kind of ad hoc emplotment by means of metaphor that is analyzed by Lakoff and Johnson in *Metaphors We Live By*.

74. "Irrelevant" in the sense that the details can be dispensed with without endangering the intelligibility of the story. See Roland Barthes, "L'effet du réel," *Communications* 11 (1968): 84–89.

75. "Two Aspects of Language and Two Types of Aphasic Disturbances," in *Fundamentals of Language*, ed. Roman Jakobson and Morris Halle (The Hague: Mouton, 1956), 53–82. I do agree with Jakobson that linguistic effectiveness is characterized by an interplay between (metaphoric) selection and (metonymic) combination. For Jakobson, see Richard Bradford, *Roman Jakobson: Life, Language, Art* (London: Routledge, 1994) and Lodge, *The Modes of Modern Writing*.

76. Which, perhaps, is just another reason we have trouble seeing metonymy, whereas metaphor keeps its freshness much better over much longer periods.

77. Not *quite* constant—but the feeling of self-evidency changes in a counterintuitive way. Whereas common sense has it that over time things can *become* more and more self-evident, one of the theses of this book is that (in historical mutations) things are born in a state of maximal self-evidency, and may become, over time, less and less self-evident.

78. There is metonymy on all levels: already in the first sentence Chabert is called "that coachmen's coat."

79. White, *Metahistory*, 40–41, 285–286.

80. Ibid., 35.

81. Ibid.

4. Spots of Time

1. Heraclitus, fragment 54.

2. See my "Een steen met een gat erin," in *Waterloo, Verdun, Auschwitz*, 176–202.

3. "Verkoop Viagra verslapt," *De Volkskrant*, Dec. 3, 2005, 3.

4. See Edward Rothstein, "Strumming the Mystic Chords of Memory," *New York Times* (April 19, 2005), http://travel2.nytimes.com/2005/04/19/arts/design/19roth.html (accessed April 17, 2006).

5. In order to have you understand metonymy I cannot avoid using metaphor. One of the reasons that so many more people know what a metaphor is than

what a metonymy is (despite the fact that metonymy is at least as common as metaphor) is that metonymy cannot be explained in terms of metonymy itself, while metaphor can be very well explained in terms of itself.

6. Strangely, whereas in the past decades museums have become more and more metaphorical, *monuments* have become more and more metonymical. Modern monuments eschew giving meaning and are predominantly concerned with just *presenting* the event they commemorate. See my "De pissende Pulcinella: Het metonymische karakter van de historische ervaring," *De Gids* 168.5 (2005): 397–416.

7. See my "Namen noemen," *TvG* 119 (2006): 242–248.

8. About Lutyens, see for example Jay M. Winter, *Sites of Memory, Sites of Mourning: The Great War in European Cultural History* (Cambridge: Cambridge University Press, 1995), 102–108.

9. Rudy Kousbroek, *Het meer der herinnering* (Amsterdam: Meulenhoff, 1985), 55.

10. Walter Benjamin, "On Some Motifs in Baudelaire," in *Illuminations*, trans. Harry Zohn (New York: Schocken Books, 1969), 160–161.

11. By this, of course, I do not wish to imply that our *mémoire involontaire* is *solely*, or even mainly, filled by what others want us to retain.

12. Unfortunately, Van het Reve did so in a newspaper essay that I didn't keep and that—as far as I know—is not reprinted in any of his books. So I reproduce his views from memory.

13. Cf. Norman Bryson's analysis of realist art in *Word and Image: French Painting of the Ancien Régime* (Cambridge: Cambridge University Press, 1981). Meanings that are *found* are trusted, Bryson says, but "meanings that are seen to be made are denied this privilege" (17). "Inbuilt into the realist approaches to art is the idea of resistance and mistrust: truth cannot reside in the obvious, the central, the stressed, but only in the hidden, the peripheral, the unemphasized" (19).

14. In fact, in Dutch you can render defamation harmless by saying: "I know who's saying it."

15. In the sense of "stored away in our memory."

16. Needless to say, by "common knowledge" I do *not* mean knowledge that is shared by everybody, but "authorless" knowledge that we (subconsciously) consider as the public secrets of our in-group. As such it might be compared with Vico's *topoi* as discussed in the previous chapter.

17. See David Lodge, *The Modes of Modern Writing: Metaphor, Metonymy, and the Typology of Modern Literature* (Ithaca: Cornell University Press, 1977).

18. F. R. Ankersmit, *Sublime Historical Experience* (Stanford: Stanford University Press, 2005), 227.

19. Aristotle, *De memoria et reminiscentia*, trans. J. I. Beare, in *The Works of Aristotle*, ed. J. A. Smith and W. Ross (Oxford: Clarendon Press, 1908), vol. 3, 1.450b20–451a2.

20. "[D]ie historische Gedanken *Vertretungen* [sind] mit den Anspruch zu *be-deuten*" (Karl Heussi, *Die Krisis des Historismus* [Tübingen: Mohr, 1932], 48).

21. Roland Barthes, *Camera Lucida: Reflections on Photography* [1980], trans. Richard Howard (New York: Hill and Wang, 1982).

22. As Sebald calls it.

23. See also what Austerlitz's history teacher tells his students (while lying on his back on the floor): "We try to reproduce the reality, but the harder we try, the more we find the pictures that make up the stock-in-trade of the spectacle of history forcing themselves upon us" (Sebald, *Austerlitz*, 101).

24. Hugo von Hofmannstal, "Das Gespräch über Gedichte," in *Sämtliche Werke* (Frankfurt, 1991), 31:74–86, 76.

5. Thirsting for Deeds

1. A colleague of Faisal Shahzad (who attempted to explode a car bomb on Times Square), as quoted in the *New York Times*, May 6, 2010.

2. "Wer bestaunt nicht lieber den wunderbaren Kampf zwischen Frucht-barkeit und Zerstörung in Siziliens Fluren, weidet sein Auge nicht lieber an Schottlands wilden Katarakten und Nebelgebirgen, Ossians großer Natur, als daß er in dem schnurgerechten Holland den sauren Sieg der Geduld über das trotzigste der Elemente bewundert?" (Friedrich Schiller, "Über das Erhabene," in *Sämtliche Werke*, ed. P.-A. Alt, A. Meier, and W. Riedel, 5 vols. [Munich: Hanser, 2004], 4:802). All translations are my own.

3. "Der Mensch hat noch ein Bedürfnis mehr, als zu leben und sich wohl sein zu lassen, und auch noch eine andere Bestimmung, als die Erscheinungen um ihnen herum zu begreifen" ("Über das Erhabene," 4:802).

4. "Das furchtbar herrliche Schauspiel der alles zerstörenden und wieder erschaffenden, und wieder zerstörenden Veranderung" ("Über das Erha-bene," 4:806).

5. See my *De pathologie van de veldslag: Geschiedenis en geschiedschrijving in Tolstoj's Oorlog en vrede* (Amsterdam: Meulenhoff, 1995).

6. "Kann denn ein großer Sünder noch umkehren? Ein großer Sünder kann nimmermehr umkehren, das hätt ich längst wissen können" (*Die Räuber*, in *Sämtliche Werke*, 1:615).

7. "Die Abenteuer des Julius Caesar und Alexander Magnus und anderer stockfinsterer Heiden lieber las als die Geschichte des bußfertigen Tobias" (*Die Räuber*, 1:495).

8. "Da ich noch ein Bube war—wars mein Lieblingsgedanke, wie [*die Sonne*] zu leben, zu sterben wie *sie*,—Es war ein Bubengedanke!" (*Die Räuber*, 1:561).

9. "Du kannst nur die Glücklichen töten, die Lebenssatten gehst du vorüber" (*Die Räuber*, 1:615).

10. "Moors Geliebte soll nur durch Moor sterben! [*er ermordet sie*]" (*Die Räuber*, 1:616).

11. "Tugend?—der erhabene Kopf hat andre Versuchungen als der gemeine— Sollt er Tugend mit ihm zu teilen haben?" "Es ist schimpflich ein Börse zu leeren—es ist frech eine Million zu veruntreuen, aber es ist namenlos groß, eine Krone zu stehlen" (*Die Verschwörung des Fiesko zu Genua*, in *Sämtliche Werke*, 1:698).

12. "Erste Äußerung seiner Selbsttätigkeit, erstes Wagestück seiner Vernunft, erster Anfang seines moralisches Daseyns"; "ohne Widerspruch die glücklichste und größte Begebenheit in der Menschengeschichte, von diesem Augenblick her schreibt sich seine Freiheit" ("Etwas über die erste Menschengesellschaft nach dem Leitfaden der mosaischen Urkunde," in *Sämtliche Werke*, 4:769).

13. "*Warum* hat er mich gemacht? Doch wohl nicht gar aus Liebe zu mir, der erst ein *Ich* werden sollte? . . . Wo stickt dann . . . das Heilige? Etwa im Aktus selber, durch den ich entstund?—Als wenn dieser etwas mehr wäre als viehischer Prozeß zur Stillung viehischer Begierden!" (*Die Räuber*, 1:501–502).

14. "Werden ihre neun Monate dran zu schleppen haben" (*Die Räuber*, 1:538).

15. "Meinen Tränen, meinen schlaflosen Nächten, meinen quälenden Träumen, seine Knie will ich umfassen—rufen—laut rufen: Ich hab gesündigt im Himmel und vor dir. Ich bin nicht wert, daß du mich Vater nennst" (*Die Räuber*, 1:610). See also "Vergib mir, mein Kind" (1:496).

16. "[D]aß zwei Menschen wie ich den ganzen Bau der sittlichen Welt zugrund richten würden" (*Die Räuber*, 1:617).

17. "Das Recht wohnt beim Überwältiger, und die Schranken unserer Kraft sind unsere Gesetze" (*Die Räuber*, 1:500).

18. "Ich will alles um mich her ausrotten, was mich einschränkt, daß ich nicht *Herr* bin" (*Die Räuber*, 1:502).

19. "Das Gesetz hat zum Schneckengang verdorben, was Adlerflug geworden wäre. Das Gesetz hat noch keinen großen Mann gebildet, aber die Freiheit brütet Kolosse und Extremitäten aus" (*Die Räuber*, 1:504).

20. Hans-Jürgen Schings, "Schillers 'Räuber': Ein Experiment des Universalhasses," in *Friedrich Schiller: Kunst, Humanität und Politik in der späten Aufklärung*, ed. W. Wittkowski (Tübingen, 1982), 1–21; Rüdiger Safranski, *Schiller; oder, Die Erfindung des Deutschen Idealismus* (Munich: Hanser, 2004).

21. "Vertigo," lecture, "Symposium on the Psychological Interpretation of War," New York, Jan. 14–17, 2004.

22. "Zu stehen in jener schröcklich erhabene Höhe—niederzuschmollen in der Menschlichkeit reißenden Strudel, . . . die unbändigen Leidenschaften des

Volks, gleich soviel strampfende Rossen, mit dem weichen Spiele des Zügels zu zwingen—des emporstrebenden Stolz der vasallen mit *einem*—einem Atemzug in den Staub zu legen!" (*Fiesko*, 1:698).

23. "Ich muß mich im Offenen dehnen" (*Fiesko*, 1:697).
24. "[D]enn der Mensch wurde aus einem unschuldigen Geschöpf ein schuldiges, aus einem vollkommenen Zögling der Natur ein unvollkommenes moralisches Wesen, aus einem glücklichen Instrumente ein unglücklicher Künstler" ("Etwas über die erste Menschengesellschaft," 4:769).
25. "Mein Geist dürstet nach Thaten" (*Die Räuber*, 1:515).
26. "Ich habe keinen Vater mehr, ich habe keine Liebe mehr, und Blut und Tod soll mich vergessen lehren, daß mir jemals etwas teuer war" (*Die Räuber*, 1:515).
27. "Lern erst die Tiefe des Abgrunds kennen, eh du hineinspringst!" (*Die Räuber*, 1:566).
28. "Nun dann, so laßt uns gehn! Fürchtet euch nicht vor Tod und Gefahr, denn über uns waltet ein unbeugsames Fatum! Jeden ereilet endlich sein Tag, es sei auf dem weichen Küssen von Pflaum, oder im rauhen Gewühl des Gefechts, oder auf offenem Galgen und Rad! Eins davon ist unser Schicksal!" (*Die Räuber*, 1:516).
29. Ron Susskind, "Without a Doubt," *New York Times Magazine*, Oct. 12, 2004. Quoted in Mark Danner, "The Secret Way to War," *New York Review of Books*, June 9, 2005.
30. "Taten wie diese überlegt man, wenn sie getan sind" ("Selbstbesprechung," in *Sämtliche Werke*, 1:632).

6. Into Cleanness Leaping

1. Quoted in Leon Trotsky, *On Lenin: Notes Towards a Biography*, trans. Tamara Deutscher (London: Harrap, 1971), 79–80.
2. Musil, *Der Mann ohne Eigenschaften*, 465. English translation: *The Man Without Qualities*, trans. Sophie Wilkins (New York: Knopf, 1995), 1:504.
3. Robert Musil, "Das hilflose Europa; oder: Reise vom Hundertsten ims Tausendsten," in *Gesammelte Werke II* (Reinbek: Rowohlt, 1978), 1090.
4. I would like to point out in this respect that my approach may be called psychohistorical in Lucien Febvre's sense that in order to understand history one should acquaint oneself with the *outillage mental* of its subjects. It is not psychohistorical, however, in the sense that I am not trying to ascertain (as, for example, Lloyd deMause does) in what respects particular styles of child-rearing surface on the level of history. In fact, I am not interested in what is the central concern of psychohistory, human motivation. Whereas the *Journal of Psychohistory* defines psychohistory as "the science of his-

torical motivation," I rather agree with Michael Gazzaniga that psychology, as the science of human motivation, is dead. Cf. Lynn Hunt, "Psychology, Psychoanalysis, and Historical Thought," in *A Companion to Western Historical Thought*, ed. Lloyd Kramer and Sarah Maza (Malden, Mass.: Wiley-Blackwell, 2006), 337–356.

5. "Nicht aus altparlamentarischen Ansprüchen, die sich etwa von Stufe zu Stufe höher gesteigert hätten, ist die Republik in England hervorgegangen, sondern aus einer anderen Reihe von Gedanken, die sich dem Parlament, wie es bisher bestanden hatte, so entschieden entgegensetzten wie dem Königtum selbst" (Leopold von Ranke, *Englische Geschichte*, 3 vols. [Wiesbaden: Harrassowitz, 1957], 2:155).

6. Runia, *Waterloo, Verdun, Auschwitz*.

7. Joseph Conrad, *Victory* (Harmondsworth: Penguin, 1970), 149.

8. Musil, *The Man Without Qualities*, 444.

9. Ibid.

10. See Scott Plous, *The Psychology of Judgment and Decision Making* (New York: McGraw-Hill, 1993), 28.

11. Musil, *The Man Without Qualities*, 509.

12. "En atteignant au seuil de sa pension, Rastignac s'était épris de madame de Nucingen" (Balzac, *Le père Goriot*, in *Comédie humaine*, 2:955).

13. Stendhal, *The Red and the Black*, trans. Roger Gard (New York: Penguin, 2002), 47.

14. Friedrich Schiller, "Etwas über die erste Menschengesellschaft nach dem Leitfaden der mosaischen Urkunde" [1792], in *Sämtliche Werke*, 4:767–783.

15. Ibid., 4:769.

16. *New York Review of Books*, April 12, 2007. http://www.nybooks.com/articles/20082 (accessed Nov. 30, 2009).

17. D. J. Bem, "Self-Perception Theory," in *Advances in Experimental Social Psychology*, ed. L. Berkowitz (New York: Academic Press, 1972), 6:1–62.

18. Timothy Wilson, *Strangers to Ourselves: Discovering the Adaptive Unconscious* (Cambridge, Mass.: Harvard University Press, 2004), 105.

19. Ibid., 106.

20. Tor Norretranders, *The User Illusion: Cutting Consciousness Down to Size*, trans. Jonathan Sydenham (New York: Viking, 1998), 187. See also Daniel Wegner, *The Illusion of Conscious Will* (Cambridge, Mass.: MIT Press, 2003).

21. Norretranders, *The User Illusion*, 220.

22. "Awareness occurs half a second after skin stimulation. But it is experienced *as if* it occurs when the brain puts out an evoked response" (ibid., 235).

23. Roger Caillois, *Man, Play, and Games*, trans. Meyer Barash (New York: Free Press of Glencoe, 1961), 23. Remarkably, *Les jeux et les hommes* was published in the same year that Hitchcock's *Vertigo* hit the screen (1958), though apparently Caillois wasn't aware of it.

24. Ibid., 24.
25. See chapter 5, n. 22.
26. Marcel Proust, *In Search of Lost Time: Finding Time Again*, trans. Ian Paterson (London: Penguin, 2003), 357.
27. Musil, *The Man Without Qualities*, 311.
28. Ibid., 513.
29. Ibid., 157.
30. Charles Rycroft, "Some Observations on a Case of Vertigo," *International Journal of Psychoanalysis* 34 (1953): 243.
31. Ibid., 247.
32. Ibid.
33. See, for example, Otto Fenichel, "The Counter-phobic Attitude," *International Journal of Psychoanalysis* 20 (1939): 263–274.
34. Quoted in Steven Sage, *Ibsen and Hitler: The Playwright, the Plagiarist, and the Plot for the Third Reich* (New York: Basic Books, 2007), 155.
35. "Peace," in Rupert Brooke, *The Collected Poems* (London: Sidgwick and Jackson, 1989).
36. Henri Bergson, *Creative Evolution*, trans. Arthur Mitchell (London: Macmillan, 1922), 172.
37. According to Aristotle this is the subject of dialectic—in fact, he regards rhetoric as the *antistrophos* to—the counterpart of—dialectic. See Aristotle, *On Rhetoric*, ed. George Kennedy (New York: Oxford University Press, 1991), 28–29n (1354a).
38. As I have argued in chapter 3, these *topoi* may be regarded as "metonymical" places.

7. Inventing the New from the Old

1. "Und wenn sie eben damit beschäftigt scheinen, sich und die Dingen umzuwälzen, noch nicht Dagewesenes zu schaffen, gerade in solchen Epochen revolutionärer Krise beschwören sie ängstlich die Geister der Vergangenheit zu ihrem Dienste herauf, entlehnen ihnen Namen, Schlachtparole, Kostüm, um in dieser altehrwürdigen Verkleidung und mit dieser erborgten Sprache die neue Weltgeschichtsszene aufzuführen" (Karl Marx, *Der achtzehnte Brumaire des Louis Bonaparte*, 19).
2. Hans Ulrich Gumbrecht, *In 1926: Living at the Edge of Time* (Cambridge, Mass.: Harvard University Press, 1997), 411.
3. Lakoff and Johnson, *Metaphors We Live By*.
4. Compare what he said to Eckermann (Feb. 2, 1827): "[E]s ist nichts außer uns, was nicht zugleich in uns wäre, und wie die äußere Welt ihre Farbe hat, so hat auch das Auge" ("Nothing is outside us that is not at the same

time within us, and just as the outside world has its colors, so has the eye")
(Johann Peter Eckermann, *Gespräche mit Goethe* (1836, 1848) [Munich:
Deutscher Taschenbuch, 1976]).

5. Vico, *New Science*, 238. See also his remark that "the wisdom of the ancients was the vulgar wisdom of the lawgivers, who founded the human
race, not the esoteric wisdom of great and rare philosophers" (384).

6. Mark Lilla, *G. B. Vico: The Making of an Anti-modern* (Cambridge, Mass.:
Harvard University Press, 1994), 129.

7. Vico, *The Autobiography of Giambattista Vico* [1725, 1728, 1731], trans. M.
Fisch and T. Bergin (Ithaca: Cornell University Press, 1944), 167.

8. Verene, *Vico's Science of Imagination*, 63.

9. Vico, *New Science*, 498.

10. Ibid., 495.

11. Ibid., 494.

12. See about the evolutionary structure of language, for example, Steven Pink-
er, *The Language Instinct: The New Science of Language and Mind* (London:
Penguin, 1994).

13. As, for example, in the Vietnam Veterans Memorial and the remembrance
of 9/11. See my "Namen noemen" and chapter 4 of this book.

14. Vico, *New Science*, 456.

15. Giuseppe Mazzotta, *The New Map of the World: The Poetic Philosophy of
Giambattista Vico* (Princeton: Princeton University Press, 1999), 145.

16. Walter Watson, "Inventio," in *Encyclopedia of Rhetoric*, ed. Thomas Sloane
(Oxford: Oxford University Press, 2001).

17. Aristotle, *Topics*, 100a30–31 (trans. E. S. Forster [Cambridge, Mass.: Harvard University Press, 1976]). Modern logic, of course, is exclusively concerned with analytic reasoning.

18. Ibid., 100a25–27. Compare Vico: Socrates "introduced dialectic, employing
induction of several certain things related to the doubtful thing in question" (*New Science*, 167).

19. Vico, *New Science*, 819.

20. Hayden White, "The Historical Text as Literary Artifact," in *Tropics of Discourse* (Baltimore: Johns Hopkins University Press, 1978), 88.

8. Crossing the Wires in the Pleasure Machine

1. "Every epoch is a sphinx who throws himself in the abyss as soon as one has
solved its riddle" (Heinrich Heine, *Die romantische Schule* (1832) [Amster-
dam: Binger and Zn, 1856], 7).

2. Henri Bergson, *Creative Evolution* [1911] (New York: Dover, 1998), 270.

3. One might say that the professionalization of the theory of history coincided with the end of substantive philosophy of history. In retrospect one has the impression that William Dray's essay in the very first issue of *History and Theory*, in which he put Arnold Toynbee through the mincing machine of the covering-law model, was a kind of exorcism. The remnants of the spirit of "speculation" were chased away in the second volume, in 1963, in a rather haughty review of the last volume of *A Study of History, Reconsiderations*.

4. Leon Trotsky, *On Lenin: Notes Towards a Biography*, trans. Tamara Deutscher (London: Harrap, 1971), 123.

5. Ibid.

6. See Donald Schön, *The Reflective Practitioner* (New York: Basic Books, 1983).

7. A notable exception is Philip Pomper's *Lenin, Trotsky, and Stalin: The Intelligentsia and Power* (New York: Columbia University Press, 1990).

8. Quoted in Slavoj Žižek, "Introduction," in V. I. Lenin, *Revolution at the Gates: A Selection of Writings from February to October 1917*, ed. Slavoj Žižek (London: Verso, 2002), 5.

9. That is, context, other, "object." Bertram Wolfe's characterization of Lenin as a "selfless egoist" is an apposite description of what narcissism is about.

10. Žižek, "From 'History and Class Consciousness' to 'The Dialectic of Enlightenment' . . . and Back," *New German Critique* 81 (2000): 117–118.

11. "Wenn wir anfangen außer uns zu wirken, dann zieht uns oft der Strom mit sich fort, wir gehen außer uns heraus, zerstören die heimische Hütte in uns, und in die Paläste die wir außer uns auftürmen, bleiben wir ewig Fremdlinge" (quoted in Arnold Labrie, *Het verlangen naar zuiverheid: Een essay over Duitsland* [Maastricht: Maastricht Uniprint, 1994], 16). Cf. Eelco Runia, "Burying the Dead, Creating the Past," *History and Theory* 46 (2007): 318.

12. Olivia Judson, "An Evolve-By Date," *New York Times*, Nov. 27, 2009. http://opinionator.blogs.nytimes.com/2009/11/24/an-evolve-by-date/ (accessed July 9, 2010).

13. Sándor Márai, *Egy polgár vallomásai* (Confessions of a bourgeois) (1935). Apparently this has not been translated into English; my translation is from the Dutch edition: *Bekentenissen van een burger*, trans. Henry Kammer (Amsterdam: Wereldbibliotheek, 2007), 185.

14. For an overview, see Hector Qirko, "Altruism in Suicide Terror Organizations," *Zygon* 44 (2009): 289–322 (thank you, Hector).

15. Jon Elster, *Alchemies of the Mind: Rationality and the Emotions* (Cambridge: Cambridge University Press, 1999), 23.

16. "Letters from Afar," in Lenin, *Revolution at the Gates*, 16.

17. Alain Badiou, *The Century*, trans. Alberto Toscano (Cambridge: Polity, 2007), 65.

18. Quoted in Philipp Blom, *The Vertigo Years: Europe, 1900–1914* (New York: Basic Books, 2008), 358.

19. Vico, *New Science*, 384. A comparable view can be ascribed to that other pioneer of evolutionary history, Johann Gottfried Herder: see *Vom Erkennen und Empfinden* [1774], in Herder's *Sämtliche Werke*, ed. Bernhard Suphan (Berlin: Weidmann, 1877–1913), 8:261, where he exclaims, "Die vollständige Wahrheit ist immer nur Tat" ("The complete truth is always only deed").

20. Victor Hugo, *Les misérables* [1862], trans. Norman Denny (London: Penguin, 1982), 721.

21. Leon Trotsky, *My Life: An Attempt at an Autobiography*, trans. Joseph Hansen (Harmondsworth: Penguin, 1975), 348. See also his remark that "a new type of man" is emerging, a man "for whom the path between words and deeds is shorter, a man who *dares*—and this type of man is a necessary precondition for a revolution."

22. V. I. Lenin, *Sämtliche Werke* (Vienna: Verlag für Literatur und Politik, 1931), 2:96.

23. Quoted in Pomper, *Lenin, Trotsky, and Stalin*, 310.

24. Ibid., 311. Quite a good description of what I have called "fleeing forward" was given by Henri Bergson: "Action on the move creates its own route, creates to a very great extent the conditions under which it is to be fulfilled, and this baffles all calculation" (Henri Bergson, *Two Sources of Morality and Religion*, trans. R. Ashley Audra and Cloudsley Brereton (1932) [Notre Dame, IN: University of Notre Dame Press, 1977], 296).

25. Trotsky, *History of the Russian Revolution*, trans. Max Eastman (London: Sphere Books, 1967), 1:307.

26. Trotsky, *My Life*, 348.

27. Ibid.

28. Cf. Edmund Wilson, *To the Finland Station*, rev. ed. [1940, 1968] (New York: Farrar, Straus, and Giroux, 1972).

29. Thomas Kuhn, *The Essential Tension* (Chicago: University of Chicago Press, 1977), xii.

30. Trotsky, *My Life*, 348.

31. Ibid., 348–349.

32. Ibid., 349.

33. Ibid., 307.

34. Trotsky, *On Lenin*, 146.

35. Ibid., 127.

36. Ibid., 124.

37. Ibid., 146.

38. Quoted in Orlando Figes, *A People's Tragedy: The Russian Revolution, 1891–1924* (London: Penguin, 1998), 390.

39. In the *Theses on Peace*, written at the beginning of January 1918. Quoted in Trotsky, *On Lenin*, 125; Trotsky's italics.

40. Trotsky's observation also draws in stark relief the difference between normal (chronological) time and the kairotic time frame of a sublime historical event.

41. Trotsky, *On Lenin*, 116.

42. Trotsky, *My Life*, 349. I use Pomper's translation, which seems to me more correct. See Pomper, *Lenin, Trotsky, and Stalin*, 267.

43. "Sie kennen kein *hic et nunc* und lassen sich nicht innerhalb der Koordinaten von Zeit und Raum situieren. In dieser Verborgenheit bewahren sie aber ihre Einmaligkeit" (Udo Hock, "Die Zeit des Erinnerns," *Psyche* 57 [2003]: 827).

44. "Repetition: A Venture in Experimenting Psychology," in *The Essential Kierkegaard*, ed. Howard Hong and Edna Hong (Princeton: Princeton University Press, 2000), 102–103.

45. In fact, I think that the Russian Revolution was just one of the episodes of fleeing forward by which in the beginning of the twentieth century the freshwater pool was salted. The other one was, of course, the First World War.

46. Vico, *New Science*, 819.

47. Michael Lewis, *The Big Short: Inside the Doomsday Machine* (New York: Norton, 2010), 119.

48. Ibid., 148.

49. Ibid., 116 (emphasis added).

9. Our Own Best Enemy

1. Jacques Presser, *De nacht der Girondijnen* (Amsterdam: Meulenhoff, 1957), motto.

2. Alexis de Tocqueville, *Souvenirs*, ed. Luc Monnier (Paris: Gallimard, 1964), 118. A slightly different translation in *Recollections*, ed. P. Mayer and A. P. Kerr (New Brunswick: Transaction, 1997), 66.

3. See my *De pathologie van de veldslag: Geschiedenis en geschiedschrijving in Tolstoj's "Oorlog en vrede"* (Amsterdam: Meulenhoff, 1995).

4. For a discussion of empiricist source-dependency: Peter Novick, *That Noble Dream: The "Objectivity Question" and the American Historical Profession* (Cambridge: Cambridge University Press, 1988).

5. David Christian, "The Return of Universal History," *History and Theory* 49 (2010): 6–27. See on the historiography of universal history the review of Raymond Grew, "Expanding Worlds of World History," *Journal of Modern History* 78 (2006): 878–898; the special issue of the *Österreichische Zeitschrift für Geschichtswissenschaften* (vol. 20.2 [2009]) on "Global history," ed. Peer Vries; Patrick Manning, ed., *Global Practice in World His-*

tory: Advances Worldwide (Princeton: Markus Wiener, 2008); and Ross Dunn, ed., *The New World History* (Boston: Macmillan, 2000). Also Marnie Hughes-Warrington, "Writing World History," in *Berkshire Encyclopedia of World History*, ed. William McNeill (Great Barrington, Conn.: Berkshire, 2004), 5:2095–2103; and William McNeill, "The Changing Shape of World History," *History and Theory* 34 (1995): 8–26.

6. There is, to be sure, a lot of theory in this new universal history, but the theories belong to the disciplines from which they are borrowed and can consequently be neither proven nor disproven by new universal history *itself*. A rival approach, "deep history"—as envisaged by Daniel Lord Smail—is theoretically much more interesting but also does not address the question that occupies me in this chapter: What *energizes* human evolution?

7. David Christian, *Maps of Time: An Introduction to Big History* (Berkeley: University of California Press, 2004). A related view has been proposed by William McNeill.

8. In chapter 6 I drew attention to the fact that though we have become what we are in a series of discontinuous metamorphoses, the *stories* about how we have become what we are are almost inevitably written in the key of continuity. Psychology, especially the branch that explores what is called "dissonance reduction," shows that there are compelling reasons that explain why retrospectively continuity reigns supreme, but that shouldn't close our eyes to the fact that life itself is at least as much characterized by faults and breaks as by the ripples of a torpid immutability. Consequently, any theory that attempts to explain human *autopoiesis* must include an epistemological equivalent to the prisms in a binoculars that turn an upside-down image into an upright one—a module, that is, that corrects our inclination to retrospectively "see" continuity where reality was unmistakably and even painfully discontinuous.

9. As was the upshot of Joseph Fracchia and R. C. Lewontin, "Does Culture Evolve?," *History and Theory* 38 (1999): 52–78.

10. Within the humanities it is still necessary to stress that evolution is not restricted to genetic change and does not imply teleology. For a discussion of the fact that even if the genotype is frozen you still can have evolution, see, for example, Eva Jablonka and Marion Lamb, *Evolution in Four Dimensions: Genetic, Epigenetic, Behavioral, and Symbolic Variation in the History of Life* (Cambridge, Mass.: MIT Press, 2005), 358. Misunderstandings about evolution as a form of teleology are addressed by W. G. Runciman: evolution is "by definition change out of a previous state into a different one, but it does not have to be change in the direction of any predetermined end-state or along any predetermined path" (Runciman, "Culture Does Evolve," *History and Theory* 44 [2005]: 8).

11. Cf. R. C. Lewontin, "Adaptation," *Scientific American* 239:3 (1978): 156–169.

12. Ernest Gellner, *Plough, Sword, and Book: The Structure of Human History* (London: Collins Harvill, 1988), 14.

13. Richard Alexander, *How Did Humans Evolve? Reflections on the Uniquely Unique Species* (Ann Arbor: University of Michigan, Museum of Zoology, 1990), 3.

14. See for example N. K. Humphrey, "The Social Function of Intellect," in *Growing Points in Ethology*, ed. P. P. G. Bateson and R. A Hinde (New York: Cambridge University Press, 1976), 303–318. See also Chris Stringer's remark that "in the case of humans it is very difficult to argue that general environmental demands have been anywhere near as important as social ones in the development of our extraordinarily large brains" (*The Origin of Our Species* [London: Allen Lane, 2011], 111).

15. R. I. M. Dunbar, "Neocortex Size as a Constraint on Group Size in Primates," *Journal of Human Evolution* 22 (1992): 469–493.

16. Alexander, *How Did Humans Evolve?*, 5.

17. Niles Eldredge and Stephen J. Gould, "Punctuated Equilibria: An Alternative to Phyletic Gradualism," in *Models in Paleobiology*, ed. T. J. M. Schopf (San Francisco: Freeman, Cooper, 1972), 82–115.

18. R. G. Klein, *The Human Career: Human Biological and Cultural Origins* (Chicago: University of Chicago Press, 1999).

19. Robert Boyd and Peter Richerson, "Group Beneficial Norms Spread Rapidly in a Structured Population," *Journal of Theoretical Biology* 215 (2002): 287–296.

20. Matt Ridley, *The Rational Optimist: How Prosperity Evolves* (New York: HarperCollins, 2010), 6.

21. The idea was first advanced by John Cairns and colleagues in a widely discussed paper in *Nature* (J. Cairns, J. Overbaugh, and S. Miller, "The Origin of Mutants," *Nature* 335 (1988): 142–145) and was initially labeled "directed mutation." For a more recent discussion see, for instance, V. V. Velkov, "New Insights Into the Molecular Mechanisms of Evolution: Stress Increases Genetic Diversity," *Molecular Biology* 36 (2002): 209–215.

22. For this example I rely on Fabian Mollet, *Evolutionary Effects of Fishing and Implications for Sustainable Management: A Case Study of North Seas Plaice and Sole* (Ph.D. diss., Wageningen, 2010).

23. And, of course, the fact that the fish is caught by net would make it rather difficult to concentrate on the smaller ones.

24. In fact, in the case of the plaice the occurrence of stress-induced mutation is an inference based on statistical evidence. The phenomenon is, however, experimentally demonstrated in bacteria like the E. coli.

25. Richard Lenski, "The Future of Evolutionary Biology," *Ludus Vitalis* 12 (2004): 67–89.

26. Cairns et al., "The Origin of Mutants," 142 (emphasis added).

27. To me "catastrophe" is a technical term referring to the generation of a kind of, or amount of, stress that cannot be coped with within the bounds of the *status quo ante*. Use of the term "catastrophe" also highlights the fact that the inventions that have made us into what we are are not the "advances" we retrospectively like them to be, but "retreats." In a catastrophe we are willfully amputating something with which we identify in order to transform it into something with which we retrospectively identify even more. The sublimely human achievement of writing was (as Plato acknowledged in his *Phaedrus*) a catastrophe for "memory," the invention of monotheism was a catastrophe for our ability to be "heroic," and so on.

28. As was the motto of the (1957) novella *De nacht der Girondijnen* in which the (Jewish) Dutch historian Jacob Presser tried to fathom the Holocaust.

29. From the ratcheting mechanism used in the socket wrench. In economics the ratchet principle refers to "the use of current performance as a partial basis for setting future targets" (Martin Weitzman, "The 'Ratchet Principle' and Performance Incentives," *Bell Journal of Economics* 11 [1980]: 302).

30. "Participants" not in the restricted sense of the men and women who were actually present in the situation, but in the much broader sense of everybody who was somehow involved in the process, including constituencies, press, civil servants, parties, assemblies, etc.

31. In a recent lecture I have argued that accomplished facts are made in what in psychiatry is called a state of "dissociation": "Of Two Minds; or, Why the Concept of 'Dissociation' Might Help to Understand History (and the World We Live In)," "Impossible Narratives" conference, New York, Columbia University, Feb. 16, 2011.

32. Quoted in Martin J. Dedman, *The Origin and Development of the European Union, 1945–2008: A History of European Integration* (London: Routledge, 2010), 133–134.

33. As Martin Stuart-Fox says in a review of W. G. Runciman's *The Theory of Cultural and Social Selection* (Cambridge: Cambridge University Press, 2009); see Martin Stuart-Fox, "Constructing a Selectionist Paradigm," *History and Theory* 50 (2011): 235.

34. Ibid.

35. Runciman has argued that human evolution is a function of how "selfish" memes replicate on a cultural and social level (ibid.).

36. The idea of the ratchet principle has an early precursor in the theory of business cycles developed by Joseph Schumpeter in the years between the world wars. Dissatisfied by the *idée reçu* that an economic system only changes "under the influence of events that are external to itself [and] that economic life is essentially passive and merely adapts itself to the natural and social influences," Schumpeter argued that each and every economic equilibrium is bound to be destroyed by entrepreneurs who try to introduce innovations. Schumpeter "felt very strongly," he said, "that [the then-

prevalent view] was wrong, and that there was a source of energy within the economic system which could of itself disrupt any equilibrium that might be attained" (Joseph Schumpeter, *Essays* [1937] [Port Washington, N.Y.: Kennikat, 1951], 159–160). Indeed, in Schumpeter's evolutionary view of economics evolution is a far cry from any form of gradual development and "more like a series of explosions than a gentle, though incessant transformation" (quoted in Esben Sloth Andersen, *Evolutionary Economics: Post-Schumpeterian Contributions* [London: Pinter, 1994], 22).

37. Quoted in Nicholas Phillipson, *Adam Smith: An Enlightened Life* (New Haven: Yale University Press, 2010), 77.

38. Consider my contention, in the previous chapter, that a catastrophic accomplished fact may be said to create complexity—at the expense, however, of increased fragility, vulnerability, and energy-consumption—liabilities that eventually are more than offset by increased robustness, versatility, and empowerment but that initially are hard to bear.

39. Ridley, *Rational Optimist*, 129.

40. Marshall Sahlins, "The Original Affluent Society," *Stone Age Economics* (New York: Aldine, 1972), 1–39.

41. John Coatsworth, as quoted in Christian, *Maps of Time*, 224.

42. Karl Polanyi, *The Great Transformation: The Political and Economic Origins of Our Time* [1944] (Boston: Beacon, 1957).

43. Eric Wolf, *Europe and the People Without History* [1982] (Berkeley: University of California Press, 1997).

44. Though, of course, afterwards, the catastrophe was "read" in terms of its results—this embodies the phenomenon called "dissonance reduction" I discussed in previous chapters. There are three broad (and often quite implicit) strategies for dissonance reduction: that we stumble upon "catastrophes" while aiming for something else (or for nothing in particular), that we engage in *reculer pour mieux sauter* and in delaying gratification, and that an elite (that *does* profit) coerces the "worker bees" to bring about situations from which they themselves don't profit. As Tolstoy recognized in his *War and Peace*, strategies for dissonance reduction are not just, or even primarily, employed afterwards, but also by the participants themselves.

45. Larry Patriquin, "The Agrarian Origins of the Industrial Revolution in England," *Review of Radical Political Economics* 36 (2004): 196–216; Robert Brenner, "Agrarian Class Structure and Economic Development in Preindustrial Europe," *Past and Present* 70 (1976): 30–75.

46. Rosemary Hopcroft, "The Social Origins of Agrarian Change in Late Medieval England," *American Journal of Sociology* 99 (2004): 1589.

47. Ellen Wood, *The Origins of Capitalism* (New York: Monthly Review Press, 1999), 80.

48. The theory of the spillover effect informs for example F. J. Fransen's analysis: "[Monnet] preferred the new territory of atomic energy to the en-

trenched interests of economics. . . . For Monnet the central goal was . . . to create common institutions with sovereign control of whatever it was they were supposed to manage" (Fransen, "On the Incongruities of Monnet's Europe," paper presented at the Biennial Conference of the European Community Studies [1999], 10–11).

49. For example, the Treaties of Paris (1951) and Rome (1957), the Single European Act of 1986, the Maastricht Treaty (1992), and the Treaty of Accession of 2003.

50. Stanley Henig, *The Uniting of Europe: From Discord to Concord* (London: Routledge, 1997), 34.

51. Quoted in John Gillingham, *European Integration, 1950–2003: Superstate or New Market Economy?* (Cambridge: Cambridge University Press, 2003), 53. See also my "Historische beslissingen en het volle verstand," *Openbaar Bestuur* 22.3 (2012): 5–9.

52. Jean Monnet, "A Ferment of Change," *Journal of Common Market Studies* 1 (1963): 204.

53. Monnet, "A Ferment of Change," 208. See also Luuk van Middelaar, *De passage naar Europa: Geschiedenis van een begin* (Groningen: Historische Uitgeverij, 2009).

54. As Helen Wallace calls it; see her "The Institutions of the EU: Experience and Experiments," in *Policy-Making in the European Union*, ed. H. Wallace and W. Wallace (Oxford: Oxford University Press, 1996).

55. Robert Cooper compares the magnitude of the changes to the emergence of the European state system after the Peace of Westphalia; *The Breaking of Nations: Order and Chaos in the Twenty-First Century* (London: Atlantic Books, 2003), 3.

56. William Doyle, *Origins of the French Revolution*, 2nd ed. (Oxford: Oxford University Press, 1988), 172–173.

57. Peter Brooks, *Reading for the Plot: Design and Intention in Narrative* (Cambridge, Mass.: Harvard University Press, 1984), 22. The episode of the Tennis Court Oath may be interpreted as the institution of a new *topos*—a *topos* that subsequently could be/had to be explored. See chapter 3.

58. It is not just a coincidence that self-determination is the quintessential theme in the most perceptive novels of the period. It defines Julien Sorel's career in Stendhal's *Le rouge et le noir* and is exhaustively explored in Balzac's *Comédie humaine*. Characteristically, self-determination is not operative just on the level of the individual but also on the level of society as whole. On a societal level it manifests itself in the way states are supposed to assert themselves. As Ranke said about nations: "Das Maß der Unabhängigkeit gibt einem Staate seine Stellung in der Welt; es legt ihm zugleich die Notwendigkeit auf, alle inneren Verhältnisse zu dem Zwecke einzurichten, sich zu behaupten. Dies ist sein oberstes Gesetz" (Leopold

von Ranke, "Politisches Gespräch" (1836), in *Das politische Gespräch und andere Schriftchen zur Wissenschaftslehre* (Halle/Saale: Niemeyer, 1925), 24.

59. By creating a regime of selectiveness in which labor was expensive, the Black Death may have contributed to technological innovation and, ultimately, to the "Rise of the West." See David Herlihy, *The Black Death and the Transformation of the West* (Cambridge, Mass.: Harvard University Press, 1997). One might also venture the hypothesis that Mao Zedong's Great Leap Forward of 1958–1960 was the "stress" that "induced" the "mutations" that made China into the supremely competitive nation it is today.

60. Quoted in Peter Gay, *The Enlightenment: The Rise of Modern Paganism* (New York: Norton, 1977), 13.

61. A chilling example is the extreme willingness to take chances that gave birth to the First World War.

62. Which may have been the reason that isolated groups like the Tasmanian aboriginals sometimes stop evolving and begin to regress.

63. Jablonka and Lamb, *Evolution in Four Dimensions,* 101. See n. 25.

64. Merlin Donald, *Origins of the Modern Mind: Three Stages in the Evolution of Culture and Cognition* (Cambridge, Mass.: Harvard University Press, 1991), 10.

65. L. Ross and R. E. Nisbett, *The Person and the Situation: Perspectives of Social Psychology* (Philadelphia: McGraw-Hill, 1991).

Index

European Perspectives:
A Series in Social Thought and Cultural Criticism

Lawrence D. Kritzman, Editor

European Perspectives presents outstanding books by leading European
thinkers. With both classic and contemporary works, the series aims to
shape the major intellectual controversies of our day and to facilitate
the tasks of historical understanding.